# A DEMOCRACY IS BORN

# A DEMOCRACY IS BORN

An Insider's Account of the Battle Against
Terrorism in Afghanistan

*Matthew J. Morgan*

**PRAEGER SECURITY INTERNATIONAL**
Westport, Connecticut • London

**Library of Congress Cataloging-in-Publication Data**

Morgan, Matthew J.
A democracy is born : an insider's account of the battle against terrorism in
Afghanistan / Matthew J. Morgan.
    p.   cm.
    Includes bibliographical references and index.
    ISBN–13: 978–0–275–99999–5 (alk. paper)
    1. Afghan War, 2001–   2. Afghanistan–Politics and government–2001–
I. Title.
    DS371.412.M67    2007
    958.104′7–dc22        2007027876

British Library Cataloguing in Publication Data is available.

Library of Congress Catalog Card Number: 2007027876
ISBN–13: 978–0–275–99999–5

First published in 2007

Praeger Security International, 88 Post Road West, Westport, CT 06881
An imprint of Greenwood Publishing Group, Inc.
www.praeger.com

Printed in the United States of America

The paper used in this book complies with the
Permanent Paper Standard issued by the National
Information Standards Organization (Z39.48–1984).

10 9 8 7 6 5 4 3 2 1

*For Murad and Sahar,*
*Whom I shall never forget,*
*And for all Afghans struggling*
*For a better tomorrow.*

1 – Panshir
2 – Nuristan
3 – Parwan
4 – Kapisa
5 – Laghman
6 – Konar
7 – Logar
8 – Nangarhar
9 – Paktya
10 – Khost

Faisabad
Badakhsan
Asadabad
Jalalabad
Takhar
Khost
Konduz
Konduz
Baghlan
Bagram
Kabul
Gardez
Orgun E
Shkin
Mazar-e Sharif
Balkh
Gouzgan
Samangan
Wardak
Puli Alam
Ghazni
Ghazni
Paktika
Sar-e Pol
Bamiyan
Zabul
Qalat
Spin Boldak
Faryab
Ghor
Deh Kundi
Oruzgan
Tarin Kowt
Kandahar
Kandahar
Badghis
Deh Rawood
Lashkar Gar
Helmand
Herat
Herat
Shindand
Farah
Farah
Nimroz

Afghanistan Provinces and Major Cities

# CONTENTS

*Preface*                                                                      ix

1. Stories of Afghanistan                                                       **1**
2. The Security Infrastructure of Post-Taliban Afghanistan                     **19**
3. Victory over Terrorism in the Presidential Election                         **59**
4. Vengeance—The Taliban Strikes Back After the Election                       **86**
5. The Assembly Elections                                                     **117**
6. Prospects for Afghan Democracy                                             **143**

*Index*                                                                        171

# PREFACE

This book is designed to relate the exciting transition of one of the poorest countries in the world to democratic governance. Leaving its tradition of the anarchic chaos and "might-makes-right" regimes of the past, Afghanistan's movement to self-governance is as revolutionary as any other in history. The change is more dramatic than the American Revolution, when the new American democracy maintained a representative form of government similar to our British roots in developing its new Constitution. The change is also more positive than the French Revolution, which resurged into tyranny and anarchy at various points. The Afghan Revolution of democratic governance, albeit aided and guided by international military and political powers, is thus one of the most historic events of our time.

Written by a U.S. Army military intelligence officer, the discussion herein provides readers a candid and frank account of Afghanistan's first presidential election and transition to democratic self-governance. In particular, I speak to the security apparatus and measures protecting the election. The election security process was a culminating defeat for the al Qaeda and Taliban terrorist insurgents attempting to frustrate Afghanistan's development into a democratic nation. This narrative on Afghan development is interspersed with firsthand, personal accounts of my ten-month deployment as an officer serving in the U.S. military in Afghanistan. Embedded with the United Nations in a civilian-clothes role, I can also speak from the perspective of a UN security officer and bring some added experience to which most soldiers are not exposed on the battlefield.

I have tried to make this "ground truth" as much as possible. So while this book is the story of the security efforts that led to the internationally acclaimed success of the historic Afghan elections process, I am also sharing my personal story and personal experiences. A firsthand account like this has the advantage of immediate relation to the events involved, but it is just one person's experience, and in that way, a "snapshot" of the moment in history upon which it is based. This book will hopefully tell the story of a nation and at the same time give you insight into the life of one soldier during his service to a country at war.

I would like to express my sincere appreciation to several people without whom this book would not have been possible. First and foremost, I must thank the many people whose stories and opinions appear throughout the book. I would also like to express my gratitude with the following authors who shared their advice freely: Cole Kingseed, Nathaniel Fick, Andrew Exum, and Anita Gandolfo (to whom I owe a special thank you). Hilary Claggett of Greenwood is an exceptional editor and has been a tremendously helpful partner throughout the entire process. Nicole Azze of Greenwood and Saloni Jain of Aptara were extremely helpful in the production phase, ensuring the book made it to the finish line. Finally, two very good friends, Jennifer Walton and Linda Nguyen, amazed me by their willingness to help, conscientiousness, and uncanny ability to identify my mistakes, making this book so much better because of their thoughtful suggestions.

# CHAPTER 1

# Stories of Afghanistan

The presidential election was a crucial milestone and culminating point in the international intervention in Afghanistan, the development and reconstruction process there, and the fight against al Qaeda and international Islamist terrorist organizations. The election would be a clear step forward for Afghanistan as a democratic nation capable of self-governance in the modern Western model. It would also be an opportunity for the public to ratify the new beginnings for Afghanistan by participating in the vote. The Taliban insurgency and its allies had decided to make the election a focal point as well. They were massing their efforts to disrupt the election, derail the democratization process, embarrass the foreign Western interlopers, and to set conditions for the reemergence of a Muslim state. The United Nations was conducting several development operations in Afghanistan in 2004, but it recognized supporting the elections as its most important role. Similarly, the international military presence in Afghanistan, led by the United States, placed the successful Afghan presidential election as its highest priority. A month before the November 2004 U.S. election, the Afghan milestone could either be a visible and substantial demonstration of progress or a serious setback for the credibility of the American government under the Bush Administration.

I spent ten months in Afghanistan serving in several different capacities as a military intelligence captain in the U.S. Army. This narrative will describe my experiences during this deployment. Being responsible for intelligence for the Afghan election gave me insights into the democratic process for the country as well as key events leading up to the election. These are some of the principal themes of this book. But first, I am going to tell the story of four Afghans whose paths crossed mine during my visit to their country: Zali Kha, a small girl in a remote province; Khoshall Murad, a young man yearning for a better Afghanistan; Siddiqa Sahar Gul, a young woman working in a system of new rights and freedoms for women; and Lieutenant Colonel Abdul Mohammed, a battle-hardened military officer desperately fighting for his new country.

## STORIES OF FOUR AFGHANS

Much of the story I will relate herein is a story of people in Afghanistan. Many people have struggled to improve their lives, and the challenge of the war against the Taliban is at the same time one of the most significant opportunities that the people have had, in some cases, in their entire lives. I was able to meet four of these people, and I share their struggles with you because they inspired me.

### The Young Girl, Zali Kha

I spent some time in the western province of Farah, which was not a Taliban stronghold. Afghanistan's western neighbor, Iran, also opposed the Taliban due to the conflict between the two competing Muslim sects, the Sunni and Shia. This led to less Taliban presence in the area. While drugs and organized crime presented major security challenges to the military forces there, the lack of a strong Taliban presence provided opportunities for development and reconstruction assistance.

In a small village outside Farah City, the provincial capital, I accompanied a civil affairs team and met Zali Kha, a girl about ten years old with a severely disfigured face due to a cleft lip. On a mission several weeks before, the team had been visiting several villages to drop humanitarian assistance equipment in January 2005. A young infantryman, Specialist Tim Johnson from the Minnesota National Guard, had seen the disfigured young girl and surreptitiously taken her photograph on his digital camera. When he returned to the headquarters compound, he approached his chain of command with the photograph to see if anything could be done to help the girl. Captain Winnie Paul, an active-duty medical officer from Hawaii stationed in Farah, approached a plastic surgeon at the military headquarters in Bagram Air Base. The surgeon, who was preparing to return to Hawaii, agreed to do the surgery for the young girl before his return home.

Having arranged the surgery, Captain Paul, the civil affairs noncommissioned officer, Sergeant David Farrands of the New York Army Reserves in Rochester, a translator, and I met with Zali Kha's uncle Mamad Tahir. He was a tall, thin man with curly, jet-black hair, a full beard, thick lips, and a receding hairline. Tahir was speaking for the girl's interests in the absence of her father, Mamad Nasir, who was away from the village at the time. The team approached the uncle and asked him whether he wanted the surgery done. He smiled a shy smile and looked at us with his eyes wide open with a sincere and pleased gaze. He replied, "Shuh," expressing the Pashtun affirmative without hesitation. As we walked through the village, I saw some children sitting against a building, and Zali Kha, really a cute little girl in a feminine traditional Afghan dress, was self-consciously covering her mouth with her hand, perhaps divining that the conversation between the foreigners and her uncle had something to do with her. What made the situation even more remarkable was that the U.S. government, through the military bureaucracy that made decisions in Afghanistan, refused to pay to transport the girl from the village in Farah to the military airport in Shindand from where she could fly to Bagram. So the soldiers in Sergeant Ferrand and Specialist Johnson's unit raised three hundred dollars from their own money to hire a taxi to transport Zali Kha and an adult male family member to the airport.

## The Young Man, Khoshall Murad

In Kabul, I met a young Afghan man who is still friends with me today. Khoshall Murad was a driver for the UN elections team when I first met him on Election Day at the ballot counting center at the south end of Kabul. I remember him on the first day we met as taciturn, an ardent Karzai supporter who did not waste words. He was thin with deep-set, dark eyes and an angular face. His hair was cut and combed neatly, a little longer than average on the top. Murad would later move to the Joint Electoral Management Body headquarters, where he would work as a security guard. Eventually, my partner and I would engage Murad as a language tutor in our efforts to familiarize ourselves with the Pashtun language. As an ethnic Pashtun, he could speak that language as well as the other main Afghan language, Dari. As I got to know Murad better, I would find that my first impression was misleading because it did not reveal his true personality. He turned out to be loquacious, outgoing, and enthusiastic almost to a fault.

He would accept no payment for his services in language tutoring, but we often gave him gifts of food and drove him home at the end of the day to save him taxi fare. We also tried to get him a job to teach Pashtun or Dari for Central Texas College, which offered courses at the base in Kabul. During the period of my deployment when we worked with Murad, my partner and I traveled in civilian clothes in a dark blue Ford Ranger pickup truck with no license plates. Driving in the outer neighborhoods of the city, the truck fit in with other dented, dirty, old automobiles crowding the streets. While we did not look the part of Afghans, our clothes and our ride likely marked us as foreign aid workers or engineers.

The first time we dropped off Murad at his home, he invited us in to see the house. It was down an unpaved road with rows of mud houses. Murad's own home was made of mud and had no electricity except for that produced by a small generator. He used this for a space heater in his room, which had a massive red carpet in the Afghan style, or what many Western people would consider a Persian rug. As we drove away, children chased our vehicle and jumped on the back. They also playfully tried to open the doors. We always kept the doors locked as a basic precaution, so the children were unable to get in. As we pulled back onto the main paved road, they jumped off the truck and went back to their games.

Murad also taught us much about life in Afghanistan. He was unfailingly cheerful, a trait for which he received some degree of ridicule from the international UN security staff who worked in the office. I found it ironic since Murad had been so aloof on the day I had first met him. His full name, Khoshall Murad, seems a great fit for his personality because the word *khoshall* means happy in Pashtun.

Murad had taught English to women during the time of the Taliban, which was a crime punishable by death. He is strongly committed to a new Afghanistan that allows more freedoms and a better standard of life for its citizens. Murad was engaged to be married, and he told me a story that showed how even in post-Taliban Afghanistan, people could be routinely detained for "un-Islamic" activities. He was in a public park in Kabul with his fiancée. Their seemingly harmless chatting resulted in a Kabul policeman fining my friend for some nominal fee. The fine was levied for appearing in public with a woman who was not his wife or a member of his family. I suspect that this was also an example of low-level graft, as I cannot imagine the policeman depositing this "fine" with the government, but I could be mistaken in this suspicion.

Murad had also shown us around Kabul and taken us shopping in districts where international visitors do not often go. I took a photograph with him in front of the Kabul Olympic Stadium, an impressive structure given its surroundings, but actually in more disrepair than most American high school athletic complexes. When it was time for me to leave Kabul, I printed the photo of Murad and myself and put it inside a binder used for Army awards. It was green plastic with a gold United States Army crest on the front, and it opened like a book. I put the photo on one side and a note of admiration for his work and ideals on the other side. The gift touched Murad deeply, and we still exchange e-mails today in spite of the difficulties for him in doing so.

## The Young Woman, Siddiqa Sahar

Another remarkable person I met was a young female Afghan secretary of a senior UN official. Her boss was Gary Helseth, the director of the UN Office for Projects and Services (UNOPS) in Afghanistan and several other countries, and as this agency assumed more control of operations, and specifically elections-related activities, in Afghanistan in early 2005, I often visited the office. The young Afghan, Siddiqa Sahar Gul,[1] was one of the most beautiful women I had ever met. She had long, dark brown hair, high cheekbones, striking brown eyes, and an incredible smile. Åsne Seierstad's bestseller, *The Bookseller of Kabul*, describes another Afghan beauty, Khadija, and the description rang true with Siddiqa. "Khadija . . . looks as if she could have posed for photographers all her life. But, according to Afghan standards, she is not very pretty; she is too thin, too narrow. The ideal Afghan woman is round: round cheeks, round hips, round tummy." When I visited the UNOPS headquarters, I would often chat with Siddiqa, asking her about where she was from and how she enjoyed her work. I thought she might be from an Eastern European country, one of the many UN workers traveling from all over the world to serve in Afghanistan. I was shocked to learn that she was Afghan, and I tried to be sensitive to the norms of the country.

When James Michener's main character in his classic *Caravans* met a young woman named Siddiqa, he was dazzled by her latent sensuality. My Siddiqa was beautiful beyond my capability to describe on these pages, but she seemed innocent and shy to the point of being incapable of flirtation. I approached her with only the harmless enjoyment that a man gets from making conversation with such a beautiful woman, and I asked her about her family and upbringing and life under the former Taliban regime.

Siddiqa shared an office with a young American woman, Alexis Bonnell, probably about twenty-five years of age, who served as the executive assistant to the UNOPS director. (Alexis' formal title was Strategic Communications Advisor, and, unlike Sidiqqa, flirtation was a hobby for Alexis.) Alexis was responsible for coordinating meetings, serving as a gatekeeper for her boss's time, and taking care of various tasks that needed to be accomplished. Her position as executive assistant to a leader high in the organization's bureaucracy reminded me of articles I had read in the business sections of magazines such as *Newsweek*, describing how entrepreneurial young professionals would find such positions to jump several rungs up the corporate ladder. Exposure to the rigors and intricacies of a CEO's daily routine—as well as contact with senior leaders in the organization—give such young professionals an edge as they move into positions of increasing responsibility. In the military, the young captain who serves as a general's aide-de-camp similarly is competitively selected for the job and often later rises through the ranks himself.

We often worked with Alexis to satisfy her boss's requests or to make requests of our own. In the final weeks of my stay in Kabul, I took photographs of the people with whom I had worked. After I took a photo with Alexis, I asked her officemate, Siddiqa, if she would like to be in a photograph.

---

[1] I have changed this woman's name in this account to protect her from any extremists who would do harm to her for her efforts as a woman working to rebuild Afghanistan.

She seemed embarrassed and did not know how to answer this question, but Alexis prompted her, "Siddiqa, you love to have your picture taken! Go ahead!"

Photos are perhaps still a bit taboo in Afghanistan. The Taliban had outlawed them because they believe that representing images of people is sacrilegious. In addition, women still cover their faces to protect themselves from male scrutiny when outdoors. But with Alexis's encouragement, Siddiqa allowed me to take her picture. I think that Siddiqa had some idea of how attractive she was by Western standards. With the United Nations and the other international presence in Afghanistan had come Western media forms that would perhaps shape Afghan notions of beauty, at least for those living in the relatively cosmopolitan capital city.

On my last day in Kabul, I visited Siddiqa and presented her with her photograph in an awards frame as I had given Murad. Although this photograph was only of her, I had learned that Afghans value photographs in spite (or perhaps because) of the Taliban's prohibition on possessing them. I suspect that Siddiqa earned somewhere around three hundred dollars a month. Even with purchasing power parity, this does not leave much money for luxuries such as personal photos. Since it was my last day, I had left my civilian dress that I had used for the last several months. I was wearing my Army uniform, the desert fatigues that had by then become common to the peoples of Afghanistan and Iraq. She asked, "Did you join the U.S. Army?" I explained to her that I had always been in the Army but had been working with the United Nations. On the facing page of the award book, I wrote a message about my admiration for Siddiqa's courage as a woman in Afghanistan doing the important work for reform. I also daringly wrote in Pashtun the word for "flower," which won me a shy but pleased smile. (Siddiqa, who was an ethnic Tajik, did not speak Pashtun, although she knew a few words and phrases and recognized this word. Since Murad was teaching me Pashtun, she and I would occasionally exchange a few phrases to help me practice. Due to Murad's instruction, I could occasionally teach her a new phrase.)

A few weeks later, when I had left Kabul for the frontier region of Khost, I would be surprised by an e-mail from an officer named Craig Gilbert, who served as a uniformed military liaison to the United Nations. He was catching up with me on how things were going, and he told me that on a visit to Gary's office, Siddiqa recognized his Army uniform and asked him to pass a message that she wanted to get in touch with me and for him to give me her e-mail address. So I e-mailed Siddiqa to ask how she was doing. She responded to me, and although her English was imperfect, it far exceeded my abilities in Afghan languages and effectively communicated her meaning:

Wow, so Nice to hear from u. Hope you doing fine down there. Yes that is right that I was trying to find any contact from u to be in touch with u thanks a lot and (*deera manana*) [Pashtun version of "thank you very much"] to sent me this mail u know on that day when u brought my photo and u went back but from that time since now I feel you and thinking about you that how kind you are and that is why I ask your e-mail address from your friend. To say thanks from bottom of my heart. Thanks again this my number . . . .

We corresponded over the next few months, and I learned more of Afghanistan from Siddiqa. She did not like talking about politics, but she did tell me much of her everyday experiences. Her father was in a deep depression, and this made Siddiqa, a twenty-three-year-old girl, the sole breadwinner for the family. Eventually, she hoped to pursue an education. She wanted a degree in computer science. There were such educational establishments in Kabul that offered courses in English and computers. I think that the unfamiliar technology was an attractive subject matter for Afghans.

At times, her e-mails saddened. " . . . Last week two singers came from Germany . . . I really like these 2 singer I mean their voices make calm when I am hearing their songs but unfortunately I can't attend in these concerts I am very sad and I hate this life that I have." There was nothing I felt I could do for her because this was the culture in which she lived. She told me that some officials in the United Nations were considering offering her a position at their office in Dubai. Since she supported her father, mother, brothers, and sister, a position with better income would be a big help. She began signing off e-mails with her middle name, Sahar. I was confused and asked her about her names. She explained, "Siddiqa my parents put this name to me it means honest and Sahar my friends call me by this name—I mean my best friends—it means Morning."

After I returned to Hawaii, Sahar and I lost the habit of writing to one another, and eventually we stopped altogether. When I tried to contact her about a year after we had last seen each other, her e-mail (which was the UNOPS e-mail account) no longer worked, and her cell phone did not work either. I am hoping that this means that Sahar is in a better paying position in Dubai, studying computer science, and sending surplus earnings to her family in Kabul.

## The Afghan Officer, Abdul Mohammed

Lieutenant Colonel Abdul Mohammed[2] was an Afghan National Army intelligence officer who was quick to share information with me to pass along to the Coalition forces. He had sources from Kabul to Peshawar, Pakistan,

---

[2] The names Abdul Mohammed and Aziz Hassan are given to protect the true identities of the Afghan National Army officers because of their relationship with U.S. government intelligence services.

and he was constantly getting reports on the enemy's plans. He was a striking figure, towering above his Afghan National Army counterparts, who for the most part were of slightly less than average height. Abdul Mohammed had a trimmed mustache and a friendly smile. He also had dark, threatening eyes that seemed to indicate his earlier military experience in Afghanistan's turbulent past. I spoke Pashtun to Abdul and his colleagues whenever I got the chance. It built rapport and brought me into their trust.

Lieutenant Colonel Aziz Hassan seemed to be Lieutenant Colonel Abdul Mohammed's right-hand man. Whenever Abdul would provide an intelligence report, Hassan was close at hand, looking over Abdul's shoulder with a ubiquitous friendly smile. Hassan did not seem to say as much as Abdul, but he loved that I spoke a few phrases of Pashtun. He was quick to respond to "*Sahar de pa khayr sha* [good morning]," "*shpa de pa khayr* [good night]," and "*khu de pah amaan* [good bye]." He was even more excited when I tried less common phrases, such as "*manana staa la ko mak tseka* [thank you for your help]" or "*khosh hala che taa sara gorum* [it is nice to meet you]." He frequently asked me, "*Tsenga-ye?*" At first, my novitiate knowledge of the language failed to register, but I quickly recovered, realizing he asked me, "How are you?" "*Za kha yum, manana, te tsenga-ye?* [I'm fine, thanks, how are you?]" I replied. He was eager to help me with my pronunciation and seemed pleased by my efforts.

In one of the quieter days after the election, he explained to me (this time with a translator assisting) that he was an ethnic Pashtun. Afghanistan is a bilingual country, where the Dari language dominates government and public discourse. Pashtun is somewhat marginalized, but it is the language of the Taliban and the wild region between Afghanistan and Pakistan where the terrorists are hiding. Only a handful of American universities even try to teach courses in Pashtun. These were among the reasons I chose to try to learn some of the language (realizing that also pursuing Dari, as well as any of the other minor languages of Afghanistan, would be a hopelessly confusing effort). Hassan was proud to tell me that his four-year-old son was already conversant in both languages, noting that they spoke Pashtun in the home because Dari was the language of the streets in Kabul. I shared with him that in the United States many Spanish-speaking families choose to do the same, preserving their ethnic heritage in the home, counting on the public to familiarize the young with English.

His talk of his family had piqued my curiosity, so I asked him whether his wife wore the burkha. There were many more women wearing the light blue symbol of Afghanistan's female oppression than I had realized. Before coming here, I had read that the southern provinces, surrounding the former Taliban stronghold, Kandahar, had more restrictive religious traditions. It was surprising to see that in the allegedly more cosmopolitan capital, Kabul, burkha-clad women could be constantly seen roaming the streets. I was equally surprised when this Afghan National Army senior officer, an avowed and complete loyalist to President Karzai and opponent of the Taliban, revealed that his wife wore the traditional garb. I suspect his Pashtun ethnicity had something to do with it, but there is no doubt that even among the part of the population most enlightened by Western standards, the burkha is commonplace.

It is interesting to observe that this repression of female sexuality seems to result in a male homoerotic sexuality that is often ridiculed by the homophobic American military. It is customary to see men holding hands in public, and the men like to talk very close and touch frequently when conversing. The close proximity in communication can be a challenge for the foreigner who hopes not to offend. In a country where the economic level is on par with the poorest countries in Africa, bodily hygiene does not meet Western standards. Walking behind a group of local national workers on Bagram Airfield, I wondered whether any had bathed at all in the past year. This apparently does not hamper interpersonal relations, however, as South African UN worker Samantha Steenkampf informed me that Thursday was "man-love day." I asked her what that means, and she responded, "Exactly what it sounds like." The Islamic Sabbath is Friday, so she explained that Thursday night permitted debauchery that could be cleansed the following day at religious services. I cannot verify this with certainty, and while my Afghan counterparts may have been comfortable with such a conversation topic, I was unwilling to risk offense by asking. In the macho American military, such a question would be grounds to break off all communication.

The repeated references to homosexual behavior comprised one of the most surprising aspects of my yearlong trip to this extremely devout Islamic country. The repression of women gives one a sense of a very repressed, asexual culture. But the experience in Afghanistan contraindicates this perception. There were numerous innocuous examples of this in watching men on the street holding hands. But more disturbing and compelling evidence came from our colleagues who had served in the south. The south of Afghanistan was the center of the former Taliban regime's power. Afghan interpreters there would gleefully sing a "Kandahar man-boy love song," expressing glee at the prospect of heading toward the city where a man can meet a young boy. Kandahar seems to have a reputation for homosexual pedophilia.

*The Bookseller of Kabul* by Åsne Seierstad provides another account of Afghan homosexual license, relating that such behavior is especially common in the southeastern provinces of the country among the militias there. The soldiers who accompanied Rory Stewart on the first part of his walk across Afghanistan, which he recounted in *The Places in Between*, seemed to have similar proclivities, indicating that it may be a common practice in the more cosmopolitan western part of the country as well. Stewart relates a conversation with one of his escorts, Abdul Haq, who was criticizing the other soldier, Qasim, for being unwilling to make part of the journey on foot:

> "Qasim is a woman, right? He can't walk. In fact, he is a queer." He turned to me to illustrate the kinds of things Qasim did with other men. "In fact," he continued, "when we get back I'm going to fuck him. Ahhh," he roared, "what a woman." Silence. Neither of us spoke for some time.

Soldiers and commanders who often spend time away from their homes and families will resort to recreation with effeminate Afghan men. In fact, members of the American human intelligence teams, who more than anyone else work with Afghan interpreters, related to me that the Afghan soldiers who work with international Coalition forces would routinely invade the domicile where the local translators reside and sexually violate the hapless interpreters. This practice is something that only happens to native Afghan interpreters, who nonetheless line up for the privilege of earning about five hundred dollars a month, an exorbitant sum by Afghan standards. (Americans of Afghan descent serving in Afghanistan as interpreters are classified as Category II or Category III interpreters, indicating their higher security clearance. These interpreters are paid in the range of eighty thousand dollars a year and have an excellent standard of living.)

This type of sexual activity is juxtaposed against one of the most misogynistically repressive cultures in the world. Women in the south are not usually seen in public; the infamous burkha is not even seen because women do not come out of doors. When soldiers (or any other outside men) arrive at a village, the women scatter. Pakistani women visiting are more likely to be seen than adult female Afghan residents. As James Michener articulately phrased it, "having removed women from public life, the Afghans realized that feminine traits were nevertheless desirable and so allocated them to men."

To return to Abdul Mohammed, I started working with him in my duties of collecting information from various organizations in the Election Security Operations Center. I asked the J2X, or human intelligence officer, from Joint Task Force Phoenix, for some background on him. Phoenix was the unit that was responsible for training the Afghan National Army, so I hoped that they would have some information that would help me gauge Abdul's reliability. Captain Jeff Hammer, the Indiana National Guardsman serving as Phoenix's J2X, told me that they had been using Abdul for about eight months and found him to be a mostly helpful and reliable source. So I continued to pass Abdul Mohammed's reports to the Coalition, along with the ones from all the organizations working in the security center. He was one of many points of contact for the reports I was fusing, but as a host nation contact, processing reports from Abdul was a more sensitive situation.

After collecting information from Abdul for some time, the Afghan colonel asked me for a telephone calling card so that one of his informants could continue providing information. The ten-dollar phone card was a minimal expense in comparison to the hundreds of millions of dollars being spent on the war in Afghanistan. So I called a senior warrant officer at Bagram in the Human Intelligence Analysis and Requirements Cell (also known as the HARC), explained the situation, and asked him for the phone card. It seemed like Abdul wanted a gesture of goodwill to show that we were placing value on the work he and his informants were doing. After all, they were risking their lives to provide the information that Abdul was reporting to me. On the other hand, in a country with a three hundred dollar per capita annual income, it seemed possible that the informant really needed the ten-dollar phone card to keep reporting. The warrant officer promised me he would send a phone card down to Bagram on the following day.

I passed the promise along to Abdul Mohammed, but the phone card did not arrive. This created some tension with my Afghan counterpart. Abdul kept asking me for the card, and I surmised that part of the problem was driving down from Bagram to Kabul. In the bureaucratic command and staff headquarters, it can be rare to venture outside the secure perimeter without navigating a very risk-averse bureaucracy. (I know many staff and support soldiers who never left Bagram Airfield at all during the 365-day tour in Afghanistan.) I called Captain Kevin Frank, a senior Navy intelligence officer serving in our United Nations higher headquarters, the Strategic Security Group, to see if he had any intelligence contacts in Kabul who could help. He promised to look into the matter to help.

Rather than resulting in a phone card, this inquiry caused the J2X of Combined Forces Command, Air Force Lieutenant Colonel David Lobue, and his Deputy, Major Dana Rucinski, to deny the request for a phone card, tell me to report to his office at my earliest convenience, and apparently stop Lieutenant Colonel Mohammed from reporting information to me. I found out that Mohammed was a contact for the CIA, which was why there was so much consternation over him reporting information to me and requesting incentives for his informants from me. This surprised me because when Abdul Mohammed provided me his first report, I asked him, "Am I the only one to receive this report or are you passing it to other Coalition contacts?" He told me that I was the only person to receive the report.

To this day, I am not sure how I could have, or even if I should have, avoided this problem. Abdul Mohammed had approached me and had begun feeding me information as all the other liaisons in the operations center had been doing. Soon after this series of incidents occurred, Abdul Mohammed told me that someone told Abdul that he was not authorized to provide information to me. (I inferred that this "someone" was Abdul's CIA "handler.") So I followed up with my superiors and Major Rucinski and requested them to send a debriefer to take information from Colonel

Mohammed. After all, he worked in the Election Security Operations Center, along with me and the other components, for thirteen to fourteen hours each day. Abdul spent his days on his cell phone speaking to his contacts and receiving information from them. I was amazed that the top human intelligence officers in Afghanistan, both military and civilian, would have preferred that Abdul's time sensitive threat information should stay with Abdul rather than reaching the field units that might need to act on it in the days leading up to the election. Of course, this experience was consistent with the critical review of the U.S. intelligence community that was being completed at the time in the aftermath of both the September 11th attacks and the faulty information leading to the Iraq war. The intelligence community is often more concerned with bureaucratic procedures and agency turf wars than actually collecting and disseminating actionable intelligence.

## STORIES OF AN AMERICAN OFFICER

Serving in the Global War on Terror was a meaningful experience in my life. After all, I left home in 1995 for West Point and had spent almost ten years studying and practicing the military craft before finally serving in combat. After September 11, 2001, our unit prepared for mobilization but never deployed. In 2002, the division received a request for two military intelligence captains to deploy to Afghanistan in support of a Special Forces unit there, but I was one of many volunteers and again did not go.

When I assumed command of the headquarters company of 125th Military Intelligence Battalion in July 2003, upcoming deployment did not seem probable. The main focus of our unit, stationed in Hawaii, was an increasingly threatening North Korea. In fact, not long before, I had spent the month of March 2003 participating in an exercise in Japan focused on the contingency of North Korea invading the South. This exercise was designed and conducted by strategic military leaders to show the Koreans that American forces were still able to counter the threat that North Korea posed even as 150,000 troops were standing by at the Iraqi border. Of course, when the invasion of Iraq began, few of us in Japan were concentrating on an exercise any longer as we watched the "shock and awe" campaign reported on CNN around the clock. For the units in Hawaii, however, after two years of the Army fighting in the Global War on Terror, it seemed that our lot was continued vigilance against the North Koreans. Perhaps strategic military leaders never intended to call on the units in Hawaii and South Korea that were focused on the Pacific region. As the Iraq war dragged on, however, it became clear that everyone would take his turn overseas.

The goal of my company was to provide service support to the rest of the battalion and to provide administrative support for the battalion command group and staff sections. While the garrison customer support was adequate, the headquarters was physically and mentally unprepared for war. The ongoing Global War on Terror, with most of the Army deployed to dangerous parts of the world, made clear that to ignore combat tasks was painfully irresponsible. Furthermore, the Jessica Lynch episode in March 2003 called attention to the consequences of a service support company woefully unprepared for the hazards of combat. Without an imminent deployment order, our unit—which had not deployed to combat since the Vietnam War—was still plagued with a challenging inertia and a garrison culture. Indeed, my personal experience reinforced the probability of continued garrison life, so I could understand the soldiers' attitudes.

It was a challenge to mobilize 200 soldiers with many diverse missions to accomplish difficult combat training tasks, especially since many of the soldiers were senior leaders or staff with other pressing responsibilities to other constituencies. Nonetheless, being constantly vigilant and ready is the main function of the soldier when not deployed to war.

I was able to accomplish incremental victories to slowly change the culture of the unit to combat orientation. This started with a major live fire exercise within six weeks of assuming command. The exercise focused on the very convoy procedures that would have prevented the capture of Jessica Lynch and her comrades. Live fire exercises are routine military training events in which soldiers maneuver with live rounds in their rifles. It is the highest risk type of training that most soldiers do, as friendly fire, one of the most pressing dangers in actual combat, is also a hazard in these intense training scenarios.

Later events, such as foot marches in rugged mountain terrain instead of on paved roads, hand-to-hand combat training, and even team sports, entailed further changes to develop a warrior spirit in the company. It was clear that the unit culture had shifted when my noncommissioned officers proposed setting up a bayonet assault course. A great combat training event that had been in the back of my mind for a while, the bayonet training was another event that supported the change without even requiring my direct influence. The company's expertise was so respected that when the deployment order for Operation Enduring Freedom—Afghanistan came, my peer company commanders asked me to run convoy live fire exercises for them to prepare them for war. My noncommissioned officers were excited at the prospect of sharing their expertise and enthusiasm as training cadre for our sister units. We trained 300 soldiers from our sister companies before their deployment, which was a satisfying experience. But it was yet more exciting when I joined those soldiers after completing my command.

The following month after relinquishing command to my successor, I deployed to Operation Enduring Freedom—Afghanistan. After coming to Afghanistan, I was surprised by the number of foreign fighters still harassing the local populace and attacking coalition military forces. If not for us engaging them there, surely Chechnyan, Algerian, Egyptian, Arabic, Pakistani, and Uzbek terrorists committed to the bin Laden fatwa calling for death to all Americans would find soft targets in our own homeland. Years after the original American invasion, the insurgency from extremist elements of the former Taliban regime as well as the presence of international terrorists presented a significant challenge to Coalition and Afghan forces.

During my first month in the country, I worked on the "Daily Intelligence Summary," a threat report that was produced each morning for dissemination to the commanders and staff officers of the 25,000 Coalition soldiers of Combined Joint Task Force-76 (CJTF-76). My title was a "Directorate of Intelligence Operations Battle Captain," but I was essentially a newspaper editor responsible for a small team of intelligence soldiers. Each night our twelve-hour shift started, and we reviewed intelligence reports for threats projected for the next twenty-four to forty-eight hours. U.S. Army intelligence is drawn from a variety of "disciplines," including human, imagery, signal, and measures and signatures intelligence. Intelligence collected from various platforms, such as communications intercept systems, aircraft, satellites, and old-fashioned interrogators, is disseminated across the American intelligence community twenty-four hours a day. My team sifted through hundreds of reports each evening to find the most relevant information, add a value-added assessment consistent with the overall CJTF-76 Directorate of Intelligence, and format it in a brief, readable document by morning. It reminded me of a newspaper because the work occurred at night, there was the constant of the morning deadline, and content and formatting issues were central to our work. Spending a month in this position gave me a good overview of the military and political situation in Afghanistan. But working behind a computer through the middle of the night, never leaving the fortress of the Coalition military compound at Bagram Airfield, soon became tedious.

Fortunately, I was tapped to serve as the Director of Intelligence for the Election Security Operations Center, which was a multiagency operations hub tasked with coordinating election security among the various security constituencies in Afghanistan. These included the Combined Forces Command-Afghanistan (CFC), and its subordinate CJTF-76, the multinational but primarily American force responsible for the south, east, and west of the country. Additionally, there was the International Security Assistance Force, a multinational and primarily European force under command of NATO responsible for the capital province of Kabul and the northern sector of the country.

The Election Security Operations Center was run by the United Nations and Afghan Joint Electoral Management Body Secretariat's Security Office, and included representation from CFC, CJTF-76, the International Security Assistance Force, the Afghan Ministry of Defense, and Global Risk Strategies (a private security firm supporting Afghan development). While the Joint Electoral Management Body Secretariat had maintained a Security Office that liaised with all of these elements throughout the election preparation process, for the month of October, the Election Security Operations Center was established to provide a twenty-four hours-a-day capability for information exchange and coordination.

The Joint Electoral Management Body has its origins in the Bonn Agreement, established in December 2001. After the fall of the Taliban, regional leaders of Afghanistan, as well as expatriates and representatives of the exiled monarch, convened in Bonn, Germany, and unanimously established the Bonn Agreement, officially the Agreement on Provisional Arrangement in Afghanistan, Pending the Reestablishment of Permanent Government of Afghanistan. The agreement called for an Emergency *Loya Jirga* (Grand Assembly) to designate a Transitional Authority to lead Afghanistan until a fully representative government could be elected through free and fair elections, which were to be held no later than two years after the *Loya Jirga*.

President Hamid Karzai, selected by the *Loya Jirga* as President of the Transitional Islamic Government of Afghanistan, issued a decree on July 26, 2003, establishing the Interim Afghan Electoral Commission to administer voter registration for the elections. The commission's responsibilities included recruiting civic education and registration staff, advising the government on the preparation of electoral law, and preparing for the elections. In order to strengthen the mechanism for overseeing the conduct of the voter registration for the 2004 general elections, the president also issued a second Decree on the same day (which would be subsequently amended on February 18, 2004) to create the Joint Electoral Management Body. The Joint Electoral Management Body consisted of eleven members, six being the Commissioners of the Electoral Commission and five international electoral experts appointed by the UN Special Representative of the Secretary General for Afghanistan. The Secretariat of the Joint Electoral Management Body was responsible for actually carrying out these responsibilities.

There were instances of tension that I observed between some workers in the United Nations system and the international military present in Kabul. Perhaps tension is too strong a word, but there were definite indications of differing perspectives. The status of detainees at U.S. military facilities in Afghanistan and at Guantanamo Bay, Cuba, was a key sticking point for several of the UN staff, as was the "illegal war" in Iraq. After the election, I would move on to be a liaison officer to the United Nations in Kabul from the Combined Joint Task Force-76 headquarters at Bagram Airfield. Gabrielle Ibarne, the UN human rights officer for one of eight UN regional offices in Afghanistan, expressed her concern over the matter. I think this was in some ways just venting, or making conversation, because she was aware that I, as an Army captain, did not have control or the slightest influence over Defense Department policy. She nonetheless insisted that if the detainees are being held, they should be charged with something, or if there was nothing to charge them with, then they should be released. The argument makes sense, but publicly charging these detainees and proving the charges would result in compromising intelligence collection methods. This legalistic approach in the 1990s tipped terrorist organizations to their vulnerabilities, and they have become so much harder to track as successful American efforts in monitoring terrorists were subsequently revealed in legal proceedings.

Major Timothy Barrick was one of the few Marine Corps officers who could be seen striding around the Army-dominated Joint Headquarters at Bagram Airbase. He was a planner serving in the CJ35, or the combined joint planning section. He had a calm, reassuring presence and rarely let the tensions around him ruffle his demeanor. He had an athletic build and slightly underaverage height. He had clear blue eyes and a bald spot on the top of his head and a slightly receding hairline. With his Marine Corps crew cut, this was not as noticeable as it might otherwise be.

Tim was consistently one of the key players in the Election Security Operations Center. Although he worked primarily in a liaison function for the American-led task force, his knowledge of Afghanistan and his strong sense of how to run the operations center contributed to the overall effort. In the course of working together, I found out that we had crossed paths a few years before. In March 2003, I was deployed to Yokota Air Base, Japan, for a strategic military exercise focused on the North Korea contingency. Tim had also deployed for that mission from his home station in Okinawa. Although working maybe a hundred meters apart, we did not interact in that earlier exercise, however, because of the large, bureaucratic nature of such joint military headquarters operations. Another Marine officer, Captain Clinton Culp, served as the long-time liaison to the Joint Electoral Management Body. His earlier mission had been training Afghan National Army forces in the rural areas of Afghanistan, and his months with the United Nations afterwards gave him a breadth of experience that made him an essential player in the Election Security Operations Center. A right-hand man for Major Tim Barrick, Clinton was confident in himself and aware of the situation in Afghanistan. He could navigate the UN bureaucracy, although he was somewhat jaded after his time with the United Nations. "I thought the military was bad," he told me, "but that was before I started working with the UN." Our UN colleagues acknowledged Clint's cynicism with a good humor, themselves often critical of UN ineffectiveness.

Tim was called a "super star" by several of the people we worked with in Kabul. Often, senior military leaders will make wild exaggerations in public settings. Any issue that has captured their current attention becomes the most important issue facing the unit (from weapons safety, to transportation efficiency, to soldiers washing their hands before meals). With the myriad of issues facing modern military organizations, the whole concept of setting priorities seriously suffers. Similarly, when recognizing the accomplishments of a particular person in a public setting, a commander will laud that individual as the best he has worked with or the best in the Army. It is difficult to envision so many concurrent top priorities and so many best people. Both of these difficulties make any sort of comparison almost entirely meaningless. It also calls into question the sincerity of a whole class of professionals for whom honesty and integrity are a defining feature of self-identity. In Tim's case, however, the compliments were not exaggerated. Aside from my personal observations, I heard candid respect paid to Tim Barrick from leaders of partner organizations such as the United Nations and foreign militaries, from junior-ranking American military, and from senior American officers in both public and private settings.

Major Barrick exemplified the process of American military support and coordination for a United Nations operation. His input largely directed what would happen, even though the election was not a Coalition military, but rather a UN, operation. Much of the election process similarly relied on international military expertise and support. The airflow planning was accomplished with the help of two American lieutenants, and many of the ballots, especially those coming from out-of-country voting in Pakistan and Iran, were delivered by military aircraft. The security infrastructure was thoroughly fashioned around the international military structure in Afghanistan, which, as I related earlier, was entirely focused on protecting the election.

My role, serving as a liaison officer from the Directorate of Intelligence of the CJTF-76 headquarters at Bagram, expanded like Tim's had. I was responsible for coordinating all information operations for the Elections Security Operations Center and conducting analysis to mitigate possible threats. There were several people I worked with in order to conduct analysis. My right-hand man was an Army sergeant first class, Eduardo Velez, who had one of the best senses of humor in Afghanistan. We also worked with several United Nations and foreign military counterparts.

After the election ended, I stayed in Kabul with the United Nations. I exchanged my tan battle dress uniform for the casual civilian attire worn by the international community in Afghanistan. I had a desk in the UN elections security office and was charged by the intelligence officers at the Bagram headquarters to collect intelligence from the various international organizations working in Kabul. I grew my hair long, dressed the part, and made connections to develop information for the planners at Bagram. A few weeks later, three UN elections workers would be captured, and this would comprise my major focus for my time in Kabul after the election. This story will follow in Chapter 4. Finally, in March 2005, I moved to Forward Operating Base Salerno, next to the border town of Khost, where I put on the uniform again to serve in a conventional role. Most of the committed terrorist leaders who lived in Afghanistan before the invasion currently live in the region of Pakistan across the border from Khost and other cities like it. Our mission would be to repel these attackers as they crossed the border from Pakistan to conduct attacks on Afghans, and this will be a major focus of Chapter 5.

The presidential election in October 2004 was the primary focus of all the security forces in Afghanistan during that time, and the Elections Security Operations Center, ultimately a UN-led organization, was the hub of those security forces. Over the years since the ouster of the Taliban in 2001, the security posture of the country had changed. It is still evolving, with the ultimate goal of minimizing reliance on international security forces in order to allow the indigenous forces to become self-reliant in preventing a resurgence of Islamic extremist tyranny in the country. Such a resurgence would certainly be sympathetic to terrorists focused on attacking the United States and its global allies and interests. While at the very top of the security priorities in Afghanistan as the date neared, the election and its security apparatus were only part of a complex security and stability network. The following chapter will expound on the international military presence in Afghanistan.

# CHAPTER 2

# The Security Infrastructure of Post-Taliban Afghanistan

The U.S. government is a dizzying bureaucracy of agencies and programs, many of which overlap one another, and the American intervention in Afghanistan is a microcosm of this massive bureaucracy. It is hard to explain the many competing and cooperating units and agencies in Afghanistan, and even harder to understand them and their purpose. When one adds the international forces and political organizations, along with nongovernmental organizations and private businesses, the situation becomes even more difficult to follow. I will try to lay out a summary here that will include the key players and their roles, while omitting the smaller and less important organizations. Such less salient groups, for purposes of both space and the limited attention of the human reader, divert from the overall goal of establishing background to describe the security team that defeated the Taliban and its allies by successfully protecting the Afghan election process.

## THE INTERNATIONAL MILITARY

There are two primary foreign military missions in Afghanistan, the American-led Coalition, and the NATO-led International Security Assistance Force (ISAF). The country is divided into regional commands as well as other functional commands. We will explore the main commands of the Coalition and ISAF and then outline the regional division of the country. Finally, we will look at the other commands and their specific areas of responsibility.

The Coalition is part of the widely touted effort to combat terrorism worldwide, and various countries, including perhaps unexpected ones such as France and Egypt, participate in the Coalition. (France had Special Forces teams operating in the south near the Pakistani border as well as embedded trainers with Afghan National Army, and Egypt had a military hospital in the headquarters at Bagram Airfield.) The Coalition was established mainly to prevent the resurgence of Taliban and al Qaeda influence, while the International Security Assistance Force had more of a nation-building mandate. ISAF was introduced in Afghanistan's capital at the same time that active combat continued in other parts of the country under a different chain of command, and this presented (and continues to present) huge challenges to civil-military coordination. ISAF is an international civil-military structure similar to the Stabilization Force (SFOR) in Bosnia. Initially, ISAF was restricted to the capital with a six-month mandate. This caused controversy over whether ISAF or a follow-up operation would be introduced elsewhere. A debate also arose over whether reliance on a security force was the best way to restore stability or whether higher priority should be given to training indigenous military and police forces. One of the major difficulties presented by ISAF is the dual military chain-of-command, with the American-led Coalition antiterrorist mission and the rotating European-led peace operation, ISAF. (ISAF was under French command at the beginning of my tour in Afghanistan, and Turkey assumed responsibility about halfway through my deployment rotation.)

Practically, the differences between the missions of the Coalition and the International Security Assistance Force are not so clear. The main point that distinguishes them is geographic areas of responsibility. The Coalition was responsible for the south, east, and west parts of the country, while ISAF oversaw the capital, Kabul, and its surrounding countryside and the north. ISAF took over the west of the country in the summer of 2005. The Coalition also engaged in rebuilding and development operations in its areas. While ISAF did not hunt terrorists with the same aggression as the American-led Coalition, in my opinion, the conventional forces of the Coalition also did not hunt terrorists with the aggression that many American citizens and members of the media believe. I expected a much more aggressive counterterrorist effort before arriving here, but this was not the case. Only specialized units and troops are devoted to these missions, and there is a demarcation between them and the majority of the Coalition forces operating in Afghanistan.

The Coalition is commanded by the Combined Forces Command (CFC), an ad hoc headquarters unit commanded by a three-star general. It is somewhat unusual that the CFC was responsible for the exact same geographical area as its subordinate command, Combined Joint Task Force-76 (known in brief as CJTF-76). CJTF-76 was commanded by a two-star general. Another unusual feature of the command structure followed from the fact that the two elements were responsible for the same geographical area; CFC has no other maneuver units to control. While this was a frustrating organizational design for many staff officers (and perhaps for the commanders as

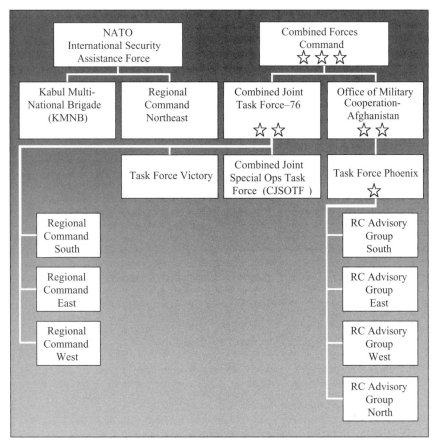

Organizational Structure of International Military in Afghanistan.

*Note:* This figure outlines the major units discussed in this chapter. It is neither an exhaustive nor exact display of all the units in Afghanistan in 2004–2005, but it gives the reader an idea of the bureaucratic challenges faced. The U.S. Embassy, "Other Government Agencies," and "Other Coalition Forces" are not displayed on this graphic because although they were important, their relationships to the other elements were not always clearly defined.

well, although I do not have the privilege of insight into their thoughts), the system did have some advantages. Even though the geographic areas of responsibility overlap, the higher CFC headquarters was able to deflect some of the political issues and coordination that would otherwise distract the subordinate Combined Joint Task Force-76 from operational and tactical concerns.

This appearance of superfluous echelons was repeated at lower levels as well. CJTF-76 (previously known as CJTF-180) commanded one United States Army light infantry brigade, which was the primary maneuver force in Afghanistan. Although there are other elements from other branches of service, other national militaries, and other agencies of the United States government, the land maneuver component was largely composed of an infantry brigade. Thus, as the American intervention in Afghanistan built up after the September 11th attacks, one three-star general supervised one two-star general, who supervised one colonel. This is different from most military hierarchies, where there are usually multiple, identical maneuver units at lower levels. (This is why these hierarchies are usually called pyramid structures.)

CJTF-76 was primarily comprised of the 25th Infantry Division from Hawai'i during my deployment, commanded by Major General Rick Olsen. The division had not deployed to combat since the Vietnam War, and the unit was plagued with a garrison culture that veterans of other units were quick and vociferous in criticizing. The 25th—or Tropic Lighting—Division had deployed to Haiti, but that brief stability and support operation did not hold the allure or esteem of Desert Storm, or even the shorter interventions in Panama or Granada, among the military's warrior culture. The end result was an infantry division with little unit experience outside of brief training events on a small, remote island without much training land available.

In garrison, it seemed one of the biggest command priorities in the unit was to ensure cars did not park on the grass on the installation, which, judging by the mass of cars parked on the grass, was apparently short on parking. The base is almost one hundred years old, and the Army's infrastructure throughout the country needs renewal, so the lack of available parking is not surprising. After deploying, traffic was another major issue for the 25th headquarters as speed traps were set up throughout Bagram Air Field. I was never pulled over during my occasional trips to Bagram, but it was easy to drive by and see some hapless military vehicle operator on the side of the road with the military police. I suppose this enforcement promoted discipline and safety at the headquarters compound, but the last thing I expected to see on a military base in a combat zone was a flashing speed sign at the side of a road telling you the speed of your car.

By the end of 2004, the CJTF-76 commander supervised three regional commanders, each a colonel in charge of a nominal brigade. This expansion occurred not so much because new forces arrived in country, but because of a "restructuring" of the existing troops in Afghanistan. First, a Regional Command East was established under the command of the divisional artillery brigade (or divarty) commander, reapportioning the command of the existing light infantry battalions, and using field artillery soldiers in light infantry capacity. This command was responsible for the turbulent "P2K" area (named for the three Afghan provinces Paktika, Paktya, and Khost), where many Taliban insurgents and al Qaeda foreign fighters flow across the border from Pakistan's North Waziristan Agency. Colonel Gary Cheek was the commander of this task force, called Task Force Thunder, and he was extremely pleased to have had the opportunity for this command. Heavy artillery is not often used in the counterinsurgency environment that characterizes the Afghan conflict, and there is no need for a theater-level artillery coordinator, which is the role that the divarty headquarters traditionally served. Thus, Colonel Cheek explained to me later in the deployment that in the months leading up to the 25th Infantry Division's rotation he had asked Major General Olsen to find a role for his headquarters. He had offered creative ideas such as overseeing the civil affairs units in the country. So when the opportunity arrived to command an actual maneuver brigade, Colonel Cheek was excited to serve and lobbied hard to make sure his headquarters was selected for the task.

This freed the commander of the light infantry brigade headquartered in Kandahar, the former Taliban capital, to focus on operations in the south, allowing him to expand into Oruzgan Province, establishing a base at the city of Tarin Kowt. A several-years-long construction project is currently underway on a paved roadway connecting Kandahar to Tarin Kowt. Thus, the infantry brigade commander assumed control of Regional Command South.

The development of the third Regional Command in the west is the most difficult to understand from an organizational standpoint, seemingly a completely fabricated and superfluous headquarters of a very temporary duration. The western province of Herat is possibly the most prosperous in the country, enjoying the flow of trade with its neighbor Iran and the protection of a strongman named Ismail Khan. A large man with a white beard, several of the enlisted soldiers had nicknamed him the "Afghan Santa Claus" because of the resemblance. Ismail Khan was the regional leader of Herat for many years. ("Regional leader" is a euphemistic term for "local warlord." While the military claims to be a candid and bluntly honest organization, political correctness is a part of the bureaucracy. However, in a briefing I attended, a three-star intelligence general justified the practice of avoiding the term warlord because he argued that such leaders must have a chance to transform themselves, and the old labels would hold them back).

Ismail Khan is well respected among Afghans for his successful efforts to repel Soviet invaders in the 1980s. At that time he developed connections with neighboring Iran that he likely still maintains today. After the Soviets finally pulled out of Afghanistan, Ismail Khan continued to maintain his power, successfully resisting the chaotic civil war that followed. Even during the regime of the Taliban, Khan was able to maintain a semiautonomous Herat Province and was able to prevent his people from being subjected to the extent of poverty and repression that the Taliban-controlled southern and eastern parts of the country experienced.

When Afghanistan reformed into a transitional representative government under the post-Taliban Bonn Agreement, Ismail Khan was a regional leader unwilling to release all of his power to a central government. Ismail Khan's violent conflict with an opposing regional warlord, Amanullah Khan, in the summer of 2004, did not help assuage Karzai's doubts about this governor. The tensions between Khan and the Karzai administration were heightening during fall 2004 as the presidential election approached. American military leaders were strongly advising that President Karzai wait until after the election to pursue any intentions to sack Ismail Khan, an authority granted to the president in the Afghan transitional government. The U.S. military hoped to avoid any instability that might threaten an already seemingly precarious election season. Karzai made the decision to remove Khan in spite of these concerns, and a transfer of power from Governor Ismail Kahn to a replacement, Governor Mohammed Khairkwah, was effected with minimal disruption. Ostensibly, the potential for instability in the west pressed for the decision to deploy another American military force to this area, which was largely untouched by international military forces.

The divisional cavalry squadron, 3rd Squadron, 4th Cavalry under command of Lieutenant Colonel Michael McMahon, deployed to Herat Province. Colonel McMahon, a West Point graduate and popular commander, was tragically killed in a plane crash in November 2004. The cav squadron is equipped with two troops of OH-58D Kiowa Warrior helicopters and one troop of ground scouts trained for special reconnaissance and counterreconnaissance efforts. The cav squadron was augmented by another company-sized element of specialty infantry, the division's Long Range Surveillance Detachment. Soon after the cavalry had assumed responsibility for the western region, a new headquarters was established, manned from excess staff officers at the CJTF-76 headquarters, to oversee the cavalry squadron. Another factor about this organizational development is the fact that plans were underway to move Regional Command West, a relatively stable part of the country not under militant Muslim influence, to the control of the NATO International Security Assistance Force within six months of the establishment of the new command headquarters. The departure of the cavalry squadron in early 2005 was followed by the arrival of portions of a military police battalion with a partial headquarters that assumed responsibility for the cavalry's mission.

During both the cavalry rotation and the following military police rotation, a brigade headquarters was commanding one battalion headquarters commanding barely more than one company of ground assets. The situation was beneficial to both the subordinate and superior commanders. A "combat command" is a highly desired "feather in the cap" for a military officer, and for the CJTF-76 commander, Regional Command West created a third subordinate brigade headquarters, making him a commander of three maneuver brigade areas of responsibility rather than one. Arguably, the initial move of combat power to Herat could have more to do with the Iranian side of Afghanistan's western border than the Afghan side.

American and civilian Iraqi casualties were escalating in the war in Iraq in the preelection summer of 2004. It was well documented in the popular media that the Iraqi insurgency was influenced by the Iranian government. Thus, the movement of American forces to Iran's other border may have been a warning signal to Iran, and more assertively, it may have allowed American military power to monitor Iranian activities with intelligence collection assets and provide a launching point from the east for any future necessary intervention in Iran. Thus, the movement of forces and the establishment of a stronghold in western Afghanistan may have had higher strategic implications. However, the logic of the establishment of the superfluous Regional Command West, ultimately to be a very short-lived part of the Coalition forces, is not as easy to hypothesize if one only considers the forces in Afghanistan. By mid-2005, ISAF had assumed responsibility for Regional Command West. With the small number of forces in the west, it would appear much more efficient if this Regional Command could be combined with the North, as it was before ISAF expanded outside of the Afghan capital. The massive staffs and headquarters organizations are already the cause of some of the most significant inefficiencies that occur in modern warfare. Especially with American and allied publics demanding to reduce the number of deployed forces, reducing unnecessary headquarters organizations would seem to be a worthwhile endeavor.

Aside from the three regional headquarters, several task forces subordinate to CJTF-76 operated throughout the country. Combined Task Force Phoenix was primarily an Indiana National Guard Brigade augmented by foreign forces from several countries including France, Bulgaria, Romania, Great Britain, and New Zealand. Phoenix, with their descriptive motto, "rising from the ashes," is responsible for training the Afghan National Army. The task force accomplishes this objective with embedded training teams (routinely known as ETTs), which consist of small groups of senior noncommissioned officers and junior officers embedded with Afghan units. These units fall into four Regional Command Advisory Groups, mirroring the CJTF-76 regional commands, with the addition of the northern command that is controlled by the ISAF. The Afghan National Army training regional commands are known as RCAGs (Regional Command Advisory Groups).

Camp Phoenix, Kabul, the headquarters for this training unit, was where I lived for most of my time in Afghanistan. Major Greg Hall was one of my roommates. He was assigned to Task Force Phoenix as a liaison officer from RCAG South. Among his major responsibilities was the coordination of logistical support to the Phoenix components in the south. Major Hall was preparing to depart on a convoy to Kandahar from Kabul, a trip of over 330 miles. First, let me note that this is a highly unusual proposition. Coalition forces general use air movement to travel this distance, which can take eight hours or even longer by road. Greg's trip ended up taking almost twelve hours.

The convoy, which was led by an Afghan National Army lieutenant, with Major Hall as an escort and observer, was not ready to leave at the appointed time in the morning. When Major Hall, through his interpreter, asked why it was not ready, the lieutenant replied, "It's the fault of my men." This is not a good answer to give to an American officer, or I suspect, to members of more professionalized officer corps of other nations as well.

Major Hall responded to him forcefully, "What the fuck do you mean it's your men's fault!" (I wonder how the translator dealt with that answer.) "You are in charge. What those men do or fail to do is your responsibility. Now take charge and let's get this convoy moving!"

When I asked Greg if the lieutenant was receptive, Greg told me that he seemed to understand. That was encouraging. American officers learn these lessons as cadets, and this lesson is crucial to the effective running of a military unit. Multiplied many times across the country, this story showed the benefits of the mentorship provided by Task Force Phoenix to the Afghan army.

This kind of hard approach to military situations is developed in the American Army through hard training experiences. Everyone in the military shares a common Basic Training experience, a caricature of which was immortalized by Stanley Kubrick in *Full Metal Jacket*. Drill sergeants in "Smokey the Bear" hats screaming at new trainees present an image that captures the sense of the Basic Training experience. Of course, my experience at West Point was not exactly the same as enlisted basic training. Cadet basic training resembles enlisted basic training in many ways, but those cadets who served in the enlisted Army before West Point (about one third of the Corps of Cadets when I was there) revealed that the West Point version is more of a "mind-fuck." Failure to complete routine tasks is often equated to killing your future platoon. You can't march in step? Your lack of teamwork will kill your platoon. Cannot be at the right place at the appointed time? Your failure to follow instructions will kill your platoon. It seems laughable, and I suppose it is ridiculous, but it creates a lot more stress when these opinions are aggressively advanced by a cadre of trainers with complete control over one's life.

It is actually a regular Army training experience that comes to my mind when thinking about the hardness that the military attempts to instill in its personnel. In 1998, I spent several weeks in the hot and humid Fort Benning, Georgia, learning the finer points of combat parachuting at the U.S. Army Airborne School. I remember vividly my first day. A grizzled staff sergeant with a black baseball cap and aviator sunglasses stepped up to the platoon of cadets, privates, sergeants, and officers. His craggy facial features reminded me of Clint Eastwood. He spoke with a slight southern twang, as it seems like many of them do. He introduced himself as the platoon sergeant, Staff

Sergeant Stebbins, and told us we would never forget him. I suppose that is true as I write this from memory almost ten years later. At Airborne School, trainees wear Kevlar helmets wherever they go. On the helmet, each person has a roster number stenciled, which reads O, E, or C and then a number. The letters signify officer, enlisted, or cadet (which could mean either college ROTC or West Point).

Staff Sergeant Stebbins derisively told us his interpretation of the C designation. "C stands for civilian. That's right, cadets. You shouldn't even be here. You are wasting our time. I just want you to know from the beginning: Cadet, I *hate* you. And, West Point, I *really* hate you."

And it got worse after that. I remember one day we had a surprise inspection. Sergeant Stebbins looked at my boots as we stood in formation after the morning physical training (PT) routine. He said they were unacceptable, and I was kicked out of the school. I should just pack my things and report to the company headquarters after breakfast. I remember getting back to the barracks room, where my three roommates, a cadet and two privates, asked why I was not packing my things. I answered, "I don't think he is really going to kick me out for dirty boots after PT." It turned out to be correct. He either forgot about it or decided that I wanted to be there enough to not pursue the issue. But I still don't doubt that my own choice to disregard the instruction to leave is the only reason I finished the school.

I remember a rare moment where Stebbins was socializing with some of the soldiers during some down time. A couple of eighteen-year-old infantry soldiers sat in the grass, and he was regaling them with a story about a bar fight. Included in the story was the dramatic conclusion, which involved him stabbing someone in the side of the head, and then the denouement, in which Stebbins and his buddies hid the body. I have serious doubts about the veracity of the story, but the young privates sat entranced. This seemed to be a moment where hardness became recklessness.

The last requirement of Airborne School was to make five "jumps" out of a C-130 or C-141 aircraft onto a drop zone in Alabama. Any sort of injury on the first four jumps would prevent a trainee from finishing the school, but once you were out the plane's door on the fifth jump, you were as good as graduated. I remember that fifth jump. I was enjoying the glide down to the ground, which is a pleasant drop until one collides into the earth at about twenty-five miles per hour. Then I heard the cadre on their loudspeakers hundreds of feet below. "Slip away! Slip away! Collision!" ("Slip" means to use the riser of the parachute to change the orientation of the wind going into the chute in order to change your direction. With the basic T10-C, or Tee Ten Charlie, parachutes at the school, this means to physically pull the riser in to yourself, which tilts the canopy of the parachute. With the more technologically advanced −10B, or Dash Ten Bravo, parachute used by paratroopers, this control is accomplished by using a drawstring.)

I scanned around to see what poor unfortunate pair of parachutists would be colliding on their last jump. And then, I felt a physical shock from behind me, and realized I was the colliding jumper! The other parachutist and I became hopelessly entangled in the risers of the parachutes. I worked to disentangle them with little success. The cadre was frantically issuing instructions using their bullhorns on the ground. Eventually, I heard the instruction, "Prepare to make a tandem landing." That panicked me even more. With the chutes stealing each other's air, there would be two soldiers landing with the support of much less than two full canopies of air. I pulled one of my own risers to my chest so that my canopy was facing completely sideways.

The wind began tugging, pulling me away. I frantically beat at the risers to release me, and finally, I shot away from the other entangled jumper. I released the riser and made a normal landing on the ground. Happy to be alive and uninjured, I just laughed. One of the instructors came over to me. "What the fuck do think you were doing up there?" I did not have a satisfactory answer, so I did not say anything at all. But I was still happy, understanding for the first time the full meaning of the saying about "any landing that you can walk away from. . . . "

It seems to me that most Army training time—and most Army time in general—is not spent in activities that are so memorable or exciting. Most of it is spent doing nothing, or something like it. This is why "Hurry up and wait" has become an Army motto, or so it seems from the regularity with which I have heard it repeated. I remember part of the last day of the school in which our platoon spent two hours in the stone parking lot. It is one of those gravel parking areas with little gray rocks. We were issued an edict: "Rocks go with rocks, and grass goes with grass!"

The platoon was divided into two groups, so that one was responsible for picking up rocks that had been dislodged from the parking lot and tossing them back into the gravel area. The second group had to pick weeds or grass sprouting in the parking area and toss the remains into the grass. If I remember correctly, the groups switched at the midpoint, perhaps to ensure that we were equally trained in rock removal and weeding, or perhaps in a futile effort to relieve the tedium. I remember remarking sarcastically to no one in particular, "Haven't these guys ever heard of weedkiller?"

An eighteen-year-old private from the 82nd Airborne Division educated me on many things that day, including resource management and the military's respect and care for its personnel. He said with a friendly smile, "Cadet, why in the hell do they need to spend any money on weedkiller when there are forty privates around?" It seemed too much of my time and the time of my soldiers in the Army was spent "moving rocks with rocks and grass with grass," although I tried to avoid it whenever possible, particularly for people working under me.

Task Force Victory, another element—like Phoenix—with a meaningful designation, was responsible for civil-military operations, also known as civil affairs. (The name "Victory" implied that the route to success was through reconstruction and development.) Civil-military operations involve the coordination between military field commands and civilian relief agencies ranging from United Nations agencies to nongovernmental organizations such as Médecins sans Frontières. Additionally, civil-military operations include dealing with local national officials and citizens in efforts at reconstruction and development. Before NATO's International Security Assistance Force expanded to the northern part of the country, the areas now known as Regional Commands North and West were controlled by Task Force Victory. Since NATO took over the northern part of the country and the new Regional Command West assumed responsibility in the west, the role of Task Force Victory has become somewhat nebulous. The civil affairs personnel with whom I discussed the matter informed me that Task Force Victory had become another superfluous headquarters without a real and necessary mission.

At the tactical level, following the deployment of Special Forces operational detachments in key areas in early 2002, the Coalition deployed Coalitional Humanitarian Liaison Cells (CHLCs—pronounced "chicklets") in several urban areas around Afghanistan. The CHLCs in many ways functioned as Civil-Military Operation Centers but did not open "store front" offices as was common practice in the Balkans and other postconflict situations. The CHLCs often operated in civilian clothes and supported the U.S. Agency for International Development by providing logistics and security. The CHLCs performed a variety of tasks including assessments, information sharing, contracting projects, and supporting combat operations. Depending on their mandate and mentality, some humanitarians cooperated with the CHLCs, while others kept them at an arm's length.

In the summer of 2002, as the mission was evolving from combat to supporting stability, the U.S. government launched combined civil-military teams called Provincial Reconstruction Teams (PRTs). Task Force Victory is currently responsible for oversight of these teams. (The thing that makes Task Force Victory extraneous is the fact that the Regional Commands actually hold supervisory authority over the PRTs. The "oversight" provided by Victory is vague and arguably unnecessary.) The teams, comprised of several different military and civilian government staff, were first established in Gardez and expanded to select cities, although there were originally none in the south of the country. In many ways, the PRTs serve as a stopgap measure in areas where more robust international presence has not been deployed and the nascent Afghan transitional government fails to hold sway. (ISAF has its own civil affairs units that carry out assistance projects and other activities within their area of responsibility in and around Kabul. However, on October 13, 2003, ISAF was approved by NATO to operate countrywide, and has expanded into the north and west since then.) The PRT's presence is thought to add to security, but the teams are largely preoccupied with their own security with the hope that the embryonic Afghan National Army will assume more responsibility.

From the Coalition's perspective, the PRTs have been a success. Officials such as former U.S. Ambassador Robert Finn and former Secretary of Defense Donald Rumsfeld strongly endorsed the success of the Provincial Reconstruction Teams. Humanitarians hardly share a positive view of the PRTs in Afghanistan. The PRTs have been roundly criticized for their mission, structure, and, now that they are in place, their lack of effectiveness. A commonly held view among humanitarians is that the PRTs "have failed to tap local resources and have botched construction projects." I have heard varying reports of the effectiveness of the PRTs. A senior and well-respected military intelligence analyst, a chief warrant officer working in the CJTF-76 headquarters at Bagram, told me that NGO criticism of the PRT arose out of "professional jealousy." But other soldiers who have served throughout the country and United Nations officials, many with military backgrounds who were arguably neutral observers, agreed that the PRT was one of the most ineffective vehicles for reconstruction in the country.

I visited the commanders of several Provincial Reconstruction Teams in different parts of the country, including Parwan PRT at Bagram, Kandahar PRT, Farah PRT, Jalalabad PRT, Khost PRT, and Herat PRT. In Farah, which is a southwestern province where there has been little international military presence, I spent some time with the civil affairs noncommissioned officer, Sergeant David Farrands, an Army Reservist from Rochester, New York. Sergeant Farrands described the progress that the PRT has been making since its establishment in November 2004. It conducted reconstruction on three schools, and had three medical clinics under construction at the time of our discussion, in February 2005. The PRT made an agreement with the Committee of Health and Agriculture, an Afghan government agency, who agreed to supply doctors and staff for the clinics if the PRT built them. The biggest concern with construction projects is staffing so that a building does not stand empty. Thus, getting cooperation from another agency with longer-term considerations is important. These reservists did nine-month tours in Afghanistan, and one of the conditions of the work of civil affairs units in the PRT is that their projects must be complete during their own deployment rotation. This has the beneficial impact of ensuring that projects undertaken have immediate and noticeable results, but it limits the ambition of military reconstruction projects. This is the role of the U.S.AID section in the PRT, which can focus on the longer-term projects.

Funding for the military projects comes from the Commander's Emergency Relief Program (CERP), which the PRT commander (an Army or Marine lieutenant colonel) can approve for amounts up to twenty-five thousand dollars. For larger amounts, up to two hundred thousand dollars, the

Regional Commander (an Army colonel), can give approval. Most projects are near-term, hoping to make an immediate impact, with many rehabilitation efforts being finished within thirty days. Longer construction may last closer to four months, but limited rotations typically restrict the amount of work that can be done. For the most part, the projects generate employment. Local contractors are solicited over television and radio if the contract is over ten thousand dollars. Of course, in a country largely without electricity, these media channels do not reach the average person. But such an average person in a country where the per capita annual income is three hundred dollars would be unlikely to bid for a ten thousand dollar contract anyway. Of course, print media would not offer any sort of advantage in advertising because much of the country is illiterate.

The PRTs find that wells, schools, and clinics are the most frequent request. Often old mosques will be converted for use as schools, but the Afghan government's provincial department of education is not responsive. It usually takes about a month to get local government approval to establish a school, even with repeated calling every few days. For these reasons, and due to the prospects of difficulty in staffing newly built schools and clinics, repairs are often preferred over establishing new buildings.

Farah PRT also delivered humanitarian assistance items for the winter, including 3,000 sweaters, jackets, blankets, and propane heaters. Even in the capital city, where I worked, eight Afghans died due to the unusually harsh winter of 2004/2005 in a refugee camp in Kabul. A couple of months before that frigid winter, I visited the camp. These refugees were the poorest people I had ever seen. Even the youngest children had very rough and dirty skin.

Jody Foster, one of the UN security officers with whom I served, visited the refugees often and brought several of us along one day. She liked to talk with the refugees with her local Afghan driver, Arash, translating. Jody explained that the refugees had fled the country over twenty years ago when the Soviets invaded. They were famed horse racers, and one of the young boys in the camp was, according to Jody, Espandi (played by Arif Herati), one of the main characters in the 2003 film *Osama*. *Osama* is not about the most famous Osama, but the story of a girl who disguises herself as a boy to work and support her mother and grandmother.

With the rise of Karzai, the tribe returned to their homeland. Jody's occasional visits included taking and sharing photographs with the Afghans. She would print them at a local shop and distribute them to those photographed. This was a great treat for them. They also loved seeing their image on the back of the digital camera after the photo was taken. The people we saw were young men and children, as all the women were segregated in the back of the camp, out of sight. There was an old patriarch who liked to answer questions and to whom the others deferred when we asked questions. He had a deformed hand, with an extra stump of a thumb and thumbnail extending from the side of his thumb.

Before we prepared to leave the camp after my first visit there, we handed out some boxes of bottled water and rations. As the people pressed forward with their hands extended, Jody decided to give the last box to the old man to distribute to those who had not yet received anything. Far more spry than he looked, the old man tucked the box under his arm and gleefully darted away to the interior of the camp. The old man turned out not to be the wise father-figure he seemed.

As we got into our vehicles to leave the refugee camp, someone from our group commented about the cruel overburdening of a cart donkey straining under the weight of its cart as the Afghans continued to load more upon it. I imagined that these people, while unfamiliar with digital cameras and other implements of modern technology, would certainly know how to load donkey carts and master the technologies their tribes had used for thousands of years. This assumption was proven wrong as we looked out the windows of our trucks as we began to drive away. The donkey was suspended in the air, flailing its legs uselessly as the overloaded cart had tipped backwards, pulling the animal off its feet. Seeing the donkey suspended, uselessly flailing its front limbs, was one of the most comical scenes of my year in Afghanistan.

Further south, my partner Eric Harbaugh had passed through an even poorer refugee camp near the southern border with Pakistan. Eric told me about his convoy through the camp. Children would run up to the convoy waving and screaming. Soldiers would throw empty plastic water bottles as the convoy passed by and the children would struggle to grab the bottles as if they were prized possessions. Eric scolded the soldiers for throwing garbage at the refugees, but the soldiers explained to him that the water bottles were highly valued among the refugees, even though they were empty. It is hard to imagine someone so poor that empty plastic bottles are items of value. The main issue of importance to people for such bottles in our country is their disposal, and that is only important to the part of society who are advocates of recycling.

In addition to poverty, effective governance in Afghanistan is an important issue. The PRT in Farah also hoped to build longer-term good governance, and to this end delivered vehicles and motorcycles for the local police force and the Afghan National Directorate of Security. It is not uncommon to find sixty police officers at a local station with only one vehicle. Unfortunately, many vehicles transferred to local security forces in this manner are irrevocably lost.

The Afghan National Police and their local affiliates have a reputation of corruption. It is common to find checkpoints charging fees to passing citizens. Sergeant Farrands related an example of this to me. He was on a patrol that encountered a suspicious checkpoint on Ring Road, the major thoroughfare that makes a "ring" around the country, also known as Highway 1. The PRT convoy sped up past the checkpoint and pulled over the truck that had passed ahead of them. The driver reported that the police asked for money, requiring that he pay twenty Afs (equivalent to about fifty cents, but with a much greater purchasing power). Afterward, the PRT soldiers returned to the checkpoint, and the police claimed that they had not been paid and were just asking citizens for money. The first of these points was likely true, but the policemen at the checkpoint were probably making more than just a request for donations.

In practice, Farah PRT did not report much coordination with other relief agencies. For one thing, only a few such organizations worked on the remote province. UNICEF is active, distributing books, paper, notebooks, and bright rubber boots to children. I was only there for a few days, but on my trip into the village areas, the brightly colored boots worn by many children clearly marked areas where UNICEF had distributed humanitarian assistance. Dakar, a Danish organization that digs wells, has built many wells in Farah, but they had not coordinated with the PRT. The German group HELP built dikes and irrigation ditches in the city of Anardarah in northwest part of the province. While there was coordination with the PRT to avoid overlapping projects with limited resources, there was no joint work conducted.

In other parts of the country, such nongovernmental organizations would often coordinate with the PRT for security, if not for actual development work. From the perspective of many members of the international humanitarian community, the PRT was the embodiment of international military presence in Afghanistan, even though these units were among the least robust and the least suited for combat operations. It is common to hear workers in such agencies, or workers in the United Nations, to refer to military presence, whether the American-led Coalition or NATO, as a "PRT." To these people, the PRT has come to mean the military presence in an area, even though the PRT is among the most innocuous and defensively oriented units in the country.

The lack of humanitarian coordination with military forces is often intentional on the part of private, civilian nongovernmental organizations. Perhaps what alarms humanitarians most is that the PRT bands together military units, including those specifically tasked with routing out terrorist elements, and civilian officials from U.S.AID. When the PRT at Herat was first established, Task Force Victory raised similar concerns over the CIA's use of the PRT as a cover for intelligence efforts directed against Iran.

At the beginning of the Afghanistan intervention, humanitarian organizations were concerned that their impartiality was called into question by the way in which the war on terrorism was being articulated. With international rhetoric suggesting that the war was one of civilization against the uncivilized, humanitarian relief groups would clearly fall into the rubric of civilization. In addition, the Coalition bombing campaign on October 7, 2001, created a dilemma for those relief agencies with close ties to the United States and the United Kingdom. The 2.4 million humanitarian daily rations dropped were a significant part of the military effort. The mark "Gift of the U.S.A." on 90 percent of the food distributed in Afghanistan made it difficult for British and American relief workers to claim their independence from official policies of their governments, especially since many NGOs are directly funded by the American and British governments. Oxfam, for example, accepted British government funds for work with Afghan refugees, although the staff preferred to maintain a discreet silence. Most agencies, especially those with U.S. affiliates or funding, were hesitant to declare neutrality in the war against terrorism; however, the lives of humanitarian workers in Taliban-controlled areas depended on the ability of the aid agencies to convince the Taliban that their neutrality was bona fide.

Nonindigenous humanitarian relief efforts and workers also felt endangered by United Nations' declarations and actions. UN Security Council Resolution 1373 "reaffirmed the need to combat by all means . . . threats to international peace and security caused by terrorist acts," and the massive bombing campaign seemed to indicate that the United Nations endorsed destructive and indiscriminate "means." Again, in November 2001, the United Nations seemed to take sides and compromise the neutrality of its sponsored relief agencies when UN Resolution 1378 expressly condemned the Taliban for allowing Afghanistan to be used as a terrorist base and endorsed "efforts to root out terrorism." Many in the humanitarian community feel that the sponsorship of or participation with military authorities can hamper the humanitarian mission. While the scope and number of organizations engaging in humanitarian assistance have increased, governments who fund relief activities have taken few measures to increase the security of humanitarian aid workers. Thus, the international community must sponsor either humanitarian interventions that employ large-scale military deployments or those where civilian aid workers are left largely to their own devices.

One potential solution for this is a privatization of security, where protection would be internally provided. UN forces, or third-country forces, provide another solution. However, the International Committee of the Red Cross (ICRC) has ruled out any armed military escorts to protect humanitarian activities for its operations. In particular, the ICRC relies on a sense of neutrality in order to promote its mission. Thus, the neutral identity—as well as the viability of the entire operation—is compromised by armed escorts for relief convoys. However, in the case of criminal behavior (in contrast to ongoing hostilities in a conflict), the ICRC does allow armed guards at workplaces and residences if no other option is available. At this point, private security options or police forces are still preferable to organized militaries in the view of the ICRC.

In addition, the military itself frequently participates in humanitarian activities that mirror the efforts of nongovernmental activists and enjoy similar status in international law to these humanitarian relief workers. Task Force Victory is predicated on such a noncombat role for the military. For instance, medical staff, stretcher-bearers, and ambulance drivers wear and enjoy the protection of the Red Cross emblem, which is not available to either the nongovernmental organizations or the United Nations. This example illustrates that the nature of the activity rather than the institutional identity of the actor defines humanitarian action according to international humanitarian law. Further, international humanitarian law requires the military to respect human rights of civilians: the "starvation of civilians as a method of warfare is prohibited" and warring parties must "facilitate rapid and unimpeded passage for all relief consignments and personnel." An occupying power acquires "to the fullest extent of the means available . . . the duty of ensuring the food and medical supplies of the population. It should, in particular, bring in the necessary foodstuffs, medical stores, and other articles if the resources of the occupied territory are inadequate." The intervention of impartial relief agencies does not relieve the occupation power of these responsibilities. However, it should be acknowledged that the challenge of delivering humanitarian assistance directly by an occupying power is different from the challenge that other parties face. Locals may theoretically resist the occupier but welcome others who come to help, making coordination with and support of neutral relief agencies important.

Two of the principal areas for military support for humanitarian operations are security and logistics. However, civilian organizations operating in a dangerous region could enjoy other potential benefits of military coordination, including information or intelligence on possible threats, contingency planning for noncombatant evacuation operations, vulnerability assessments of the civilian group, training, protection, and advising. Ultimately, security for emergency situations seemed to be the most important role of the PRTs from the perspective of international relief agencies.

In spite of differences with some members of the humanitarian community, the international military presence needs to be closely linked with the reconstruction of Afghanistan. Improving the economic and social atmosphere will be instrumental in developing a strong, friendly democracy, and preventing the resurgence of a failed or extremist state that will invite terrorist patronage. Unfortunately, examples abound of failures to effectively "win hearts and minds," to use the old phrase from the U.S. Army's earlier experience in Vietnam.

For example, there was a chaplain in Kandahar who wanted to convert the Afghan people to Christianity. I felt that the story was reliable; it was related to me on a visit to Kandahar by an Iowa infantry National Guardsman serving in the Kandahar PRT, who provided security for the chaplain's missions and observed his efforts firsthand. While this may seem a pious missionary endeavor, it is problematic for several reasons. First, the Afghan people are religious to a point well beyond the modern Western citizen of any religion. Like people of traditional medieval times, religion rules their life, combined with a series of irrational superstitions. Thus, efforts toward religious conversion would meet strenuous resistance and arouse feelings of hostility from the tribes. Second, it is illegal for Afghans to practice Christianity. Only under the protection of the U.S. Army and Operation Enduring Freedom could the chaplain possibly distribute crosses and other religious paraphernalia in one of the most conservative regions of the country. Any civilian missionary would surely have been killed many months before. The great offense with which the Afghan people view the imposition of a foreign religion would seriously undermine the U.S. national interest by confronting the Afghans' own legal system. Finally, the conversion of indigenous people is not the role of the military chaplaincy. A chaplain's role is to minister to soldiers who would otherwise not have religious ministry available. Additionally, the chaplaincy is a multireligious program that is not only Christian. Of course, this sort of behavior validates the criticisms of Islamist observers who feel that the Global War on Terror is a return to the medieval crusades as Christian warriors attempt to establish conversion by the sword.

Another major component of Coalition forces in Afghanistan is Combined Joint Special Operations Task Force (also known as CJSOTF, pronounced SEE-jay-SO-tef). Discussing this task force will allow an opportunity to extend the discussion of relating to the Afghan people. Originally, President John F. Kennedy established Special Forces units to conduct unconventional missions, and they are well-known for training indigenous forces across the world. In Afghanistan, the Task Force Phoenix National Guard brigade is responsible for training Afghan soldiers, and the Special Operations Task Force is not involved in this traditional role, except to train Afghan Special Forces units. CJSOTF in Afghanistan is at the point of the spear, operating in the most difficult and dangerous areas of the country. They are responsible for capturing or killing many of the most active and dangerous insurgents in the country. Among some people who have worked with them, the task force does not enjoy a good reputation for "quiet professionalism" and diplomacy, which are often-heard watchwords of American special operations forces.

Rather than specially qualified soldiers, many stories seemed to indicate merely a group of infantry soldiers with more aggression and less discipline. Since this task force operates with "relaxed grooming standards," wearing beards and quasimilitary uniforms, it is possible that a diminution of discipline would follow. The Global War on Terrorism has resulted in an expansion of special operations missions, and age and rank standards have been dropped to increase recruitment of these soldiers from the conventional force. I received several anecdotal accounts from a variety of sources who had firsthand knowledge of incidents involving these elite soldiers in Afghanistan.

Special Forces enjoy quite a bit of autonomy and independence when compared with more conventional troops, and have occasionally abused this power. As I indicated, I have secondhand access to these stories, and perhaps the worst is being shared because it is more interesting. The routine and effective missions of CJSOTF no doubt have contributed to the progress of the security situation in Afghanistan. However, several examples indicate problems that can arise.

One of the officers I worked with in elections security had previous experience working with French Special Forces in the south of the country. Captain Eric Harbaugh was a 2000 West Point graduate and worked in supply with the infantry brigade responsible for the south of the country. From October 2004 to March 2005, he served as my partner in a civilian clothes role embedded with the United Nations elections project. At the time of his experience with the Special Forces units, he was assigned to provide logistical coordination for French Special Forces in Spin Boldak, a border village near the southern border with Pakistan. After several months, American Special Forces arrived to assume responsibility for part of the territory down there. Eric accompanied the French team with the American Special Forces as they conducted a familiarization tour for the transition of authority. Eric, two French soldiers, and two American Special Forces soldiers arrived at a small outlying village for introductions with the village elders.

Typically, in Afghanistan, there is no interaction with women who are not members of one's family. Robert Kaplan wrote in *Soldiers of God* that the only indication he ever had of the presence of a woman in the Pashtun households he visited was the quality of the food. (Bad food meant there was no woman around; good food indicated there was an unseen woman somewhere in the household preparing it.) Even in the relatively cosmopolitan capital, women wearing the burkha, covering every inch of their body (except the hands), are common to see. Further south, where this incident occurred, when a military or other convoy carrying foreign men approaches, women older than twelve years of age will leave the streets, enter their buildings, and close the windows. It is very rare for a foreign male to even see a woman in the traditional Pashtun villages in the south of Afghanistan. When the Special Forces transition team and their interpreter arrived at the village, they found one old woman at the gate. She did not open the way and told the team that the men in the village had left for a local *shura* (council meeting). The two American noncommissioned officers pushed past the woman and entered the compound. The women and children in the village scattered and ran when the men came in. The American SF soldiers were amused, chasing the women and laughing, trying to introduce themselves and shake hands. The women ran away from this unwelcome male contact. Finally, one of the two tired of the chase and got his partner to stop. When the five soldiers left the threatened and frightened Afghan women, they likely had poisoned relations with Westerners and that village for years to come. Imagine the outrage that Americans would feel if foreign men came in and agitated their vulnerable women and children, frightening them in the absence of the providers and protectors. A traditional society like the Pashtuns would find this outrage so much the more appalling. Since I was not there to witness this event in person, I must rely on the validity of the account I received from the witness. I do not believe it is exaggerated; Captain Harbaugh did not find the occasion at all amusing and was himself sincerely outraged by the behavior he observed.

In February 2005, an official report came in that Special Forces soldiers in Shindand in the western province of Herat shot fleeing Afghans. The Afghans were suspected of emplacing an improvised explosive device, but they had no weapons. It seemed from the report that there had been some sort of violation of the rules of engagement. Eric Harbaugh was reading it with me, and both of us felt that this was another example of reckless behavior in the field. I visited Shindand a few weeks after the report had come out, and my curiosity got the better of me. When I asked a major in the military police unit stationed at Shindand about the report, he told me that a commander's inquiry had been conducted. A commander's inquiry is an official investigation nicknamed a "15–6" after the regulation that directs how to conduct the inquiry. The 15–6 had found mitigating circumstances and that no soldiers were at fault in the incident. But it was also clear from the investigation that the Afghans were not emplacing an explosive and were not insurgents. Another incident in Kandahar was averted when a senior noncommissioned officer lost his temper and started to beat a prisoner until an American officer, the CJTF-76 southern task force's brigade operations officer, Major Duke Davis, who happened to be nearby, told him to desist.

Combined Joint Task Force-76 and its constituent elements were focused on counterinsurgency, reconstruction, and development, and fell under the purview of Central Command (Centcom), the regional combatant command under the command of General John Abizaid. The U.S. Special Operations Command oversaw the hunt for al Qaeda leaders. A military unit simply called "Other Coalition Forces," or OCF, commanded by the Joint Special Operations Command, conducted these missions, while the remainder of the Coalition forces in Afghanistan focused on other matters. The Other Coalition Forces include those specialized and secretive forces that conduct the most dangerous and important missions.

It amazed me how unfocused on and indifferent to this search CJTF-76 was. On the other hand, the Other Coalition Forces—along with the "Other Government Agencies," or OGA—were able to demand priority on any of the various intelligence collection platforms in the country. In this way, their mission was the priority of the various military units in Afghanistan. For instance, the first major terrorist leader was killed by CJTF-76 forces during my time in Afghanistan in August 2004. Rozi Khan had been the police chief of Kandahar Province, and for months since the 10th Mountain Division had left Afghanistan in April 2004, catching Mr. Khan was a top priority. A midlevel Taliban leader, I wondered if all the emphasis on Khan was too much. Who was this character that we wanted to capture him so urgently and that we had pursued him over such a long period of time? He was not a significant figure in the deposed Taliban government. To all apparent knowledge, he posed no threat to Americans except for the fact that we had placed ourselves in harm's way by entering his country. Although a thug and a brutal murderer, Rozi Khan did not seem to merit the strong command and intelligence attention he had received. A cat with nine lives, as he was called, reports of his death had surfaced and resurfaced over the months of our time here. It was hard to even verify his physical appearance, and detainees were used to confirm his death.

The picture of his corpse was presented in the morning command briefing the day after his death. While there was nothing that seemed to me offensive about the picture—it was the man's face in silent repose—the commanding general of CJTF-76, Major General Eric Olsen, made it abundantly clear that such a photograph was inappropriate for his daily briefing. When I heard about his tirade as he yelled at the assembled staff officers about the offensive photo, it occurred to me that only weeks before, a picture of Saddam Hussein's sons, Uday and Kusay, in a similar position of repose, had been disseminated in the press. Perhaps General Olsen, who had been promoted to generalship a few years before by President Clinton, did not approve of the hard approach of the Bush Administration. In addition, it seemed that in the environment that followed Abu Ghraib, General Olsen, likely similar to other field commanders, was extremely sensitive to the appearance of impropriety.

But the general was also a bit unpredictable. A few months later, he would "cancel Christmas" by banning the posting of any Christmas decorations or paraphernalia in the headquarters building. When one of the staff officers in the command headquarters, an infantry captain named Mark Van Gelder, told me about this decision, it reminded me of news reports about schools back in the states changing their Christmas holidays to "winter season celebrations" and removing mangers and other religious articles from public view. The general's reasoning was not exactly the same; he argued that front line soldiers in outposts throughout the country could not enjoy the holiday, so the headquarters area should be similarly austere. The Christmas ban was later rescinded after the command sergeant major—the senior enlisted soldier in Afghanistan—appealed to the general to change his decision.

To return to the Other Coalition Forces, the primary terrorist hunters in Afghanistan, a rotating battalion from the 75th Ranger Regiment was the largest of the Other Coalition Forces, but others complemented that unit. Although Other Coalition Forces is a name used to hide the unit designation of these elements, to my knowledge, this piece of information is not classified; it is just hidden. Classification can only protect information that is disseminated. The security around the unit designation information is extremely paranoid; the soldiers do not wear their unit designations, grow their hair long so that the notorious Ranger haircuts do not give away their unit identity, and go only by the moniker, "Other Coalition Forces." On the other hand, when the Ranger football star Pat Tillman was killed in action, the Army and the 75th Ranger Regiment repeatedly publicized the Rangers' presence in Afghanistan.

In spite of the secrecy around OCF, the press corps announced a regular synopsis of their activities: the search for Osama bin Laden and al Qaeda key leaders continuing, with limited success. There were occasional important developments, such as the capture of the 9-11 architect, Khalid Sheik Mohammed, in March 2003. However, Osama bin Laden and most senior leaders remained at large after several years of American military efforts. Perhaps, as Theresa Hines Kerry claimed to a Democratic presidential campaign gathering in September 2004, Osama was hidden in some Pakistani prison, awaiting an opportune time for the Bush Administration to announce his capture to best improve its reelection chances. Farfetched as this outrageous claim was, we even heard some intelligence from seemingly reliable Pakistani sources attesting to that very story. Most of us dismissed such reports as common sense prevailed.

The information sharing between our task force and these OCF units was limited, but it varied in my experience over my time in Afghanistan. I worked with several of them in different parts of the country, and the degree of information sharing seemed to depend on the particular intelligence officer with whom one was working at the time. Information could be "lim dis," or limited distribution for operational reasons, and not be shared at all. Or it could be shared anyway. Overall, the Other Coalition Forces were one of many examples of disunity of command among the international military forces in Afghanistan. Between the Coalition that was directed by the U.S. Central Command, the International Security Assistance Force directed by NATO, and the Other Coalition Forces directed by the Joint Special Operations Command, there were three major units in Afghanistan that were not even accountable to the same commanders in Washington, DC. This was one of the major challenges of the international military effort in Afghanistan.

## OTHER SECURITY ORGANIZATIONS

The Other Government Agencies, a moniker earlier reserved for the Central Intelligence Agency, according to Chris Mackey's *The Interrogators*, included a collection of civilian government organizations working in Afghanistan during my rotation there. The CIA was certainly the primary member of the Other Government Agencies, but others included the Federal Bureau of Investigation, the Drug Enforcement Agency, and the Defense Human Intelligence (HUMINT) Service.

The FBI's role in Afghanistan was to assess and respond to threats on the U.S. homeland that might arise due to the presence of terrorists in Afghanistan. To this end, the FBI also stationed people at the American

Embassy in Pakistan. Much of the work of the FBI officers in Afghanistan involved tracking threats to Americans living abroad in Afghanistan. The FBI investigated the bombing of the American security company DynCorp in Kabul in August 2004 and a suicide bombing in Kabul in November 2004 that led to the death of a female American translator.

The Drug Enforcement Agency was focused on the opium industry in Afghanistan. At the time, the United States was not focused on drug eradication, but Great Britain was providing significant counterdrug support to the Afghan government, and the United States was providing limited assistance. The role of the Drug Enforcement Agency increased more recently as narcotics became an increasing concern of American policy.

The Defense HUMINT Service was formerly abbreviated DHS but changed this acronym to DH after the Department of Homeland Security was created. Defense HUMINT has a collection capability similar to that of the CIA. It falls under the Defense Intelligence Agency, or DIA. Officers in Defense HUMINT primarily conducted "strategic debriefing," which involves talking to American military personnel to collect information to satisfy high-level strategic intelligence requirements. They also told me that they met with other contacts to collect information. The officers consisted of civilian clothes military personnel as well as civilians. The people working in this agency were some of the most helpful people I met in the intelligence community in Afghanistan. They provided information whenever needed and went out of their way to assist the missions of other units serving in the country. This was a significant difference from the CIA, who were extremely unresponsive to requests for information. Most adjacent units in Afghanistan had liaison officers embedded, and even CJTF-76's liaison to the CIA, an intelligence major I had known for the past several years, told me that it was difficult to get any information from them. Seeing the almost paranoid security precautions of the CIA made it easy for me to understand the information sharing problems in the American intelligence community identified by the 9-11 Commission.

Another major group of international security forces in the country are the private contractors that support various interests in Afghanistan. The growing presence of private military forces in global conflicts was documented by Peter Singer in 2003 in his book *Corporate Warriors*. DynCorp was responsible for the security of President Hamid Karzai and for key leaders of the U.S. Embassy. Global Risk Strategies provided assistance to the United Nations in distributing Afghanistan's new currency and planning, securing, and running the presidential election. They also guarded the American Embassy. Kroll Security Services provided similar assistance for the national assembly elections. Blackwater was widely publicized for its role in Iraq when four of its contractors were killed outside Fallujah in a reprehensible attack in which the men were burned alive and their charred corpses hung over the road. Blackwater also served in Afghanistan, where I met several of its employees working with the CIA in the border region. Military Professional Resources, Inc. (MPRI) provided retired military officers who served in staff and advisory positions in the command structure.

These private military companies can provide several advantages to the United States government. First, they provide augmentation and relief to an overstretched military. Second, there is less public attention to harm to these contractors than there is to military casualties. The 1,000th American military casualty in Iraq was a milestone in late 2004 that reinvigorated opponents to the war and was widely publicized in the American media. On the other hand, casualties among these private firms are much less publicized and do not have the traction that military casualties do to undermine the war effort. The United States military learned about the necessity of public support on the home front during the Vietnam War. North Vietnamese Colonel Bui Tin, who received South Vietnam's surrender on April 30, 1975, said in an interview in the August 3, 1995, *Wall Street Journal* that the U.S. antiwar movement was "essential to our strategy." American strategists are cognizant of the impact of a casualty averse public opinion on the war, especially since deaths of nineteen soldiers in the Black Hawk Down incident in Somalia in 1993, after which the entire American force was quickly withdrawn by the Clinton Administration. Third, there is little oversight of these private contractors, as documented in the October 6, 2003, *Washington Times*. After cutbacks throughout the 1990s, the CIA had very little operational capability, and that capability is strictly monitored by congressional oversight. Short-term private contracts can significantly expand the capability of the CIA without having the same type of budgetary scrutiny to which the expansion of permanent case officers is subject.

However, these advantages also imply serious drawbacks because lack of accountability can lead to irresponsible actions on both large-scale and individual levels. In October 2004, a BBC correspondent reported that he saw a member of President Karzai's DynCorp security detail slap the Afghan Transportation Minister during a visit to the northern city of Mazar-e-Sharif. This report, along with complaints from visiting European diplomats, caused the U.S. Department of State to issue a public criticism of DynCorp's harsh methods.

Global Risk Strategies was another key player in Afghan security that proved to be an unconventional, but valuable, source of information. The purpose of Global Risk was to augment the UN international staff with operators who could venture into provinces that were off-limits to the United Nations because of the precarious security situation. This provided a unique benefit for Coalition intelligence analysts because it also resulted in experienced former military officers or noncommissioned officers being in locations where the Coalition had no presence or intelligence collection. (While the United Nations did not go to many places because of an aversion to possible risks, the Coalition did not have similar qualms. But the shortage of soldiers in the country resulted in limits in the amount of places where the Coalition could be located.) Once the election ended and the Global Risk Strategies team left the country, many Coalition analysts began to ask me for the information being collected by Global. Of course, there was no information once the contractors had left Afghanistan. The fact that the information was missed seemed to be an indicator that it was valued.

James Offer was a young, confident contractor with Global Risk Strategies. With clear blue eyes, a slightly receding hairline, and a crisp British accent, James had met with me at the weekly threat meetings leading up to the time when the Election Security Operations Center was activated. He had introduced himself to me as James, but I discovered after a while that James more often went by the nickname "Joffer." He explained to me, "There were fifteen lads named James at preparatory school, so I just mixed James and Offer, and that's why I am called Joffer."

Joffer was responsible for the daily Global Risk Strategies Situation Report (or "Sitrep"). The man who assembles the Global Sitrep does not have an enviable job. Global representatives do not have the resources or precision of American military intelligence agents. Thus, the incidents related in these reports often lack details including the time they occurred, the specific location, or where the information came from. The latter problem is perhaps the most significant. It is often impossible to confirm whether an incident happened at all as the Global Risk representative in the field hears rumors distorted as the information is passed from one person to another and passes this along with all-too-often little scrutiny of its accuracy. So Joffer had to compile these reports from across the country into a daily report that averaged about fifteen pages. In the days after the election, the daily would shrink to under ten pages on most days, as threat reports receded and the movement of ballots became the key issue.

Joffer's title was the Global Risk Strategies Information Officer, although he had previously served as an Operations Manager. James Offer left the Irish Guard infantry regiment of the United Kingdom Army in 2001 after five years of service. He was a graduate of the military academy at Sandhurst and had been a captain when he left the military. After two years of working in London, Joffer felt restless. After a Friday phone call to a friend from Global Risk Strategies, Joffer found himself in Afghanistan on Sunday, in charge of a Russian helicopter responsible for distributing the new Afghan currency in northern Afghanistan.

Joffer was very helpful to the intelligence process in the Elections Security Operations Center and to the Coalition intelligence staff by providing the Daily Sitrep. When there were information gaps, he was quick to inquire about missing details from his regional or provincial operators. Altogether, the election constituent organizations were very impressed with Global Risk Strategies and the pool of talent they brought to Afghanistan.

al Risk, more aggressive private security contractors did
ˑeputations for their demeanor. I experienced DynCorp's
ฉirsthand when I was walking down the street in Kabul
ᴜ.S. Embassy to the CFC headquarters. I was dressed in nonde-
ˑˑpt civilian clothes, but it was clear from my dress and my face that I
was a Westerner visiting the country. Nonetheless, these civilian security
contractors sighted me in their weapons as they drove by in spite of my
appearance as an apparently harmless Western civilian. My pistol was secreted on my person and not visible. I had never before had a loaded weapon
pointed directly at me, but it was apparently the standard procedure of these
convoys to direct their weapons at all bystanders as their convoys passed. I
imagine the practice of sighting all passersby is not something that endears
the American intervention to locals or builds goodwill.

While in my civilian clothes role in Bagram or Kabul, it seemed more
likely to me that I should be shot by an American contractor or soldier than
by an Afghan or Arab terrorist until I moved to the border regions where
terrorist rocket attacks on American outposts were fairly common. During
my time in Kabul in civilian clothes, I had both contractors and soldiers
point weapons at me as I was driving or walking near their convoys, and
the trigger-happy and unaccountable civilians were more of a concern to me
than the risk-averse soldiers. If I felt this way, I can understand apprehension
among Afghan civilians, who to visiting Americans, and even to each other,
are often indistinguishable from dangerous Taliban extremists.

Driving accidents were also a serious concern for both military and contractor vehicles in building rapport with Afghans. The driving in Afghanistan
is no-holds-barred, with American military drivers the most aggressive on
the road. Without traffic signals or other guidelines of any sort, the traffic in
the city of Kabul, with a population between two and four million, is hard
to describe to a Western audience. Afghan drivers routinely make left turns
from the right lane at a crowded intersection, and gridlock is common. At
the center of most gridlock is a member of the Afghan traffic police, attempting to direct traffic. With a population that is mostly illiterate and with a
rule of law that is just beginning to take hold, there is no traffic law of which
I am aware. It is common to see Afghan drivers driving on the wrong side
of the road on a divided highway or kicking up clouds of dust passing in
the median. Since most people often ignore the police, it is difficult to blame
the ineffective traffic police for the gridlock, even though twenty minutes
of waiting in bumper-to-bumper traffic to get to an intersection will often
reveal a policeman at the center of things. Finally, road conditions across
the country are abominable. In Kabul, the road seemed like merely a series
of potholes at the height of the winter freeze. In Farah, there were no paved
roads outside of the provincial capital, and the dirt roads necessitated repeated replacements of the shocks on the military's pickup trucks. In Khost,
the mudslides in the early spring made the road extremely difficult, and

there were several points at which I was surprised we didn't get stuck. A wide wadi filled with water intersects the road, and even the Toyota Corolla sedans popular in Afghanistan cross this running water, which reaches the top of their tires.

In spite of the anarchic driving style, there are surprisingly few traffic accidents. Perhaps the unpredictable driving of one's neighbor causes a driver to attend completely to driving. In the West, our attention is diverted by cell phone conversation, daydreaming, and other distractions. In Afghanistan, drivers cannot afford such diversions because an unexpected and dangerous event is even more likely. The lack of traffic education results in unclear standards and conventions. For instance, turn signals can be confusing. If a car pulls off to stop on the right side of the highway in the United States, the driver will signal with his right turn signal, or occasionally with his emergency signals. In Afghanistan, it is common to see a car stopped to the right side of the road with his left turn signal blinking. I would approach such a car with caution, expecting him to try to merge into traffic at any minute. Similarly, when we were about to pass a vehicle on the left, it would turn on its left turn signal, seemingly indicating it was going to make a left turn. After a few months of driving around Afghanistan, I learned that these signals indicate not that a car is going to make a move in the direction indicated. The signal means that it is clear to pass on that side.

Afghanistan has a few other unique driving conventions. At busy urban intersections, it is common to use your double emergency blinkers to indicate you intend to drive straight through the intersection. (Left signal means left turn; right signal means right turn; both signals mean straight ahead.) In highway driving, cars will flash their headlights when passing or when a passing car is approaching from the opposite direction. The headlights mean get out of the way; the approaching car is not going to yield. Finally, it is common to sound the horn with a series of light beeps when passing or approaching another vehicle to alert him of your presence. This practice is particularly helpful. On three separate occasions, my car was nearly run off the highway while passing a large, slow-moving jingle truck, which decided to aimlessly drift into the middle of the road just as my vehicle approached or began to pass.

Jingle trucks are the main method of transport for industrial supplies in Afghanistan. They are large, usually with an open container on the back, and are commonly seen on the Ring Road highway that encircles the country and moving in an around the capital city. The trucks are called jingle trucks because they are decorated with dangling ornaments that jingle as the truck moves. The trucks are painted with vivid and fanciful designs, so despite the brown and bleak atmosphere of Afghanistan, the people seemed to like bright colors and decorative additions. Many CIA analysts, who had likely never seen one of the trucks, wrote "jingha trucks" in their daily spot reports, and maybe this was a pidginized form of jingle, spoken in Afghan Dari or

Pashtun, but my partner and I thought it was probably a misunderstood translation that was turned into a bad habit.

I traveled between Bagram Air Base and Kabul City often throughout much of my tour in Afghanistan, and I was initially surprised to see that dirt was the main commodity hauled in these trucks. Hauling dirt hardly seemed to be worth the fuel and the wear and tear on the vehicles (most of which had seen better days). In spite of Afghanistan's not insignificant land mine problem (it is the most heavily mined country per square mile in the world), mines are not so pervasive that people never venture off the road or conduct construction or dig dirt. Afghanistan is one of the five poorest countries in the world. It highlighted to me how poor the country is to see dirt as the major transported commodity on the roads I observed on my trips around the country. Dirt, however, is popular for the military, international community, and local government because it is used to fill Hesco barriers, which are large cartons that provide security around bases or compounds. I am not sure to what extent the dirt transported in these trucks is also used for the building of mud structures, which seem to be the most common type of buildings in the country, or in making bricks for slightly more stable and modern buildings. It is also a possibility that the mounds of dirt in the back of jingle trucks are used for less scrupulous purposes; smuggling illegal arms or the harvest of the opium crop would be hard to detect underneath a pile of dirt among a large number of such trucks traversing the country.

While, for the most part, drivers seem especially alert, pedestrians are unexpectedly careless and unaware of what is going on around them. The admonition to "Look both ways before you cross the street," was apparently not a point of emphasis in the upbringing of Afghan children. Children and adults wander about the streets without much regard for the reckless driving rampant in Kabul. They are also very tolerant of cars driving by at high speeds in close proximity to them. It is only the caution of drivers or very good luck that prevents more pedestrian accidents. I think there are two possible explanations for the apparent carelessness of the Afghan pedestrian. First, the culture there is much more tolerant of an invasion of "personal space" than Anglo-American cultures. Men walk hand in hand, stand close together, and frequently touch. All of this notwithstanding a level of personal hygiene that is consistent with a lack of indoor plumbing in much of the country. The different sense of personal space makes a car brushing by more tolerable. Another factor that might explain the pedestrian behavior is the fatalistic belief that God's will dictates everything. Much more than determining the behavior of people walking through the streets, this belief system results in a different view of life from the American perspective. If an Afghan is asked if he will be at a meeting the following day, he will respond with—rather than "Yes"—"*Inshallah* (God willing)." People are much more likely to mentally put their fate in God's hands, and to some extent, it seems like this results in pedestrian carelessness.

Military drivers are even worse than the locals. Military convoys in the city frequently use "nontactical vehicles," or NTVs, which are most often large sports utility vehicles, but are also other makes such as pickup trucks. Military drivers call their style of maneuver "tactical driving," which is a precaution to minimize the time spent in a dangerous environment. Practically, this results in aggressive, even reckless, driving at speeds well above the flow of traffic. While the commonplace gridlock can mitigate the speeds and aggression with which military convoys can move, there are plenty of opportunities for damage. On the other hand, European components of the NATO ISAF drive much more cautiously because they patrol Kabul in large and ponderous armored vehicles, signifying a severe risk aversion. These giant vehicles—once I even saw a convoy of three tanks—do little for the pavement condition of Kabul's roads, which, as I have described earlier, are not in the best shape.

The American private security firm DynCorp is especially well known for its people's reckless style of driving. Far more aggressive than even the typical U.S. Army driver, DynCorp employees speed through town, weapons pointed out the vehicle at the ready. Charged with protection of President Hamid Karzai, the vigilance of these contractors is understandable. However, with the social development and counterinsurgency nature of the mission in Afghanistan, the antics of DynCorp are certainly not helping to win hearts and minds of Afghans. Civilian casualties are viewed as acceptable collateral damage, and are likely not even documented by the firm, which is not as accountable as the military units in the country.

The resentment against DynCorp literally exploded in the weeks leading up to the October presidential election. In one of the most serious attacks of 2004, a car bomb tore apart the side of one of the guesthouses used by DynCorp personnel, killing several of the American contractors. At first, it was difficult to understand why this target was selected. The guesthouse was right next to a Joint Electoral Management Body building formerly used as a voter registration center. Analysts believed that surely the attack was aimed at that building, a fulfillment of the militants' anti-election threats. However, further research revealed the careful planning and surveillance, extensive explosive materials used, and proficiency with which the attack was carried out. It became clear that targeting the DynCorp guesthouse was no mistake. Rather than Islamist extremists, the attack was most likely carried out by criminals related to or contracted out by the family of one of the accidental victims of DynCorp's careless aggression.

DynCorp exhibits the worst of the aggressive posture that Americans have taken to the streets of Kabul and the other urban areas of Afghanistan. But I cannot say that I am blameless either. Several convoys in which I have driven or rode have been involved in traffic accidents. My first experience involved a two-vehicle convoy moving down Kabul's main strip, Jalalabad Road, when I first arrived in Kabul in September to begin working in the Election

Security Operations Center. We were taking a soldier to Kabul Airport to move back to Bagram by helicopter. I was driving the second vehicle, and it was my first time to brave the dangers of Kabul traffic. The lead vehicle was being driven by a young sergeant who served as a driver for the operations section of CJTF-76, and he was used to the city and the routes. He was engaging in "tactical driving" down the highway, and I followed as best I could as he sped through traffic, weaving in and out of traffic. Driving aggressively was indicated by the threat level, which was high due to the concentration of reports of extremist planning to disrupt the approaching election. But it went poorly for an Afghan driver who was not expecting us to be heading down the road so fast. He pulled out onto Jalalabad Road from a side street, and his front bumper was crushed and shattered into a blend of glass, plastic, and metal. I had a prime view from my position behind the lead vehicle.

Unfortunately, there is nothing Coalition forces can do for local drivers in such cases. Unless there is a danger to someone's life, military drivers are told to keep moving at all costs. As a matter of fact, during my time in Kabul, I coordinated parking passes from all of the major military compounds in order to expedite my movement through the inspection process at their gates. The CFC headquarters, also known as Kabul Compound, issued me a parking pass, which came with an accident notification letter written in English, Dari, and Pashtun. It said something to the effect of the following:

> YOU HAVE BEEN INVOLVED IN AN ACCIDENT WITH A COALITION VE-
> HICLE. WE ARE WORKING TO MAKE AFGHANISTAN A SAFER PLACE FOR
> EVERYONE AND REGRET THIS ACCIDENT. FOR YOUR SECURITY AS WELL
> AS THE SECURITY OF THE PERSONNEL IN THE COALITION VEHICLE, WE
> CANNOT STOP TO SPEAK TO YOU RIGHT NOW. PLEASE CALL 237-5151
> TO FOLLOW UP ABOUT THIS INCIDENT.

The phone number given was the number to the military police of Kabul Compound. While many Afghans are illiterate, the capital city likely had more drivers with the ability to read such a letter than most areas of Afghanistan. However, the phone number given was a Defense Switched Network (DSN) phone number, so no one could dial it from a civilian phone. Since the average Afghan citizen could not enter an American military compound, much less ask to use an American military telephone inside one, the letter could never actually result in a phone connection producing restitution for any damage caused by an accident. In trying to discover the rationale behind issuing this letter to hundreds if not thousands of American military vehicle operators, I was never able to determine whether this was intentional so that Afghans involved in an accident would be temporarily placated, or if it was due to thoughtlessness on the part of the individuals who developed, executed, and approved the accident letter program. I never used the letter myself as it seemed a way to add longer-term frustration to an immediate grievance.

In this case, the collision was probably the Afghan's fault. He hit the American SUV near the rear wheel, but the comparative rates of movement left the Afghan with the most damage by far. The point of impact seemed to indicate that the Afghan driver, who was also turning from a side street onto a main road, had carelessly driven into the passing military vehicle. However, as I pointed out to our driver, our excessive rate of speed ultimately led to the accident.

A few weeks after the election, I was working embedded with the United Nations' electoral office in a surreptitious civilian-clothes role. My superiors at Bagram sent me a young Marine corporal to serve as a driver and security guard for several weeks. His specialty in his home station of Okinawa was driving large military trucks, so I was happy to turn over the wheel of our blue Ford Ranger to him. His tenure as my driver was mostly unmarred by accidents, with one exception. Kabul does not have traffic lights; the city does not enjoy electric power at all hours. So many major intersections have traffic circles to regulate traffic. My young Marine decided to cut off a large jingle truck that was trying to merge out of the circle. As we continued around the circle, the truck struck us against the rear side of our pickup truck. I calmly told the Marine to keep driving; there would be no benefit to stopping, and the damage was likely minor anyway. He was upset that the truck hit us, but I doubt that it was possible for the Afghan to see us because his driver's seat was very high off the ground, and the Marine's maneuver brought our pickup extremely close to the turning truck.

Another incident occurred in December 2004. We were visiting some sites in Kabul with a United Nations Development Program employee, a female journalist from Singapore named Dora Cheok, who was sitting behind me in the passenger's side back seat. My partner was driving and realized he made a wrong turn near the King's Tomb in Kabul. He started to back up to turn around, and a taxi smashed into the side of our front driver's side headlight. The taxi and his fares exited the vehicle, perhaps expecting us to do the same. Again, these Afghans hit us, and although backing up in the middle of the road was not the best idea, it was a side street with little traffic, and the taxi should have seen it clearly if he had been paying attention and driving at a reasonable speed. There were clearly no injuries and the damage to both vehicles was slight, so I suggested that immediate departure would be prudent.

We drove off, and a few minutes later were surprised by Afghan persistence as the taxi drove up behind us, with its occupants waving and beeping the horn. When we didn't pull over, as the taxi clearly wanted, it actually began to ram our vehicle from behind! This was a surprising turn of events, but my partner thought of an easy way to evade this nuisance. We were approaching the Afghan presidential palace, which blocks off traffic at what would otherwise be a large and busy part of Kabul. International military can pass through the checkpoint toward the palace, but aggressive and angry taxi drivers have no such access. So we slowed and approached the checkpoint, guarded by an Afghan National Army patrol. The taxi frustrated expectations again as it pulled in front of us when we slowed down, preventing us from entering the checkpoint. Eric and I agreed that this was actually a rather clever move. The Afghans exited the taxi, and we simply took a right turn and took off again.

But the taxi driver's determination was not to be thwarted. He leaped into the back of the pick-up truck as we pulled away. Leaving his taxi and his fares behind, the driver began using his fists to hit the roof of the truck's cab and the rear passenger side window. Unfortunately, this was the window where Dora was riding, and the violence of the situation would certainly have escalated if the driver had broken the window and endangered her. As it was, his actions were harmless, and although alarming, the situation was at the same time somewhat comical. My partner lowered his window and shouted in a loud and commanding voice, "Get off the vehicle!" I observed that it was unlikely that our unwanted passenger understood English. Eric countered wryly, "I think he gets the idea." The Afghan was unpersuaded, and we drove on with the rampaging driver on the back of the truck, to the amusement of bystanders.

This time, we decided to drive to a U.S. Army compound, where the guard force would handle this fellow. There would also be sufficiently skilled translators to explain that he would not be able to get any money for his trouble and convey apologies for the whole incident. But the driver's gesticulations and shouts calmed, and as traffic pressed, and we slowed down, he jumped out of the back of the truck. He ran along side us for a short time, grabbing the rear view mirror by my window and spoke to me in his native tongue. All I could do was shrug and look apologetic. At this point, his mien had changed from enraged to beseeching, but there was nothing we could do for him. He finally gave up keeping pace with the pickup truck, and was left behind, slightly damaging the mirror as it pulled out of his grip. At this point the poor driver was a few miles from his taxi, which he had abandoned in front of an Afghan National Army checkpoint. Doubtless his vehicle and his livelihood were lost, whether his fares decided to steal his car or whether the Afghan National Army soldiers manning the checkpoint otherwise disposed of it.

My own accident is of course the one about which I feel the most remorse. I had a late afternoon meeting at the U.S. Embassy, and at this time, my Marine was not with me. The other captain serving with me as my partner was in Wisconsin on R and R leave, so I was on my own. It was just one of those days with really bad traffic. I was using my partner's pistol, while he was on leave, because the Army never issued me my own weapon for this mission, and I took it out and put it on my lap because the traffic was so tight. I was inching through the bumper-to-bumper traffic, and finally I reached Abdul Haq Circle, the traffic circle that turned into Jalalabad Road, where our previous accident with the Marine corporal had occurred.

As I moved out of that traffic circle, a blue sedan struck the right rear side of my vehicle. An Afghan traffic policeman waved me to the left, which was an obvious move, because to continue with the car's front bumper pressed against my side would have scraped the vehicles against one another. So I moved to the left and continued forward. The Afghan passengers got out of their car. As I kept driving, I heard one of them attempt to open my rear passenger side door. Of course, he had no luck with that effort because we always drive with the windows up and the doors locked. Like the two previous situations, an Afghan civilian vehicle struck our pick up truck, and like the other traffic circle incident, there could only be the slightest degree of damage to either vehicle. As a white person wearing civilian clothes and traveling alone in an unmarked car in the middle of the crowded traffic in a rapidly approaching twilight, I felt vulnerable and had no intentions of stopping to get into a traffic dispute. My rudimentary command of Pashtun, a language that these Afghans may or may not have even spoken since Dari is the predominant language in Kabul, was insufficient to communicate anything of value. So I did not think too much of driving away.

Several hundred meters down the road, a car suddenly pulled in front of me from the shoulder. It was the same car that had struck me as I was coming out of the traffic circle! The four Afghan civilians, along with the traffic policeman, emerged from the vehicle and came up to my truck. They were yelling in their native language and again trying to open the front and rear passenger side doors of my vehicle. I lowered the passenger side front window about an inch, and said in English, "You hit me!" Under the circumstances, I imagined that the departure of a victim of a traffic accident without any demand for remuneration would be ideal for the perpetrator of the accident. But the light color of my skin and my inability to speak the language marked me as a foreign government agent, international aid worker, or private reconstruction contractor. Any of which possibility might yield a healthy payoff for the enterprising Afghan who finds himself in a traffic dispute.

The Afghans did not seem too impressed by my protests, and they still wanted me to exit my vehicle or to allow them access, as they indicated by gesture and by continuing to try to open my locked doors. One of the Afghans spoke English well enough to communicate to me the authority of the traffic cop, pointing to the cop and saying, "International police man! International police man!" Once it was clear to them that I was not suffi- ciently impressed by their efforts or the policeman's authority, the policeman wandered off to a group of other policeman in sight further ahead at the side of the road. Already outnumbered by five to one, with the four Afghan occupants of the sedan and their accompanying policeman, I would soon be more outnumbered and definitely outgunned as well. For while these Afghans appeared unarmed, the police would likely have something that would more than match my partner's pistol that I was carrying. Allowing myself to get drawn into a traffic dispute without a common language and placing myself at the mercy of Afghan jurisprudence and due process would not be an acceptable possibility.

At this point, to the surprise of the Afghans remaining behind as the policeman went for reinforcements, I drove off again. This time, aware that pursuit was likely, I took off at a high rate of speed. The sun had set by now, and it was dark. Traffic was a little lighter, but it was still necessary to weave in and out of traffic. Here, I reach the part of the story I don't like telling friends at cocktail parties. But for you, the reader, I will tell the whole story. A car in front of me suddenly came to a stop, as apparently a car in front of him was making a left turn. If my bearings were correct, this turn was into the same side street where I had earlier experienced my first Afghan traffic accident when some hapless Afghan shredded his front bumper against the lead vehicle of my convoy to Kabul Airport.

I slammed on my brakes, but I skidded into the car in front of me. I had absolutely no sympathy for the Afghans who were pursuing me, who had hit me, then demanded some sort of redress of grievance as if hitting someone guaranteed them a payoff, so long as that someone was from a richer country. But for this poor man and his passengers, I felt extremely remorseful. Stopping because someone in front of him was stopped, perhaps without sufficient notice, this car was rear-ended without warning. I was certainly at fault. Again, there appeared to be no injuries to anyone, although both vehicles were damaged this time. I took off again, pulling around the poor car in front of me. Alone in the middle of a combat zone and a country with no guaranteed rule of law, with likely pursuit of armed Afghans behind me, I was now committing that most odious of traffic violations: hit and run. The road ahead was clear by now continuing away from the heart of Kabul. A bicycle road across the road in front of me, and again I skidded and swerved as I pressed my brakes, but fortunately I avoided hitting that man. I sped down the road with no further incident and returned to the military compound, where I immediately went to file a report on the incident and turn the vehicle in for repair, for a slight scrape on the side from the sedan that hit me and a dent in the front from my collision with the other car. That was the most disturbing traffic incident I was involved in, and I am glad that no one was injured and that I was not pressed more violently by the police or the original Afghans who wanted to engage in the traffic dispute.

Altogether, driving in Afghanistan is a dangerous and emotionally charged experience. While it is impossible to avoid damage to all civilian vehicles, it is fortunate that I never experienced an accident where someone was seriously injured or killed. The inherent risks of traveling in the country make it difficult to settle any accident in a satisfactory manner, which only adds to the problems for both sides.

## THE DEPARTMENT OF STATE

A final part of the international security apparatus is the United States Department of State, as embodied by the U.S. Embassy in Kabul. This was by far the most secure compound I entered in the country, with the most forbidding barriers and the most thorough checkpoint procedures. Ann Jones in her *Kabul in Winter*, an account contemporary to my time in Afghanistan, revealed that the embassy had a nickname among the international community in Kabul: "Fort Paranoia."

It is common to read in the news media critiques of American "empire" and a concern over American domination across the world. It is a perspective common to both the right and the left, with right-wing commentator Patrick Buchanan having written a book entitled *A Republic, Not an Empire*, and with the left-wing frequently deploring the inexorable expansion of American power. This perspective is probably exemplified by Chalmers Johnson's *The Sorrows of Empire*.

If Afghanistan is one of the latest protectorates of the American empire, then the United States Ambassador to Afghanistan Zalmay Khalilzad was a highly qualified proconsul. He was popular among the Afghans, his native people. He was often said to enjoy even more popularity than President Karzai. Afghans frequently approached the Ambassador when he visited outlying parts of the country and requested his help with their problems. The Ambassador had been said to run Afghanistan, and my personal experience does not, for the most part, contradict this.

It is not insignificant that the weekly "Country Team" meeting at the Embassy had representatives from all of the American agencies listed above reporting to Ambassador Khalilzad. The CIA Chief of Station, the senior officer from the Drug Enforcement Agency, and even the three-star general commanding CFC sat around the long table in the conference room outside the Ambassador's office. In my six years as an officer in the military, I have been to many staff meetings. The major duty of a staff is to provide the commander with the information he needs to make decisions. The meeting thus proceeds, with each staff officer providing an update on his or her area of expertise, and the commander listens and asks questions or makes judgments on the staff input. Ambassador Khalilzad's meetings ran a bit differently. As the discussion moved around the table to each staff officer, Khalilzad would often provide his insights and new information that he had obtained from meeting with various Afghan officials with whom he maintained strong relations. The meeting was thus the opposite of my experience in hundreds of military command and staff meetings. In Ambassador Khalilzad's Country

Team meetings, the Ambassador chairing the meeting provided information to his staff rather than the other way around.

It was not easy getting to the U.S. Embassy meetings. I have already described the strange and massive government bureaucracy that is being reproduced in Afghanistan, although I hardly feel I am doing justice to the overlapping and interconnecting headquarters, staffs, and special support organizations that provide roles for the thousands of support personnel stationed in Afghanistan. Nonetheless, negotiating the bureaucracy is the best way to get information and resources needed to do one's jobs and satisfy the needs of one's superiors. The Embassy, with its central role in the Afghan development effort, was clearly a place to go for support in Kabul.

My first stop at the U.S. Embassy was to pay for meals consumed by U.S. military soldiers at the United Nations. The United Nations contracted out a caterer named Esko services, managed by an excellent German chef named Robin Pankl and a staff of Filipino assistants. The Department of Defense could not pay Esko according to their regulations, but they could transfer funds to the Department of State, which could issue the money to me and Captain Harbaugh to pay Esko. This is how we ended up driving across Kabul with seven thousand dollars in cash to pay Mr. Pankl with money drawn from the U.S. Embassy's coffers. It was also an introduction to the Embassy, where I would develop some useful information for my superiors at Bagram Air Base.

For CJTF-76 and CFC-Afghanistan, the Afghan elections process was primarily run by their planning sections. Major Tim Barrick, whom we met in Chapter 1, had been planning future operations for the headquarters at Bagram for the five months leading up to the operation. As the foremost expert on the election, he transitioned to his role in the Election Security Operations Center in September 2004 in part, I think, because that the election was such a priority for the Coalition forces that future planning was put on hold for part of the planning staff. Major Barrick left Afghanistan in October, several days after the election. He was replaced by a Marine aviation major named John Forti and later an Army infantry major named J. B. Vowell. After the presidential election process ended, one of my major responsibilities in Kabul was to provide Majors Forti and Vowell with information they needed to plan for the security of the following national assembly elections.

It occurred to me that the contacts I had made with various UN agencies in Kabul, including the Joint Electoral Management Body, were not the only possible sources of information to which the planners at Bagram would not have access. I made contacts with other international organizations, aside from the United Nations, such as the European Commission, which had an office and an elections expert in Kabul as well as nongovernmental organizations, such as The Asia Foundation, which was significantly involved in the development process and the election in Afghanistan. I visited Dr. Deborah

Alexander, a political scientist who served as the Ambassador's senior elections advisor. I first met Dr. Alexander at the Joint Electoral Management Body weekly security meetings in September as the various security constituencies prepared for the election. A diminutive, sharply dressed woman probably in her late fifties, she struck me as a smart, friendly professional.

As my superiors in Bagram prepared to develop plans for the spring elections, opening sources of political information was a priority. I explained my need for information to Dr. Alexander and asked if there were any regular meetings or working groups at the Embassy where I could sit in to get updated information on the elections. I was surprised when she referred me to the same meetings at the Joint Electoral Management Body where I met her. After all, these meetings occurred in the same room where my own desk was. She also suggested that I go to the Combined Forces Command weekly election planning meetings. A representative from Bagram already attended those meetings (one of the majors to whom I reported). In addition, CFC was an extraneous echelon that did not get tactical information from military forces (this was reported from the soldiers on the front lines back to Bagram, who then reported it to CFC) or political information from liaison with the Afghan government and other political actors (the Embassy did this, although my contacts with the United Nations were better than anyone else since I had a permanent office there). So I was not much better off from her suggestions, although Deborah invited me to come see her anytime I needed anything.

Two weeks later, I did need information and returned to Deborah's office. She was nowhere to be found, so I asked the man in the cubicle next to hers if he knew where she was. A dignified gray-haired man in a conservative business suit, the placard on the wall next to his desk said JUDGE PATT MANEY. Judge Maney told me that Deborah was on leave, but he invited me to sit down and talk. He told me he was a county judge in the First Judicial Circuit in northern Florida and was temporarily assisting as the Senior Political Sector Advisor in the Afghan Reconstruction Group of the Embassy, to which Deborah was also assigned. I explained to him who I was and what I was doing. At the time, I needed some information on the election that Major Forti had requested. Judge Maney provided all the information he had and was happy to hear that I was from Bagram. He was a brigadier general in the Army Reserves, and he explained that his current position in the Embassy was a result of his being recalled for active military service. He was in charge of coordinating the Inauguration Ceremony and needed some assistance from Bagram in arranging security. I promised to put him in touch with some officers who could assist him. Judge Maney suggested that two weekly meetings at the Embassy would help me with future information, so I became a regular, but usually silent, attendee at the Ambassador's Political Core meeting on Monday mornings and the Country Team meeting on Wednesday mornings. These meetings also provided an opportunity to meet other members of the Ambassador's political team. In my experience, smaller discussions before and after a meeting can be as important as the meeting itself.

These meetings became a helpful conduit of information. As I explained already, Ambassador Khalilzad was one of the most informed Americans in the country on a variety of political matters, so he regularly provided up-to-date information on the status of the election, and my superiors were extremely happy with the information that they received that would have taken days or weeks, if ever, to reach them through the normal channels of the bureaucracy. Not wearing a uniform allowed for anonymity not only at the United Nations, but also in these Embassy meetings, where uniformed lieutenant colonels and colonels regularly attended. In spite of my civilian clothes and unmilitary haircut, I was cognizant of my rank, and always introduced myself to the Embassy officials as an Army captain working with the United Nations on the elections, and was liberal with the use of the words "Sir" and "Ma'am."

General Maney introduced me to Ambassador Khalilzad at one of the weekly Country Team meetings and to his Deputy Chief of Mission (DCM), Richard Christiansen, at one of the Political Core meetings. The Ambassador welcomed me with a friendly smile, and Mr. Christiansen was quick to ask for my input from my contacts with the United Nations. I answered his question with information I had recently received during a UN meeting. He expressed his appreciation and asked me to continue to provide updates. To get answers to my questions, discussions before and after the meetings were as helpful to me as the meetings themselves, where I never asked questions, and only very occasionally contributed when senior UN officials had disseminated information to me that the Embassy had not yet received. (Junior officers in meetings of colonels are like children according to the old adage . . . best seen and not heard.) My few moments of contribution occurred after a few weeks of attending the meetings to understand what sort of information the Ambassador's staff had and what they needed. I usually contributed at meetings when the Ambassador was absent, which occurred for a few weeks in November and later during the Christmas and New Year holiday season, when he returned to the states for his vacation.

On the Monday morning after Deborah Alexander's return from her holiday, she was surprised to see me at the Political Core meeting. I gave her a friendly smile and a wave from across the conference table. I greeted her the next Wednesday as we walked up the stairs together toward the meeting. She asked me why I was there, and I told her that Mr. Maney had invited me and that my superiors at Bagram were very pleased with the information they were receiving. She informed me that the military's representative at the meeting was the three-star general in command of CFC-Afghanistan, so my presence was not needed. I suggested that not every piece of information that the general received could be expected to wind its way through the hundreds of staff officers that served in its headquarters to make it to the operational planners at Bagram whom I was supporting. I also noted that their requests for information could be better satisfied by me, and that these meetings were helpful to find information for them.

She then accused me of barging into a classified meeting uninvited and hiding my identity as a military officer to those present at the meeting. I informed her in a calm voice that both Ambassador Khalilzad and DCM Christiansen had welcomed me to the meetings and reminded her that General Maney had invited me. She said that General Maney had no authority to invite me to these meetings, and I imagine she disregarded or disbelieved my point about being welcomed by her superiors. At this point, she realized that she was yelling at me in the corridor right in front of the Ambassador's office, and she said, "I am not going to talk to you about this any more." I suppose my temper had gotten the better of me, so I only could respond in a quiet voice, "Good."

The next time I saw Major J. B. Vowell, he asked me about a shouting match with Deborah Alexander in front of Ambassador Khalilzad's office. I told him there was no match, although I did admit that Dr. Alexander had been shouting at me in front of the Ambassador's office. He gave me some wise advice in the military bureaucracy: "Do not antagonize civilians who have regular meetings with generals." Fair enough. I told Major Vowell I was in-between in a rock and a hard place. I could either discontinue going to the meetings, which would satisfy Dr. Alexander, or continue going to the meetings and risk her ire. He told me to figure it out. He needed the information from the meetings, but he told me I was to be a "quiet professional" and to have no more confrontations with Deborah Alexander. So the next time I saw General Maney, I mentioned that I was under the impression that Dr. Alexander was not very comfortable with my presence at these weekly meetings. He told me not to worry about it, and that he had invited me. I said that Deborah told me that he did not have the authority to invite me to these meetings. He smiled, chuckled, and said not to worry about it. I continued attending the weekly updates at the Embassy, and Dr. Alexander did not speak to me after that.

Some of Deborah's colleagues in the Embassy had told me that she was a very secretive person and tended to enjoy her monopoly on information. In a conversation after one of the later meetings, I asked one of the political officers about a cryptic comment Deborah had made during the meeting. I said it was not very clear what she was referring to, and wondered if this political officer understood the background. The woman responded to me that Deborah had been intentionally mysterious. "The only person who can get information out of Deborah that she doesn't want to share is the Ambassador." So my difficulties might have come from a midlevel functionary trying to protect her turf. My partner, Captain Eric Harbaugh, suggested that it might have involved a conflict between the Defense Department and the State Department, which was a popular subject in the media. Tensions between then Secretary of State Colin Powell and Defense Secretary Donald Rumsfeld were well publicized in the media at the time. Eric felt that I was reliving this conflict in the persons of the career State Department political scientist, Deborah Alexander, and the Army general, Patt Maney. Eric thought that the more accommodating Ambassador and Deputy Chief of Mission—as well as the other helpful junior political officers I had met at these meetings—were just less inclined to play the anti-Defense Department politics than Deborah. Regardless of which political game she was playing, or if it were a combination of both possibilities, it was just one more barrier to getting the job done in a dangerous environment.

After having reviewed the maze of organizations and agencies that I dealt with in Afghanistan, I do not want to leave the patient reader under the impression that navigating U.S. government bureaucracy was the main battle any officer in Afghanistan was fighting. There were, and still are, very dangerous people in Afghanistan. These people were bent on violently opposing Americans at every possibility. Their sole livelihood was doing harm to Americans and the nascent Afghan government and its supporters among the populous. The next three chapters will relate the struggle against this terrorist threat as Afghanistan prepared the way for its first ever democratically elected government.

# CHAPTER 3

# Victory over Terrorism in the Presidential Election

Afghanistan's election posed a serious challenge to the security forces trying to facilitate the development of governance in the country. The process was a dramatic, culminating event in the struggle over Afghanistan in many ways. First, in the months leading up to the election, al Qaeda and Taliban threats and plans indicated a momentous offensive for the election, reminiscent of Tet in Vietnam, to demoralize the Afghan people and Coalition nations. Second, in the two weeks before the election, the Coalition, and to an even greater extent, the Afghan National Army and the Afghan National Police, mounted an aggressive security campaign, discovering and capturing an incredible amount of explosives and terrorists preparing to conduct "spectacular attacks." Election Day itself was a series of unexpected events, from a crisis over the indelible ink to a threatened candidate boycott. Interim President Hamid Karzai may have caused some of the current controversy over the election by taking a hard line with warlords in the preceding months. His opponents, chief among them former warlords themselves, seized on the opportunity to discredit the process in order to gain leverage with the new government, threatening the fragile democracy. This chapter will discuss these events as terrorists and their opponents in the international and Afghan militaries mobilized before the election. I will relate a detailed account of the election threats, the terrorist attacks and interventions against the terrorists, and finally the controversy of Election Day itself.

## THREATS TO THE ELECTION

The time before the election was characterized by an intense stream of threat reporting from multiple sources of intelligence. These reports were clear about the terrorist forces' desire to disrupt the election. It could be argued that the terrorists did not place as much importance on the election as did the international community in Afghanistan and the central government. However, the threat reporting contradicts such an assessment. Both the Taliban and al Qaeda had reason to place significance on Afghanistan's first democratic election.

Perhaps at this point it would be helpful to comment on the distinction between the Taliban and al Qaeda. These two elements represent the largest threat groups in Afghanistan. The Taliban was the ruling regime since the mid-1990s. The word Taliban itself signifies student, or scholar, and the movement derives from the study and application of Islamic teachings and the *sharia*, or religious law. Their extreme implementation of Islam was well known throughout the world as news reports on the subjugation of women and the mutilation of thousands-of-years-old Buddhist statues circulated. The regime's destruction of two ancient Buddha statues in 10021 in the central Bamiyan region of the country, was based on their belief that the relics, which stood 180 and 121 feet tall, were idolatrous icons of an infidel religion. If not the most extreme and repressive regime in the history of the world, the Taliban were certainly the most extreme and repressive rulers in modern times. Their overthrow was an event long awaited by many of the Afghan people.

Al Qaeda, on the other hand, is not primarily an Afghan movement and organization. This group consists of foreign fighters who infiltrated Afghanistan by the thousands after the Taliban established its rule. Mostly of Arab descent, al Qaeda also included Chechens and Muslim North Africans who had combat experience often originating in the battle against the Soviets in Afghanistan in the 1980s, but also in more recent violent campaigns in Palestine, Bosnia, Chechnya, and Kashmir. New recruits were generated by attracting young Muslim men to the Taliban's Afghanistan by the lure of the pure spiritual life under the Taliban's application of *sharia* law and the possibility of finding a devout Muslim wife. These recruits were then taken to terrorist training camps and instructed and led by the veteran cadre of al Qaeda. After the initial American-led invasion, leaders and key operators of both the al Qaeda terrorist organization and the former Taliban government fled to the wild, untamed regions of Pakistan known as the Northwest Frontier Province, the Federally Administered Tribal Areas, and Baluchistan. These areas, where Pakistani forces had little control and international military forces in Afghanistan could not go, provided a sanctuary from where these threat groups were able to prosecute a war against the new Afghan government and their foreign protectors.

Afghan hospitality was legendary, and it was perhaps partially the cause of the American presence in the country. Shortly after the September 11th attacks, President Bush had given an ultimatum to Mullah Mohammed Omar and the Taliban leadership: " ... Tonight the United States of America makes the following demands on the Taliban: Deliver to United States authorities all of the leaders of al Qaeda who hide in your land." Aside from the symbiotic relationship enjoyed between the Taliban regime and the tens of thousands of Bin Laden's al Qaeda Arabs living in the country, the Taliban also were beholden by the principle of hospitality. The Taliban was not only a religious movement, but also a resurgence of Afghanistan's oppressed majority ethnic group, the Pashtuns. Among the traditional tribal practices of the Pashtuns is the convention of *Pashtunwali*, which has a strict code of conduct requiring duties of a host to guests seeking hospitality. Henry David Thoreau argued in 1849 that the American people must make moral choices even if it cost them their own survival: "This people must cease to hold slaves, and to make war on Mexico, though it cost them their existence as a people." The Taliban seem to have made such a choice in refusing to turn over Bin Laden in the aftermath of the 9-11 attacks. Many observers feel that the traditional moral duty of Afghan hospitality was a serious part of this fateful decision.

I learned a lesson on this core cultural value on the road, a place where so many lessons of Afghan culture can be learned. I have never been an expert at driving in snow. I was quick to let my partner, a native of Kansas, take over during the winter season. I had learned to drive in Port Orange, Florida, so I was ill equipped for the icy, snow-covered roads of Kabul. I have noticed several things people take for granted since my return from Afghanistan. Since moving to Boston, for example, I notice that trucks will travel across the city's roadways after a heavy snowfall, dropping salt and dirt to melt the snow and provide traction on the roads. Afghanistan, whose paved roads are in horrible conditions where they even exist, has no such luxury.

The normal rigors of driving on snow-covered roads were exacerbated by the potholes of Kabul's road network and the icy coating that normally dissipates with salt treatments in the United States. Even Eric, who had grown up through some harsh winters, got our truck stuck as we traveled to a Thanksgiving dinner at a United Nations guesthouse. So I had no delusions as I drove down Flower Street alone early in January. Eric was in a meeting at the Elections Office, and I had business at the American Embassy, so I was traveling by myself.

The ice was so thick that the road was not flat, but inclined and declined with formations of ice and tightly packed snow. At several points, my truck just began to slide sideways. As I came to a particularly narrow pass between cars parked on both sides of the road, I was about to discover the meaning of Afghan hospitality.

However, as I drove my pickup truck through downtown Kabul, I was not thinking of Afghan hospitality. I was focused on preventing the truck from sliding left and right so it would not crash into the Afghan merchants' and shoppers' cars parked on the sides of the street. In spite of using four-wheel drive in first gear, my truck slid into a mass of ice from which I was unable to extricate it. I was stuck.

Alone, stuck in the middle of Kabul, was not a good position in which to find myself. As I tried to extricate the truck from the ice, getting out and looking at the formation of ice and snow in which I was caught, I was a bit concerned. I tried to move the truck in various directions with no luck. In the best scenario, it seemed I would have to call in some American forces for assistance. They would have difficulty moving down the narrow road as well, and having them drive up in force to help would not be the best maneuver to blend in as a neutral member of the international community in Kabul. In addition, such assistance would probably take a few hours to arrive. At worst, some Afghan criminal or extremist might try to take advantage of my vulnerable position. After all, I was down the road from Chicken Street, where several NATO soldiers and a female American translator had been killed by a suicide bomber weeks earlier. And it was still unclear to me if the election worker abduction would result in further kidnapping attempts. Altogether, these risks were improbable at the time as the onset of winter had reduced the amount of jihadi activity in the country, but the worst-case scenarios did concern me at the moment.

Then I experienced the Afghan hospitality that had preserved Bin Laden from destruction a couple of years earlier. Afghan men came up and began to push me out of the snow. A few of them pantomimed movements with their hands to indicate which way I should turn the wheel. I imagined that their experience in the harsh conditions of the Kabul roads had given them much more insight than I had to extricate myself from this icy mass. Even with the help of the Afghan passersby, it took another thirty minutes to finally get out of the large icy buildup. As soon as the truck was free, I got out and thanked all those who had helped me and still remained. We carried emergency rations and bottled water in the truck as a precautionary measure. I took this stock of supplies and gave it out with *deera manana*'s [thank you very much] to the men who had helped. Aside from my appreciation to get out of my situation, the duty of the guest to show appreciation to the host is an important part of the *Pashtunwali* code.

To return to the election preparations, the Taliban, who view themselves as the rightful rulers of Afghanistan, considered the election and its preparations to be an illegitimate process to further usurp their rightful position and authority in Afghanistan. The regime was initially welcomed for rescuing the country from the disastrous civil strife that followed in the years after Soviet invaders were repelled. However, its harsh rule, brutal repression, and radical theology quickly undermined any mandate the Taliban had enjoyed. They most likely never acknowledged this dwindling popular support.

The *Loya Jirga* (grand council) that selected President Hamid Karzai as the interim president was perceived by Taliban loyalists as an American proxy, a sign of further domination by the United States after overthrowing the Taliban regime. Karzai was widely viewed throughout Afghanistan as closely influenced by the Americans. (In my opinion as an outside observer, this view was fairly accurate, even more so in the beginning years of the nascent government.) Karzai's American DynCorp private security detail, movement on U.S. military aircraft, and close relationship and frequent appearances with U.S. Ambassador Zalmay Khalilzad contributed to this popular perception. The sum of all this is that the Taliban were determined to disrupt the election at all costs, hoping to prevent a further solidification of their dispossession of authority in Afghanistan and what they saw as an increasingly permanent American influence in the country.

Al Qaeda similarly recognized that the election was key terrain in their strategic goals. Still operating in the tribal region in the Waziristan agencies of Pakistan and neighboring areas, the foreign terrorists recognized the opportunity that the election represented. These fighters are first rabidly anti-American. While Osama bin Laden's *fatwa* (religious declaration) in 1998 had already called for all Muslims to "kill Americans wherever possible," American incursion into Afghanistan and Iraq has only increased their desperation to strike back.

Additionally, al Qaeda recognizes that the failure of democracy in Afghanistan is its best hope to return to a state sanctuary for its aspirations of international terrorism. A State Department report in late 2004 analyzed the possibilities available to al Qaeda for sanctuary in the aftermath of its expulsion from Afghanistan. The report considered and dismissed several alternatives across the Muslim world, arguing that the Pakistani tribal area was still the best viable option in spite the pressure from ongoing Pakistani military operations. With the Pakistani military pressing al Qaeda from the east, and no viable alternatives in the Middle East, Southeast Asia, or northern or eastern Africa, the terrorists needed to do something to break the West's hold in their former stronghold. The election presented the best opportunity to do this. Showing the international community and Afghans that Afghan society was unprepared for democracy would be the best way to return to the conditions of a failed state that would allow al Qaeda's reemergence in Afghanistan.

While the Taliban hoped to discourage people from voting through intimidation and violence in the weeks leading up to the election, al Qaeda's methods are more extreme and dramatic. Catastrophic attacks on Election Day would allow them to advance their cause and would fit their pattern of operations. Finally, in addition to the local strategic concerns in Afghanistan, al Qaeda was hoping to influence other strategic goals as well. With violence in Iraq increasing in the run-up to the American presidential election, voices of dissent in the United States and the international media suggested that January 2005 was an unrealistic timeline to hold Iraqi elections. A failure to hold a safe and effective election in Afghanistan could have derailed the process in Iraq. Further, al Qaeda must have felt encouragement from their success in the 2003 Madrid bombing to influence the election of a major Western democracy. A chaotic and destructive failed election in Afghanistan would be the best way al Qaeda could have fanned the flames of criticism of the plans for Iraq in the coming months. Such an accomplishment would have been a serious blow to the Bush Administration, whose policies al Qaeda views as a major hindrance to their ability to reestablish a stronghold from which to launch future attacks.

A review of threats in just the month leading to the election can confirm the importance with which these terrorist groups viewed the event. These reports came in from across the country on a daily basis. The following is only a sample of this threat stream. Other events, such as night letters, where the Taliban would leave threatening letters in popular gathering places, and local intimidation, were taking place on a regular basis. I am going to walk you through the threats that American intelligence was receiving to the Afghan election in a chronological sequence. Tracking these threats, alerting the responsible actors across the major security constituencies, and conducting pattern analysis were my and my team's major roles before the election. The following threat reports occurred in the month prior to the October 9, 2004, presidential election.

## The First Week

A good starting point in looking at these threats is with a video released the month before the Afghan election that attracted international media attention. Osama bin Laden's top lieutenant, Ayman al-Zawahiri, appeared in a videotaped message released on Thursday, September 9, 2004, on the Arabic-language TV news network al-Jazeera, saying southern and eastern Afghanistan are controlled by the *mujahideen*. "East and south Afghanistan is an open battlefield for the *mujahideen*, while the liars are hiding in the big capitals," he said, a Kalashnikov assault rifle resting on the wall behind him. "The Americans are hiding now in trenches and they refuse to come out and meet the *mujahideen*, despite the *mujahideen* antagonizing them with bombing and shooting and roadblocks around them. Their defense focuses on air strikes, which wastes America's money in just stirring up sand."

The video followed a pattern of al Qaeda tapes released near the anniversary of the September 11, 2001, attacks. On September 10, 2003, they released a video of bin Laden walking in the mountains with al-Zawahiri providing an audio message. On September 9, 2002, al-Jazeera broadcast a videotape of bin Laden, who praised the 9-11 hijackers. The 2004 release was significant because videotaped messages have been rare since the 9-11 attacks. The reference to *mujahideen*, instead of al Qaeda or Taliban, may be an attempt to win sympathy for their cause in the Muslim world. The cause of the *mujahideen*, who successfully repelled the Russian invasion in the 1980s is likely more sympathetic than either al Qaeda, who had targeted

Muslim civilians in numerous attacks in the past few years, or the former Taliban regime, who practiced an extreme variant of Islam and was unable to secure normal diplomatic relations with even many Muslim countries. Extremist night letters, notes left to threaten the people or inspire them to jihad against the Coalition military or the government, were often addressed to the *mujahideen* of Afghanistan.

I spoke with one of my Afghan National Army counterparts about the significance of the term *mujahideen*. Lieutenant Colonel Aziz Hassan, the logistics officer from the Afghan Army assigned to work in the Election Security Operations Center, and I had a conversation on the subject that lasted some time. The term *mujahideen* is viewed with reverence among Afghans. Thinking of Chalmers Johnson's book *Blowback*, describing how the CIA created al Qaeda by supporting the anti-Soviet *mujahideen* in the 1980s, I asked Colonel Hassan what the term meant. I explained to him that some Americans think of it as a synonymous term with al Qaeda, except that it hearkens back to the struggle against the Soviet invasion two decades ago. Hassan told me I could not be more wrong. *Mujahideen* is the noble Islamic warrior, not the terrorist. I then asked about former Herat Province Governor Ismail Khan, who had earned some credibility among today's Afghans as a *mujahideen* for resisting the Soviets in the 1980s and then the Taliban in the 1990s. Hassan told me I was again wrong. Khan forsook the honor of that title when he refused to comply with the central government led by Interim President Hamid Karzai. Perhaps not all Afghans were as discriminating in the meaning of the term as the progovernment military officer. Nonetheless, the terrorist leaders were thus wise to appeal to this heroic term, which appeals to a broad base of Muslims, some of whom are less loyal to the interests of the Afghan government than my Afghan officer counterpart.

Following al-Zawahiri's tape, reporting came in regularly warning of the determined Taliban forces hoping to violently unsettle the historic election. A look at the four weeks of reporting before Election Day indicates that specific, credible threats were being posed against the government across the entire country. On September 11, there was a report of a planning meeting to disrupt the election in the city of Jalalabad with missiles, improvised explosive devices, and car bombs. Such reports of planning meetings were very specific in the issues discussed at the meeting as well as attendees, times, locations, and other details. Additionally, the Director of Security for the United Nations Joint Electoral Management Body reported sophisticated surveillance activities in Kabul and Jalalabad and increasing community complaints in Kabul from citizens living near potential bombing targets, such as international organization offices and safe houses. On September 12, a report was received of terrorist leader Zer Mohammad targeting the election in Jalalabad and Kabul. Additionally, in the violent southern province of Zabul, authorities learned of confiscation of voter registration cards, assault of voters, and active intimidation. A report came in describing the intentions of a Taliban Commander in Ghazni Province to prevent females from voting and to intimidate election officials by calling them directly. On September 13, enemy surveillance of Kabul and Bagram was observed. On September 14, Afghanistan's National Directorate of Security revealed Taliban plans to disrupt election in Naw District, Helmand Province, along with specific details of the planning meeting in which these plans were refined. On September 15, the Konar Province Taliban leader, Najibullah, argued among his colleagues that their previous harassing attacks on outlying American outposts should be replaced with more concentrated efforts against targets in the major regional city of Asadabad. He explained that such plans would be more effective in discouraging people from voting. Further surveillance of Bagram and Kabul was noted. On September 16, a terrorist named Naim Jan was planning a Kabul suicide bombing in the days before the election. In addition, a plan was discovered to move four trucks to Kabul as remote-controlled improvised explosive devices. Senior Taliban leaders Kabir and Haji Din Mohammad met in Jalalabad to plan attacks to undermine the election. Reports from Logar Province revealed that Taliban fighters were taking advantage of a limited Coalition presence in that area to stage there for election attacks. And it was reported that the terrorist group Hezb-e-Islami Gulbuddin was obtaining Afghan National Army uniforms to gain access to election-related targets. On September 17, the Joint Electoral Management Body in Kabul reported on a third incident of suspicious surveillance of its compound in a week. The private contracting firm Global Risk Strategies revealed a report of a planned rocket attack on the JEMB office in Wardak Province.

### The Second Week

The following week continued this reporting stream. On September 19, plans were reported for terrorist attacks in Kandahar using jingle trucks to smuggle rockets and other munitions into the city. On September 19, it was also revealed that Hezb-e-Islami Gulbuddin was joining forces with the Taliban in Konar Province to better concentrate their efforts. A senior leader meeting of forty-five terrorist leaders took place in Chaman, Pakistan, to discuss plans for the election. On September 21, it was revealed that some terrorist leaders felt that Coalition military forces would be the center of gravity for election security and that targeting these forces would be the best way to disrupt the election. Ironically, the United States military and its allies would have greatly preferred this approach. Protecting civilians and vulnerable election sites would be extremely difficult, and locating terrorists and insurgents is also a challenge unless they choose to reveal themselves. The report that the terrorists would seek out Coalition military was an encouraging report in an otherwise daunting stream of antielection threats.

Another report of Taliban in Nangarhar Province revealed plans to disrupt the election. On September 22, a report noted ten prospective female suicide bombers leaving Jalalabad City for training in Pakistan to target Jalalabad during the election. This report was unusual because suicide bombing was rare in Afghanistan and using females for combat was virtually unheard-of. The prediction ultimately did not come to pass. Another report of Taliban and Hezb-e-Islami Gulbuddin cooperation arrived, based on the results of a conference between the groups in Pakistan. The Taliban also held an anti-election meeting in Nuristan Province to refine plans there. Nuristan is a remote, untraffricable area in the northeast of the country. It is isolated by severe terrain and by a population that is independent and alien to Afghan culture. Nuristan has a nickname of "Kafiristan," which means the land of unbelievers. This is because it has a traditional animist religion that resisted conversion to Islam more than any other part of Afghanistan. I heard it called the "Wild West of Afghanistan" by members of the international security community in Afghanistan, a country which itself is often compared to the wild west.

Finally, on September 22, it was reported that Afghan government officials feared election attacks in Oruzgan and Zabul Provinces to the south. These two provinces were among the most loyal to the former Taliban regime, or at least to the strict Islamic way of life practiced under the Taliban. They were active insurgent hotbeds. Oruzgan was the homeland of the Taliban Supreme Leader Mullah Mohammed Omar, and Zabul was a violent border province. It was said that Mohammed Omar would visit his homeland occasionally. It was even rumored that American soldiers entered a mosque while the Taliban leader was at prayer, but they had not noticed him. Since no photographs of Mohammed Omar exist, this is entirely possible, but it seems unlikely that such an event would actually have happened. The prospect of American soldiers entering a mosque while locals were praying seems unlikely. Such a coincidence is also a statistical improbability. The members of the senior Taliban leadership were in hiding and rarely ventured out in public much less in public in occupied Afghanistan. Additionally, patrols by American soldiers into any given part of the frontier regions of the country were rarer than anyone would have liked to admit. The convergence of two such events was more likely rumor than fact.

On September 23, further plans were revealed for disguised attacks, this time using police uniforms. A Taliban meeting in Quetta, Pakistan, reached the decision to threaten local elders about the election and kill those who failed to comply. Taliban in Kandahar planned a car bomb attack on Election Day. A senior leader meeting in the southern provinces discussed how best to target the election. Finally, in the east, extremist leaders discussed strategy for Konar and Nuristan Provinces. The movement of Taliban fighters from Pakistan to the southeast provinces of Afghanistan was reported, and the source of the report stated that their goal was to disrupt the elections. On September 24, a report arrived on an al Qaeda car bomb plan on Election Day. Another report of Taliban-disguised attacks arrived. It was also reported that Qari Amadullah, the Taliban intelligence chief, was going to lead attacks on the election in Ghazni and Bamiyan Provinces. This report did not seem likely as these central provinces had not experienced as much insurgent activity in the past. If true, the report represented the Taliban's effort to extend its reach during the election. Ghazni Province was a major target area for improvised explosive devices along Highway 1, or Ring Road, which runs through the province, but it was not a home of as many insurgents as those in the south or southeast, and it was not as easy to reach from sanctuaries across the border in the Pakistani tribal areas. Bamiyan Province was even more removed from the insurgent campaign. The area is populated by the minority Hazara population, a Shiite Muslim people distinguished by their Asiatic features. It is separated from its neighboring provinces by forbidding mountainous terrain, and the people living there, religiously and ethnically different from the rest of Afghanistan, were previously targets of violence and oppression. It was not a likely place for terrorists to be able to hide, and its remoteness made it unlikely that they would concentrate efforts there. Bamiyan is known outside of Afghanistan for housing the Buddhist monuments that the Taliban destroyed. These statues were the largest images of Buddha in the world, and the grievance that the Taliban held against them included not only that they were icons of an unIslamic religion. It was also believed among Taliban Muslims that depicting the image of a person is unholy, so these statues were a giant affront to this belief. It is due to this belief that Mullah Mohammed Omar has never in his life allowed his photograph to be taken, a fact that has complicated the manhunt for him.

## The Third Week

The third week's reporting made increasingly clear that urban centers would be targeted during the election. On September 25, a report of Taliban infiltration from Logar to the Kabul Capital Province was observed. Additionally, fighters moved to Kandahar to target the election. On September 26, there was a report of two terrorists planning attacks in the days before election in Kabul. The Haqqani terrorist network planned to attack Coalition forces in Khost Province to disrupt the election, and they were receiving additional funding for their antielection efforts. Jalaluddin Haqqani was the Taliban's former minister of tribal affairs and has been a pivotal figure in the insurgent resistance following the American invasion in 2001. Haqqani was a renowned Pashtun fighter during the resistance to the Soviet occupation and served in the post-communist government in the early 1990s. Shortly before the fall of Kabul to the Taliban, Haqqani defected from the government and swore allegiance to the Taliban. His intervention allowed the Taliban to consolidate their military gains in Nangarhar Province, the most populous area of the eastern part of the country. This was where Jalaluddin lived with Osama bin Laden and other senior leaders of the al Qaeda terrorist organization that moved to Afghanistan after the Taliban took power. Bin Laden was friends with Haqqani, and Haqqani is credited with orchestrating bin Laden's escape through the Tora Bora Mountains in Nangarhar. Like many of the central leaders of the Taliban, Jalaluddin was aging. His insurgent network, known as the Haqqani network, had moved to several medium-sized cities across the border from the P2K area (Paktia, Paktika, and Khost provinces). Haqqani's sons directed the network, and Siraq Haqqani was primary among these subordinate leaders. It was reported that Siraq himself was moving across the border to Paktika to supervise antielection activities.

On September 28, twenty Arabs were reportedly moving to Kabul to disrupt the election, and rocket attacks were planned against Coalition forces in Naray to disrupt the election. On September 29, terrorists were preparing new improvised explosives in Kandahar to disrupt elections, and others in Logar and Kabul were planning attacks. On September 30, a meeting in Kohat, Pakistan, resulted in plans to disrupt the election in Kabul and Nangarhar. In Kandahar, a plan to attack government officials to cause chaos before the election was revealed. Fighters under a leader named Mullah Assidullah planned to disguise themselves and shave their beards in Zabul Province to gain better access for election attacks. On October 1, we received information on a plan to assassinate President Karzai in Bamiyan Province and for motorcycles to be used as vehicle-borne improvised explosive devices in Kandahar. The Afghan Ministry of Defense warned about infiltration of terrorist elements from Logar Province into Kabul Province. Another report warned of al Qaeda and Taliban targeting the election with mass casualty attacks.

## The Final Week

The final week in the run-up to the election continued to provide more urgent and more focused threat reporting. On October 2, it was reported that the Taliban planned to attack schools in the election run up. Schools were often the location of polling sites, so targeting them would intimidate voters and signal that these areas would be unsafe on Election Day. Additionally, it was reported that two car bombs had arrived in Kabul from Peshawar, Pakistan. Finally, another report came out on plans to disrupt the election in Logar and Kabul Provinces. Logar Province was on the southern border with the capital province of Kabul. Kabul was an obvious target for election-related attacks. A city of two to four million people, it presented great opportunity to substantively disrupt the election and conduct a large-scale, spectacular attack. It also contained most of the international presence in the country, including media representatives, so activity in Kabul would be more likely to attract press coverage. Logar was not a hotbed of Taliban activity, so the relatively smaller Coalition presence in that province made the area more permissive. At the same time, Logar bordered the provinces to the south and east that housed large numbers of insurgent fighters and populations sympathetic to their cause. After the repeated reports about strikes based from Logar and southern Kabul province, I developed a detailed analysis presenting this threat to the CJTF-76 intelligence headquarters and sent it to them over the secret Internet (siprnet). A couple of days later, Major Tim Barrick informed me that his colleagues in the planning section had developed a "con op" (contingency operation) to target the possible terrorist hideouts in these areas. The operation would need to include the NATO International Security Assistance Force because ISAF was responsible for Kabul Province, and thus a joint con op would need to take place. Tim told me that the operation was awaiting approval from ISAF, then under the command of a French general. The following day Tim let me know that the operation was going to be cancelled because ISAF would not participate. Without ISAF's involvement in their area of responsibility in southern Kabul, there would not be sufficient coverage of the threat locations to make the operation worthwhile. At the time, given the threat reporting, not conducting the op seemed to be taking an unwarranted risk. As it turned out, Logar and Kabul both experienced election-relation violence, but not on the scale feared due to the election-day security mustered by both international and Afghan forces.

On October 3, it was reported that the Taliban planned to attack Kabul-Nangarhar Road and Bagram before the election. Jalaluddin Haqqani was reportedly going to disrupt the election in eastern Afghanistan. On October 4, a report indicated a terrorist named Chariq was to receive explosives on October 6 to target U.S. forces during the election period. The Taliban were planning a large number of suicide bombings in cities throughout Afghanistan. The Taliban also planned to dispatch fighters from a training camp in northern Afghanistan to Kandahar to target the election. It was reported that rocket attacks were planned against election sites in Ghazni Province. A Taliban commander was placing explosives in Ghazni to disrupt routes to polling sites. The Taliban were also planning to kidnap government officials and Coalition forces to disrupt the election. On October 5, reports indicated the Taliban-planned bomb attacks and international worker kidnappings before the election. Jaish-e-Muslimeen, a Taliban offshoot, was planning to disrupt the election. Al Qaeda had plans for car bombs to disrupt the election. In Pakistan, there was training in sabotaging ballot boxes with unknown liquid or powder substances. An organization called Jemyeta Mullah bought ten cars to use as car bombs in the southern provinces. The Taliban were planning to attack the city of Qalat on October 6 to scare people so they would not vote. On October 6, Mullah Abdullah, an Iranian in Kandahar, was reported to be planning to sponsor car bomb attacks during the election in Kabul and Kandahar. Another leader named Qari Ahmadul-lah was preparing to organize attacks in Ghazni Province. Militant fighters were reportedly moving from Pakistan to the city of Gardez to disrupt the election. Another report indicated that the Taliban were going to allow the Haqqani network to spearhead antielection activities. And Hezb-e-Islami Gulbuddin had two car bombs to target Jalalabad during the election. On October 7, a report revealed that Taliban and Hezb-e-Islami Gulbuddin planned to conduct rocket attacks in Kabul on Election Day. Additionally, Taliban were planning attacks in Ajristan District, Ghazni Province. The Taliban had moved rockets outside of Qalat City to attack before the elec-tion. The Taliban were confiscating and forging voter registration cards to gain access to polls for attacks. On the day before the election, October 8, a phone call to the U.S. consulate in Peshawar, Pakistan, indicated that suicide bombers were going to target Afghan polling stations. A truck bomb was planning to attack a polling station in Kandahar. There was a report on a Taliban meeting of leaders from the southern provinces for election attacks. There was another report further north that remote-controlled explosives were going to be used in Konar Province to disrupt the election. Finally, in Zabul Province, a reliable report indicated that Coalition forces were disrupting Taliban efforts to conduct antielection attacks.

Throughout these reports, we received indications that many terrorist leaders felt that the Coalition military was the key to disrupting election security. These fighters hoped to concentrate attacks on the Coalition forces in order to divert their attention from protecting vulnerable election loca-tions. The details of the reports outlined above confirm this assessment, and specific attacks against Coalition troops also provide evidence that this approach was indeed the strategy of the terrorist leaders.

This impressive stream of threat reporting confirmed a Taliban effort to disrupt the election. While it could conceivably have been part of a misinformation campaign, the credibility of the Taliban rested on shaky ground if they were intentionally making so many false threats. Additionally, reliable sources reported on movement of forces, planning meetings, and other preparations with credible specifics. The election was an opportunity for the Islamic extremist elements in Afghanistan and across the border in Pakistan, but they were unable to capitalize on it. We will look at why the terrorists failed to achieve any of the major victories they had planned.

## SECURITY AND INTERDICTION RESPONSE

As the American campaign season was underway, with a deteriorating situation in Iraq, it was common to hear pundits in the news media or the political world argue that there were insufficient forces in Afghanistan and that those forces present were spread too thin. It is true that there are far fewer forces in ratio to the population than in Iraq, Bosnia, or Kosovo, and that many areas of Afghanistan rarely, if ever, see a Coalition patrol. However, it is also true that the complete failure of the massing of Taliban effort to ruin the election demonstrated the effectiveness of the Coalition presence as well as Afghan security forces.

The limited terrorist group activity contradicted our expectations from the multiple-source reporting stream targeting the elections that I described in the last section. At least three possible reasons were proposed by intelligence analysts in Afghanistan to explain the unexpected lack of terrorist activity on Election Day.

First, it was suggested that extremist groups did not in fact care about the election. However, this countered the evidence of previous voter registration terrorism, the threat reports, and the prevailing assessment of threat groups. The voter registration process was characterized by terror throughout the countryside of Afghanistan, particularly in the southern and eastern parts of the country. Prospective voters were threatened with night letters and other more direct threats. Major attacks were conducted, but these seemed to only strengthen voters' resolve in the affected regions. The terrorist voter registration effort seemed to presage further electoral violence and to announce terrorists' hostile intentions toward the election process. The threat reports in the previous section can be interpreted most simply as presenting, in their totality, a strong extremist focus on disrupting the election. The assessment of the threat groups themselves also contradicted an assessment that they did not care about the election. Al Qaeda would have loved to disrupt the election in order to bolster their anti-U.S. violence and media campaign in Iraq and damage Western interests in Afghanistan and credibility throughout the world. The Taliban felt that the election represented an illegitimate process that had usurped their rightful position as Afghanistan's ruling government in order to establish an un-Islamic, puppet government that supported the infidel United States.

Second, the threats could have been part of an organized misinformation campaign. This would explain earlier threat reporting, but it caused the terrorist groups to lose face among the Afghan people and the international community. While menacing disinformation is a viable strategy to intimidate prospective voters, the exaggerated threat reports did not serve Taliban long-term interests. The Taliban proved themselves almost laughable in Afghan society when dire predictions in threatening night letters failed to come to pass. The response of regional leaders, reported in the October 20, 2004, *New York Times*, supported this assessment. "A defeat definitely," said Haji Shir Muhammad, governor of Helmand, a southern province where the Taliban insurgency has remained active. "They told all the world, we will not let the election happen, but they failed." Yusuf Pashtun, the governor of the southern province of Kandahar, the spiritual home of the Taliban and their former capital, had predicted that a violence-free election would mark a turning point in the insurgency. "If the election goes without a major attack, a phase of the struggle will be over," he said in an interview on the day before the election. "They warned that they would not let the election happen."

It is more plausible there was some sporadic effort at misinformation, exacerbated by normal exaggeration in reporting and intense Coalition and local national intelligence collection efforts focused on the election. Indeed, one thing you must expect when dealing with Afghans is a certain degree of exaggeration. Our military intelligence experiences bore this out. Afghan author Khaled Hosseini wrote in *The Kite Runner* of "*laaf*, the Afghan tendency to exaggerate—sadly, almost a national affliction; if someone bragged that his son was a doctor, chances were the kid had once passed a biology test in high school."

The third explanation, interdiction successes, seems to be the most plausible of the three. The serious Coalition and Afghan security effort over the weeks leading to the election resulted in the capture of numerous radicals planning antielection violence as well as caches of weapons and munitions.

From an operational standpoint, the election period can be considered to have begun with the first movement of ballots on September 21 (although other election activity, such as registration, occurred much earlier). On the same day the ballots began to travel across the country to stage for Election Day, a joint Afghan National Directorate of Security and local police operation resulted in one arrest and two mines seized in Afghanistan's third largest city, Jalalabad, in Nangarhar Province. Two days later, in Jalrez Dis, Wardak Province, a remote-controlled mine was discovered under a bridge and removed without incident. A counternarcotics operation against a heroin factory resulted in the arrest of seven criminals, including an extremist militant who was later detained by the Coalition.

The Kabul City Police prevented a disastrous potential attack, or series of attacks, by seizing a ton of explosives on September 26. The driver of the truck was arrested. The following day, in the Taliban sanctuary in the south, the Coalition military arrested five suspected Taliban commanders. In west Kabul, an improvised explosive was discovered and detonated on a road. On September 28, security forces arrested a man in Kabul for carrying explosives and associated detonation equipment. Interrogation revealed that the man intended to use the explosives in a crowded area of Kabul.

On September 29, several events took place that foiled plans to conduct antielection violence. First, in the capital, Afghan security forces discovered over 300 pounds of explosives, six rockets, and sixteen artillery rounds. To the south of the capital, in Puli Alam, Logar Province, two terrorists trying to plant an explosive to destroy President Karzai's campaign office were killed when the bomb detonated. Security forces also discovered six mines and grenades in Mohammad Agha District of Logar Province, which they assessed were intended for use during the election. In Kandahar City, an explosive device was discovered and detonated. The following day, in

Bari Kot, Nangarhar Province, a motorcycle bomb detonated, killing two individuals riding, but failing to damage any target. In Farah Province, a local national turned over a significant amount of munitions including five HN-5 Chinese shoulder-fired antiair missiles and over 1,400 mortar rounds.

On October 1, an Afghan citizen turned over a cache of mortars and grenades to Coalition forces in Paktika Province. The following day led to the discovery of a large cache of heavy machine gun rounds and rocket-propelled grenades in the northwest part of Ghazni Province. The cache was destroyed. Another explosive device was discovered in Kandahar City, only nine meters from the one that was interdicted on September 29. On October 3, another explosive device was discovered on the main highway in Kandahar City and removed without incident. In Kabul, a car bomb was removed near the university.

The week before the election was frenetic with threat activity, but Coalition and indigenous security forces actively met most of these challenges. On October 5, Coalition forces discovered a militant observation post near the border between Kandahar and Zabul Provinces. The Coalition fired mortars at the position, and the fighters dispersed. Militants staged a bombing against police in Atghar, Zabul Province, killing six policemen. Explosives blew up on a back road in Kandahar City and in a culvert under a newly paved road in Kandahar City, with no injuries. Three separate mortar and rocket attacks took place against Coalition forces, in Logar, Ghazni, and Paktika Provinces. A motorcycle bomb failed in Kandahar City when the motorcycle lost control and slid into a ditch. The two terrorists riding dropped the rocket, and it exploded, killing them both. Two caches were found by Coalition forces, including seventy rocket-propelled grenades in Sar Hawaza and almost a hundred rounds for various large weapons systems turned into Bagram Airfield by a local citizen. The Afghan National Army discovered a cache of two mortar rounds and thirty-three boxes of heavy machine gun ammunition in Kandahar City.

On October 6, there were some attacks with limited success. In Puli Alam, Logar Province, two rockets were fired at Siyedan School, which had been a voter registration site, although it was not a polling center. Classrooms were damaged, but no one was hurt. Several mortars were fired into the city. There was also an attack on District Headquarters in Sar Hawzeh, Paktika Province, wounding three local nationals. There was an explosion at a polling center at Jaghland Jadid Girls' School, Baghlan Province. In Musjjid Amad Zai, in Kabul, polling center staff were assaulted, and three poll workers were wounded.

In the northern city of Faisabad, Badakshan Province, there was an unsuccessful bomb attack against President Karzai's running mate, Zia Massoud, the brother of the late national hero of Afghanistan who was killed by al Qaeda days before the September 11, 2001, attacks. Badakshan is a remote area of the country, the far northeast that extends as a long finger to border with China. Most of the province is inaccessible throughout much of the year because of harsh, forbidding temperatures and weather in this high elevation area. Faisabad is one of Afghanistan's major cities, and it connects the outlying province to the rest of the country.

Ahmad Shah Massoud, revered today as the National Hero of Afghanistan, was assassinated on September 9, 2001. Two men posing as journalists detonated a bomb, killing Northern Alliance commander Massoud. They were pretending to interview him, and in their suicidal attack they were able to decapitate the leader of the Northern Resistance. At the time, Massoud's murder seemed to be an attack by the Taliban to remove their strongest opponent. A couple of days later, however, with the September 11th attacks, it seemed like al Qaeda was likely behind the assassination. Conspiracy theorists have even accused the U.S. government of the murder. Paul Wolf of the Canadian Centre for Research on Globalisation articulated such a point in his 2003 article, "The Assassination of Ahmad Shah Massoud." The serious conspiracy theorist must have at the same time a cynicism that requires suspicion of even the most obvious realities and a naïveté that requires willful ignorance of other obvious realities. To conduct such an assassination, the United States would have had to know about the September 11th attacks far enough in advance to plan and execute Massoud's assassination and have been able to retain the services of Islamic extremists willing to blow themselves up. While the government is powerful and large, I do not think it is realistic that there are so many heartless agents in the government to have allowed the September 11th attacks to happen with their full knowledge and to keep this information from all of the post-9-11 investigators that wanted to discover causes behind the attacks. Additionally, the American government does not have the ability to influence suicidal Muslim terrorists to do America's bidding. Such men have sworn themselves to oppose Americans wherever possible.

Admittedly, the United States enjoyed several benefits from Massoud's death. First, the Afghan people were united behind the idealistic image of a fallen leader and strengthened in their resolve against the Islamic extremists widely believed to be behind the attack. Second, a strong, independent, violent, and brutal warlord was removed from influencing the future of Afghanistan, leaving the way for Hamid Karzai to become the father of his country. Karzai was beneficial from several perspectives. Friendly to American interests, he could find alignment between Afghan and American interests. In addition, Karzai, an ethnic Pashtun, could unify the majority of the country that shares the ethnic (and in many cases, religious) background of the former Taliban regime with the ethnic minorities that supported Massoud. The alternative would have most likely led to further bloodshed because the historically oppressed but numerically greater Pashtuns would likely not have accepted an Ahmad Shah Massoud presidency. Massoud would likely have aggravated this possibility for violence by his own violent methods. Thus, his role as a martyr was the best possible contribution to Afghanistan as it moved from warlike resistance to Taliban oppression to attempting to piece together a peaceful coalition government. Karzai further capitalized on Massoud's popularity by replacing his contrarian vice presidential running mate, Fahim Khan, with Zia Massoud, whose name recognition could win Karzai support among the ethnic minorities that backed his opponents.

The attack on Zia Massoud was the most serious offensive on October 6, 2004, winning international media attention. However, on October 6, there were also incidents of successful counterterrorism. In Ghazni Province, a booby trap was discovered at the election official's home and removed without incident. A rocket was fired at a police vehicle, resulting in an arrest and recovery of the rocket launcher. In Kabul City, an improvised explosive device was found and removed without incident. In Maydan Shar, Wardak Province, an improvised explosive was discovered and disarmed by the National Directorate of Security near a main road. In Maruf District, Kandahar Province, seven militants were killed by Afghan security forces. In Gardez, an explosive was found under the Khost-Gardez Bridge.

The following day also saw limited attacks. In the northern city of Konduz, an improvised explosive blew up on the road between Konduz City and the airport, but there were no casualties. In Rehkhar, Kabul Province, an Afghan National Army patrol was engaged with small arms, but there were no casualties. In the provincial capital of Lashkar Gar in the southern Helmand Province, two hand grenades were thrown by terrorists on motorbikes in front of the Police Headquarters. There were no injuries or damage. A Coalition outpost in Helmand received a rocket attack, but there were no injuries or damage. In the city of Orgun-E, Paktika Province, which borders Pakistan, three rockets were fired at the town, damaging a customs building. In Kabul, two rockets hit outside the International Security Assistance Force's Camp Warehouse. There were no injuries. A rocket was also fired at the Coalition headquarters encampment at Bagram Airfield, but there was no damage.

The day saw several attacks thwarted. In Wardak Province, improvised explosive devices were found and destroyed by the Coalition. The explosives were found between a mosque and a school, and their purpose was assessed as an attempt to injure people waiting in polling lines. They had a two-kilometer range remote-control capability. In Chapr-e-Har District, Nangahar Province, the National Directorate of Security conducted a raid on a Taliban group in the process of conducting a rocket attack against Jalalabad City. Two rockets were seized. In Jadid, Baghlan Province, a rocket was discovered outside of the police station and was recovered by Afghan National Army and Coalition forces. A Lewis Berger construction crew discovered an improvised explosive on the Kabul to Gardez road. In Qalat, Zabul Province, six mortar rounds were fired within the city limits with no damage, and five suspects were apprehended. In Kandahar City, a car bomb was found in a white Corolla and destroyed by Coalition forces before it could do any damage. In addition, Coalition forces confiscated an antiaircraft gun and a heavy machine gun while on patrol. In Mizan, Zabul Province, small arms fire broke out. Coalition forces pursued the perpetrators into the bazaar and detained two individuals and confiscated thirteen rocket-propelled grenades.

Attacks and interdiction continued on the day before the election, October 8. In Kabul, a rocket impacted in the parking lot of the American-led Combined Forces Command compound, wounding one person. In Logar Province, two rockets were fired at the Coalition and the Joint Electoral Management Body office, but there was no damage. In Jalalabad, three rockets were fired, wounding two people. In Cahar Cineh, Oruzgan, a 2-5 Infantry Battalion patrol engaged a group of militants with small arms fire. In Deh Chopan, Zabul Province, a rocket-propelled grenade was fired against Coalition elements. South of Jalalabad City, two eighty-two-millimeter mortars exploded on a main road. In the border city of Shkin, an explosive detonated along a main road, but there was no damage. In Asadabad, Konar Province, an Afghan National Army patrol was ambushed. In Logar Province, a polling site at Baraki Barak was attacked, wounding one worker. The local JEMB office decided to open the site on Election Day anyway. In Logar Province, the Chark polling site was attacked by five militants. When the Coalition investigated, two rocket-propelled grenade launchers were found and seized.

There were a number of prevented attacks on the eve of the election as well. The most prominent of these attracted media attention when a fuel truck filled with explosives was stopped before entering Kandahar City. Two Pakistani drivers were taken into custody for attempting this spectacular attack. The importance of the aversion of this plan should not be underestimated. Such a massive explosion could have killed hundreds of people and certainly would have demonstrated to the world through the international press that the Taliban still exercised a strong and destructive influence in their former capital city.

In southern Deh Rawood, the capital of Oruzgan Province, an explosive was discovered and destroyed one kilometer from a polling site. In rural Oruzgan, several improvised explosives were discovered along the road from the small towns of Charchina and Kijran. Oruzgan is a remote province in the south, cut off from the rest of the country by rugged mountainous terrain. As I mentioned in the previous chapter, construction on a road from Kandahar to Tarin Kowt (a major city in Oruzgan) is currently underway, which should bring some commerce by connecting Oruzgan to the rest of the country. Another change was the division of Oruzgan into two provinces. Oruzgan itself had been divided into a northern and southern section, with impassable mountains preventing communication between the two parts of

the province. The Karzai Administration decided to form the province of
Deh Kundi from the northern section of Oruzgan Province. A region cut off
from another poor and remote region of the country, Deh Kundi was like a
world on its own.

I remember a story of an American patrol into a village in the area.
The soldiers were led by their company first sergeant, a senior noncommissioned officer who had risen through the ranks over a twenty-year career
in the Army infantry. The first sergeant was an African American, a race
with whom most Afghans had no experience before the American invasion.
When the patrol met the village elders, the Afghans asked the Americans,
through the Americans' translator, "Are you Russians?" The Russians had
fled Afghanistan in 1989 after their failed decade-long invasion. This remote
village had apparently not received this fifteen-year-old piece of news. The
first sergeant exploded in disbelief: "What? Man, have you ever met a black
Russian?" Of course, the Afghan had never met a Russian of any color, but
knew something of an invasion by way of some rumor from several years
ago.

In Jalalabad City, two terrorists, Haji Mohammad and Ahmad Shah, were
arrested smuggling mines. The explosives, an eighty-two-millimeter mortar
and two antitank mines, were disposed of by Coalition forces working
with the local police. At Bagram Airfield, a cache of rockets and mortars
was discovered near past points of origin for rocket attacks. In Khogiani,
Ghazni Province, two antitank mines were found by police and removed.
Helmand Province in the south had several finds, following early morning
explosions reported by the United Nations personnel stationed there. In
Nawa, twelve remote-controlled explosives were captured, and two men
were arrested. In Lashkar Gar, three 107-millimeter rockets on timers, aimed
at the home of a local official, were discovered and two militants were
arrested. In the north, a large cache of forty-three antipersonnel mines,
sixteen rocket-propelled grenades, and other munitions was discovered in
Kaligal, Konduz Province. In Jalalabad City, police arrested two terrorists
with a dozen explosives. In Samar Khel, Nangahar Province, police arrested
a suspected suicide bomber near Torkham City Gate. In the capital, two
caches were found: twenty rocket-propelled grenades in Kabul District 4
and twenty-seven rocket-propelled grenades in Kabul District 6.

On Election Day, four rocket attacks occurred in Wardak Province. One
polling station was moved as a result, but there was no damage and voting
continued. In Ismail Khan Village, Wardak Province, a JEMB convoy was
attacked by machine gun fire, but there were no injuries. In Logar Province,
the Baraki Barak polling station was attacked. Two border checkpoints
monitoring the Afghanistan/Pakistan border were attacked with rockets.
Northeast of Deh Chopan, Coalition forces from the 2nd Battalion of the
35th Infantry Regiment reported that two mortars impacted within 500
meters of their position. In southeast Paktia Province, two rockets and one

rocket-propelled grenade were fired at a polling station. In Qarah Bagh, Ghazni Province, there was an explosion near an election worker's house. In Farah City, Farah Province in the west, a police checkpoint was attacked. South of Kabul City, an Afghan National Army convoy received small arms fire, but there were no injuries. In Oruzgan Province, a convoy moving from Langar polling station to Tarin Kowt was attacked with small arms and rockets. The police and Coalition responded, and no ballot boxes were jeopardized. In Konar Province, Dag polling station was attacked with machine gun fire, but voting continued. Six rockets and a rocket-propelled grenade were fired eight kilometers north of Asadabad in Konar Province. The governor's house received one rocket, and one rocket landed between the police chief's house and women's polling site. In Shamulzia, Oruzgan, two eighty-two-millimeter mortars were fired at a polling station, but there was no damage. In Gardez, a polling center in the city received two 107-millimeter rockets, and a rocket-propelled grenade was fired at police headquarters. At the Coalition outpost Camp Blessing, there was a rocket attack; the Coalition returned fire with mortars and heavy weapons. In southeast Paktia, three 107-millimeter rockets flew over a village. In southern Helmand, near the Pakistani border, a polling station received small arms fire and mortars. In Kandahar, a tractor drove over a land mine planted two kilometers from a polling station, killing two civilians. This incident has not been definitively connected to the election because it remains uncertain whether the mine had been recently planted to target the polling site. Since it was near a polling station on a main line of communication, it was likely an election-related attack, although the result did not have anything to do with the election.

Election Day security also resulted in several prevented attacks. In Badghis Province, police discovered an improvised explosive on the road and removed it. In Deh Chopan, Zabul Province, police removed a mine from the road. In southeast Deh Rawood, 2nd Battalion of the 5th Infantry Regiment discovered a 107-millimeter rocket pointed at a polling site and defused it with the cooperation of local police. On Bagram Airfield, six grenades were discovered daisy-chained together and removed without incident. In District 4 of Kabul City, a cache of seven rocket-propelled grenades was discovered. In Marghab, the chief of police detonated an explosive device found on a main route. In Gardez, two terrorists in a white Corolla unsuccessfully attempted to bribe an Afghan National Army guard to gain access to a polling area and were apprehended.

The election period saw a significant increase in terrorist activity, although it did not result in the destructive and extravagant attacks threatened and expected. In part this was due to the militants being unable to mass the capability that they had hoped for, but a large part of the explanation comes from successful security operations conducted during the run-up to the election. Coalition efforts resulted in numerous finds of munitions and detainment or killing of militants. A lower key and perhaps even more widespread effect against the enemy forces involved the Afghan security efforts. The Afghan National Army, Afghan National Police, and local police forces were responsible for a significant number of successful interdictions. In addition to those of which we are aware, it is likely that other security successes took place among Afghan security forces that we may never know about because of their less sophisticated tracking and reporting systems. Finally, the co-operation of private citizens who provided essential intelligence on hidden weapons caches deprived radical fighters of the munitions they needed to attack the election process.

## ELECTION DAY SYNOPSIS

In addition to the security threats posed by extremist militants and the attacks they planned and executed during the election period, political events transpired to threaten the election. Throughout the day, reports of fraud and intimidation arrived. While minor, these incidents marred an otherwise successful election, provided fodder for an aggressive media watchdog apparatus, and set the stage for ugly confrontations from opposing candidates. The four main candidates included Interim President Hamid Karzai, an ethnic Pashtun, his leading opponent, ethnic Tajik Yunis Qanuni, the Hazara candidate Haji Mohammad Mohaqiq, and the Uzbek general, Rashid Dostum. While there were many other candidates, only these four broke into double digits.

Several incidents of fraud were reported on Election Day, and anecdotes and rumors continued to drift in throughout the day. In Darreh Chest Village, Bamiyan Province, some people tried to vote with others' registration cards. When the District Electoral Commissioner refused to allow this, he was assaulted. The site was temporarily closed, and the police arrested four assailants. In District 8 of Kabul City, a local man complained to Global Risk Strategies officials that Qanuni's supporters were armed and expressing support for their candidate. He also said that many Qanuni supporters were permitted to vote without proper identification. In Districts 4 and 10 of Kabul, incidents of staff corruption, in which staff reportedly filled out ballots for voters or told them whom to support, were reported. In District 9 of Kabul, two polling sites reported guards and Afghan election workers threatening to shoot voters if they did not vote for Qanuni. Presidential candidate Haji Mohammad Mohaqiq entered at least two polling sites in Mohammadi District, Parwan Province, and asked voters to vote for him. Polling staff asked him to leave, and he began to abuse the staff. The second site closed for thirty minutes as security handled the situation. Outside a polling station in Abodakri Sediq, Jawzjan Province, about fifty people staged a demonstration in protest of polling staff instructing them to vote for Qanuni. The police broke up the demonstration. It is likely that many of the corrupt staff were also supporting Karzai. On October 19, *The Los*

*Angeles Times* cited presidential candidate Yunis Qanuni, who told a story of a minor presidential candidate going to vote and having a poll worker tell him to check the box next to Karzai's name. The candidate indignantly replied, "Look up. I am Mr. Said Abdul Hadi Dabir, one of the candidates!"

The most famous and disturbing reports of fraud involved the indelible ink that was supposed to prevent multiple voting. It was already well-known that many Afghans had secured more than one voter registration card. Some estimates suggested between 10 and 20 percent duplicate registration. United Nations officials did not attribute the multiple registrations entirely to corruption, however. There is an Afghan expression, "Having is useful," implying that people like to be prepared with things, just in case they are needed. Punching holes in the registration card was to be the primary method of preventing multiple voting, but due to the commonplace practice of multiple registrations, the Joint Electoral Management Body developed a plan to use indelible ink on the left thumb to prevent multiple voting.

The ink soaks into the cuticle of the thumb, and it is not possible to wash off without fading over time. Afghan National Army officers in the Election Security Operations Center showed us their thumbs, and our own eyes contradicted complaints of washable ink. However, reports arrived from numerous places, including Kabul, Kapisa, Parwan, Panshir, and Wardak Provinces, of staff using the wrong type of ink or marking the thumbs incorrectly. A broadcast on CNN even inadvertently and unknowingly revealed the incorrect procedure being used behind the reporter as she commented on the election process. It is possible that some of these incidents were intentional, but it is unclear whether corruption in favor of any particular candidate, or corruption at all, was the intent. Taliban fighters had threatened to cut off the thumbs of anyone bearing the indelible ink marking, so it is possible that well-meaning election workers made the mark easier to remove and thus harder to detect in order to protect voters in their areas. Nonetheless, whether well intentioned or planning for fraud, the ink clearly resulted in illegal voting. When I visited the Central Region Counting Center on the south side of the capital, the Regional Security Director, an American ex-marine named Chris Farrell, told me that on Election Day, his drivers boasted of voting for Karzai several times. When they said they were planning to go back and vote again, Chris and the other Westerners asked them to please not do so. Of course, my friend Khoshall Murad, the ardent Karzai-supporter, was one of the people of whom Chris spoke. This is only one story of many, the like of which were spread by visiting international news media applying critical scrutiny to the nascent Afghan democracy's first election.

These incidents formed the backdrop for a coordinated candidate protest that occurred fairly early in the day. Fifteen candidates met with the Joint Electoral Management Body at about noon on Election Day to share their concerns. At the meeting, the candidates declared a boycott of the election, saying that it was irreparably tainted. What the Taliban and al Qaeda had failed to do, the legitimate political opposition in the race seemed to be accomplishing. The election was deemed a failure in several early news media reports, and what had seemed at first a minor incident with the indelible ink became a serious cause for alarm.

The day after the election, the Joint Electoral Management Body's Chief of Operations, an Australian named David Avery, briefed the Security Center on the protest. He said that the opposition candidates' sincerity was viewed with suspicion by the JEMB. First, there was a large number of journalists and other media personalities present, indicating that the candidates had arranged the meeting for the media rather than for actual grievances. (On the other hand, genuine grievance might have motivated the candidates to seek journalists to document their protest and thus ensure that it received attention.) However, the ink issue, although it had received traction in the press, was not even the concern raised by the candidates. The leader of the opposition, Yunis Qanuni, stated that he did not care about the ink issue. Finally, the issues raised were rehashes of grievances from the past several months. It is likely that the candidates planned the protest at least a few days ahead of time and that the ink issue was not part of the motive for the meeting.

In spite of the turmoil on Election Day and allegations of corruption and fraud, a high voter turnout and a groundswell of popular support seemed to show that the election was a success. Although some initial media reports were negative, and the candidates were threatening boycott, the situation would improve in the following days. A special investigating team would be appointed to look into the fraud problem. However, with his mandate compromised by the suggestions of fraud, President Karzai had not won the unblemished victory that conventional wisdom had predicted.

## POLITICAL CONSEQUENCES

In the days following the election, candidates continued to voice protest over the election procedures. Latif Pedram, a minor presidential candidate and poet who had lived in self-imposed exile in Europe during the Taliban regime, was quoted on Iranian state-run radio saying that Afghans should fight until the fall of the next government. The other candidates called loudly for a new election. It is unclear what they hoped to gain by calling for a new election. With Karzai so far ahead of any opposing candidate, the delay entailed in a new election would buy them some extra campaigning time, but it could hardly be expected to change the results. Even had Karzai failed to win 50 percent, as seemed possible during the lengthy vote tabulation, there would already be a second election round with one of the challengers.

The candidates were likely using the protest as a subterfuge to advance their own political ends. At their most benign, the candidates hoped to leverage Karzai in order to maintain their own political influence. Karzai's sacking of his running mate Fahim Khan, his refusal to give assurances to Qanuni in a preelection deal, and his removal of Ismail Khan as the governor of Herat likely provided an incentive for other warlords to take matters into their own hands to preserve their power bases. Thus, it is likely the candidates did not want or expect a new election, which would have been logistically prohibitive for JEMB to conduct. However, by discrediting Karzai's election, they hoped to force the same sort of coalition government he had run from the beginning, where opposition leaders such as themselves were placed in key positions of authority instead of Karzai's more recent proclivity to remove opponents from their positions of influence. At its most dangerous, the situation threatened to devolve into the warring fiefdoms that existed before the Taliban regime, or even more radically separatist efforts. With leading opposition candidate support emerging along regional and ethnic lines for the Hazara Mohammed Mohaqiq in the central highlands, Uzbek Rashid Dostum in the far north, and Tajik Yunis Qanuni in the intermediate north, the situation was threatening to become unstable. Even though these warlords were not strong enough to oppose both the central government and Coalition military, their regional resistance to the national government could make things extremely difficult for what was still a very vulnerable developing nation.

The early protests and media reaction indicated that the perceived political legitimacy of the election might present a security problem in the future. The impact of negative media coverage has already been seen in demonstrations, violence, and the threat of violence. The extent of both local and international media criticism of the election and the extent to which the criticism influences the populace, could have led to stability problems for the new, and transitional, government. Fortunately, the media narrative turned positive fairly soon. The influential American Ambassador, Zalmay Khalilzad, was able to mute or soften many of the candidate protests and head off the calls for a boycott. According to inside sources who related to me about the nature of these talks, Khalilzad was quick to point out the balance of power in a government with executive and legislative branches. He warned candidates that attempts that threatened to undermine the entire system of government would leave them excluded from prospective roles as active members of the opposition who would shape the future of Afghanistan after the coming round of parliamentary elections. The establishment of a special investigating body also seemed to assuage some of the concerns about legitimacy, but the candidates seemed to want to leave themselves an option if they did not like the results. For instance, Qanuni outrageously asserted that any correct count of the vote would leave him in the lead.

Opposition leaders still left themselves the option to call into question the legitimacy of the government and to mobilize popular support, perhaps along ethnic or regional lines. This possibility would lead to difficulty for the administration as it attempts to combat narcotrafficking, warlordism, and the continued threat posed by militants staging in Pakistan. While Karzai was a long favorite for this election, some of his opponents, former warlords themselves, may have seen an unacceptable American influence in his victory. These former warlords may yet return to their earlier style of actions, especially if the new government attempts to reduce their power bases. Some indications of this were seen in violence from Qanuni and Mohaqeq supporters on Election Day. It is already strongly suspected that there was advance coordination among the fifteen opposition candidates who protested fairly early on Election Day. It is likely that these candidates were planning alternative solutions to the problem of losing the election. The dangerous possibility loomed that disenfranchised regional leaders might decide that violent action would be another justified response to what they could believe in their own minds to be an unjustified process and outcome.

The controversy resulted in a delay in counting as the Joint Electoral Management Body considered the protests over election irregularities. While ballots were being reconciled, counting of actual candidate votes was delayed. Some in JEMB felt that the delay was a mistake, inviting civil unrest due to the people not receiving the results of the election and enflaming media scrutiny by indicating that authorities were uncomfortable with the process to the extent that they suspended counting. Allegedly, Secretary-General Kofi Annan himself called to the United Nations' Assistance Mission Afghanistan and ordered counting to begin. In the end game, the tallying postponement was not a problem because counting the votes was such a long process that the delay of a couple days was not noticeable.

## CONCLUSIONS

Altogether, the presidential election was a stunning success for Afghanistan. While there were incidents of fraud and intimidation, the election certainly ran as smoothly as could be expected considering the decades of armed conflict and the impoverished level of economic development. Additionally, the Taliban, in conjunction with the most notorious international terrorist organization in the world, failed to achieve any noticeable effects at all to disrupt the election. This blow to the enemies of freedom in Afghanistan was one from which it was hard to recover.

An important point about the election is the extent to which indigenous security forces contributed to the successful security outcome. In addition to the enthusiastic and energetic cooperation of Afghan agencies such as the Ministry of Defense and the Ministry of Interior and their constituent groups, local citizens also provided intelligence, turned in munitions, and came out in large numbers to participate in the election. As discussed earlier, President Karzai was widely viewed as influenced by American interests and leaders. Some of his opponents had campaigned in large part on the excessive ties Karzai has to the United States. In this way, Karzai's success in the election can reasonably be seen as an Afghan popular endorsement of American policy and presence in Afghanistan.

In many ways, the election was a large step forward both for Afghanistan and the Global War on Terrorism. A more routine election in Australia took place on the same day. Like President Karzai, Australian President John Howard received a strong endorsement from his electorate. Both of the elections on October 9, 2004, were encouraging for Americans, because both countries had tied themselves closely to the United States and its interests in the War on Terrorism. In both the nascent democracy of Afghanistan and the more industrialized and mature democracy of Australia, the voting public gave a strong mandate to leaders who have made courageous decisions in the fight against the opponents of freedom.

# CHAPTER 4

# Vengeance—The Taliban Strikes Back After the Election

The months following the election were a period characterized by sporadic and impulsive lashing out from a now demoralized and depleted insurgency. At the same time, international military, U.S. Embassy, and United Nations workers were taking or planning leaves as their major effort had finally culminated and the Western holidays of Thanksgiving and Christmas were approaching. This time period lacked the coordinated activity of the previous month during which Taliban and associated forces had massed their efforts for the election. However, between Murphy's law—that famous martial axiom, "What can go wrong, will go wrong"—and the violence of a country still untamed by central authority, the aftermath of the election remained eventful.

Immediately after the election, the major focus was security of ballot movement and counting houses. Since Election Day was such a setback for the terrorist groups, attacks on either of these targets seemed unlikely. Nonetheless, the international and Afghan forces vigilantly protected these potential targets. The Taliban lost their major opportunity to disrupt the election through intimidation attacks in the week before the election and to make a statement to the Afghan people and the world by conducting a spectacular Election Day attack. A major counting center attack would be too little, too late, and it was assessed as a dangerous, but improbable, course of action. It also seemed unlikely that the Taliban possessed sufficient logistical sophistication to interdict ballot delivery successfully, especially given their absolute failure to do so before the election. A more likely threat to counting centers would be a scenario in which discontented candidates or their supporters might mount attacks on the centers in order to further discredit the election and gain a personal advantage. Destroying a large quantity of ballots in the intervening weeks before it was possible to complete counting them would add further uncertainty to an already contested election.

In the aftermath of the dramatically successful election, militant elements in Afghanistan seemed demoralized and disorganized. As the Muslim holy month of Ramadan began, insurgent activity declined, bucking the trend of a spike in militancy during the holy month. In the days after the election, some isolated rocket attacks in Kabul City took place to no effect. Most likely, militants who had been unable to accomplish anything during the election period due to the high security conducted these attacks. However, the militants were disorganized and unable to concentrate their efforts at any decisive place or time.

In the initial days after Election Day, our work in the Election Security Operations Center focused more on emergency response to nonviolent contingencies. In the remote northern province of Badakshan, a UN aircraft crashed on October 12, 2004, and called for emergency assistance. The temperatures in this area, at one of the highest elevations in the world, were dangerously cold. The crew, lacking the training and procedures of military aircrews, did not have the requisite equipment to survive such a contingency. The United Nations requested military assistance, and we coordinated this support. I obtained satellite images of the areas where the crew had crashed and where they later moved to. They chose to leave their plane to find a lower and warmer elevation from which rescue would be easier. Captain Clinton Culp coordinated with the pararescue jumpers (PJs), an elite Air Force Special Operations unit trained for just such types of high-risk rescues. These airmen parachute into the crash location, provide the downed crew with needed supplies, such as food, water, temporary shelter, warm blankets, and clothing. Then they coordinate the extraction with advanced communication equipment. Parachuting at an elevation of 10,000 feet is a highly dangerous and unusual maneuver, aside from the rugged terrain and the forbidding weather. So even for the highly trained PJs, this rescue was challenging and risky. Communications with the UN crew were spotty at best, and as I mentioned, they did not bring the needed supplies to survive the wait for a rescue in this harsh climate.

When the Air Force rescuers arrived at the designated location, there was no sign of the UN crew. We were not able to get through to the crew to verify the location after the rescuers arrived, so the PJs conducted a search of the area. After two days, without finding the UN crew, it was necessary for the PJs themselves to be extracted. Only after the PJs returned did the stranded UN crew reestablish communications contact. They informed us that they had found shelter with a local Afghan resident. We were able to get more accurate coordinates for their location and arrange an extraction. This time, since they were safely located with the local Afghan, the risky parachute insertion was not needed.

During midafternoon on October 20, an Afghan elections worker responsible for civic education was driving across the remote and winding roads of eastern Farah Province. He was accompanied by three policemen and one driver. One of the policemen accidentally fired his weapon in the moving vehicle, hitting the civic educator in the upper arm. Throughout the afternoon, the Election Operations Security Center buzzed with activity to try to save this man's life. The operations team coordinated with the men in the car via cell phone to discover their location and determine which type of aircraft or ground rescue could reach them. At the same time, the medics of Ex-Med, the private medical firm contracted out to the UN elections project, got on the cell phone to try to coach the Afghans to stop the bleeding and to receive continual updates on the injured worker's condition. Chris Morris, a rough-around-the-edges former British Special Forces medic, was the leader of the Ex-Med medics and personally collected this information. In the meantime, I was crossreferencing the names of villages being passed from the men in the car to try to determine their exact location. After arriving at their location, I used a "chat" over the secret Internet to discuss possible landing zones (LZs) for a rescue helicopter with the imagery analysts at Bagram. They did imagery analysis based on the size and slope of the open terrain around the road where the car was driving.

Finding a common framework with the Afghans in the car was difficult in order to arrive at a clear picture of where they were. The easiest possible solution would be to have the car stay where it was because we had arrived at a confident idea of its location. However, I informed the operations team that the closest safe landing zone was ten miles away, based on my input from the imagery analysts. The operations guys coordinated with Task Force Wings, the aviation brigade task force, who assured them that there was a closer LZ, only three miles away. The satellite imagery showed an open patch of ground close to the river that ran near the winding road. This was an obvious choice, so of course, I had inquired about it with the imagery team. Unfortunately, the open ground was smaller than it appeared, the slope was not sufficiently flat for a safe landing, and the area near the river might be too soft to support a landing. So I explained why this seemingly more advantageous landing zone should be ruled out in spite of its more favorable proximity. Although the situation was becoming more urgent for the bleeding Afghan, who had been losing blood since the afternoon about five hours earlier, the dark of night only made the safe choice of LZ even more important.

To compromise, the aviation decision-makers decided to use a C-130 fixed wing aircraft to scout their preferred landing site. The C-130, along with a UH-60 medical evacuation (medevac) helicopter, departed from Shindand Airfield in Herat Province at around 8:00 P.M. The C-130 located the closer landing site and they judged it sufficiently safe for the rescue landing.

Around midnight, the medevac chopper crashed. The Afghans awaiting rescue were dialoguing with the Operations Center on their cell phone. "The helicopter fell," one of them said. Was this his way of saying that the aircraft had landed? After a few minutes, it was horribly clear that "fell" meant crashed. Another medical rescue helicopter was dispatched, and the wounded Afghan was saved, but the pilot of the first rescue bird did not survive. I will never forget the following morning, when I saw Chris Morris, a hardened veteran of one of the most elite military organizations in the world, weeping desperately for a fallen American helicopter pilot.

Further south, frustrated Taliban forces, rather than the dangers of chance, were able to take vengeance on election officials as insurgents successfully assassinated Dr. Abdul Satar with an improvised explosive device at about eight o'clock in the morning on October 18, 2004, a week after the election. Dr. Satar was the District Electoral Commissioner of Yaja Khel District of the Paktika Province, bordering Pakistan. The attack killed Satar and the other four people riding in the vehicle. One was a driver, and the other three were bodyguards. Satar was well-known in the local community for his active support of the registration and elections processes.

The device appears to have been a double stack antitank mine and was believed, after investigation by Coalition engineers, to have been remote-controlled. Some type of pressure release was also found. The mines were planted inside a culvert under the road next to a mud wall. Locals later reported that, near sunrise, they saw two men near the site of the incident who were joined by two others an hour later. Upon further investigation it would appear that the four men were hiding behind a small mud wall about one hundred yards from the point of detonation.

The attack was the fifth attempt on Dr. Satar's life in six months. First, a similar explosive device was detonated against his car. Later, a bomb was discovered in his house. Then, an ambush was prepared for him two months before his death, which he had luckily avoided by taking a different road. A bomb was then later detonated at his clinic. This information was not tracked in any of the several UN Security headquarters at Kabul. I pressed several different agencies, and found that there was no systematic tracking of this type of threat information against specific UN officials throughout the country. There were several reasons that prevented this systematic tracking. First, the security staff at most UN agencies were not as resourced and professional as necessary to maintain large databases of such information. Second, the information itself was not reported in a timely or reliable manner. Communication systems were not in place for local areas to report such information. If an international UN worker was involved in an incident, it was possible to count on receiving information, but the reporting from local Afghans was just not as robust. For local indigenous leaders such as Abdul Satar, violence has been a way of life for decades. Passing along information on such incidents just did not occur to many of these workers.

Satar's nephew, Mullah Yaqoob, had an important position in the local Taliban insurgency. Perhaps in frustration over the failed attempts to disrupt the election, or perhaps only to settle an old score, the nephew set a bomb, having his fighters detonate it as Satar and his driver passed by in the UN-owned Russian jeep. Mullah Yaqoob was apparently responsible for many madrassas in Northern Katawaz, and had long been an active Taliban supporter. The general consensus elicited through discussion with elders, local Joint Electoral Management Body personnel, and the provincial governor was that, although the act itself may not have been carried out by Mullah Yaqoob, he was most probably involved in some way in the incident. Although Dr. Satar was not involved in election-related activities when the explosive detonated, the incident appeared to have a clear political overtone.

The American military unit located in the area was 3rd Battalion of the 3rd Marines, nicknamed "America's Battalion." Marines provided a small but robust portion of the overall Coalition forces. The Marines, a much smaller branch of service than the Army, do not deploy for the normal twelve-month rotations that have become habitual for hundreds of thousands of Army soldiers. Usually, a Marine unit is in place for six to seven months. For the most part, the quality of the individual Marine and the individual Army soldier is about the same. I served as an attachment to a Marine unit in Afghanistan in the spring of 2005 and have worked with Marine officers and noncommissioned officers from time to time over the six years of my military career. The similarity between the organizational cultures of Army and Marine units is striking.

There are two observations on which I can comment about Marine officers. First, there is an inordinate amount of service pride among the Marines. This is no surprise to anyone who knows a Marine. They take it very seriously. A smaller service, they consider themselves elite, and perhaps with good reason. This is admirable, but to be completely frank, this pride can turn into arrogance and can get a little annoying after a while even to a young Army officer who does not focus so much on interservice rivalry. The second observation is the quality of the officers. I remember working with hundreds of officers over my career. There were outstanding, mediocre, and poor officers. While an outstanding Marine officer is not necessarily better than an outstanding Army officer, the Marines seemed to have less variation in the caliber of their officers. Rather than a range of outstanding to poor, my personal experience with Marines gravitated from outstanding Marine officers to somewhere in the middle, but it is difficult for me to remember dealing with a poor Marine officer. I really can think of only one such occasion in six years of military service.

Another practical difference of the Marine battalion is that it is larger, perhaps as much as 150 percent larger, than its Army light infantry counterpart. This allows for the projection of more combat power across more area of the battle space. After the death of Abdul Satar, Lieutenant Colonel Norm Cooling, the commander of 3/3 Marines, set up a headquarters, or tactical operations center (TOC) in the vicinity of Yaja Khel. He and his staff officers and subordinate commanders then proceeded to conduct a police-style investigation into the assassination. Colonel Cooling, a native (and proud) Texan, told me that the key to their eventual success would be the establishment of a permanent presence in the area. This was different from the usual approach of combat and stability operations in Afghanistan, which consisted of roving patrols. Cooling felt that a consistent Marine presence would give locals assurance that they would not be abandoned before the terrorists were apprehended. Indeed, Cooling told me that he announced a stated policy to the locals: "We will not be leaving until all of these guys are captured or killed." He wanted confidence so that leads could be developed, but I inferred that he also wanted to project enough of a threat to prevent any sympathetic locals from providing temporary sanctuary or support to the attackers.

The improvised-explosive device (IED) is one of the most feared devices on the modern battlefield as it has developed in Afghanistan and Iraq. The IED is similar to a landmine in that it is a form of indirect contact rather than direct contact with an enemy. It is different in that there are several ways in which it can be emplaced and detonated, but it usually has the capability of targeting a specific objective in conjunction with some sort of remote trigger system. Hunting IED makers and users has always been a big priority for Coalition forces. American military convoys are usually a prime target for these types of attacks, and the individuals and munitions that go into the IED process are a significant problem. Thus, the assassination of Dr. Satar left 3/3 Marines a great opportunity to not only bring ruthless murderers of an important local official to justice, but also to prevent future such attacks in their own area of responsibility to which American Marines and soldiers might one day be subjected.

After two weeks, the Marines had rolled up four of what was apparently a five-man IED cell that had been operating in the area for months. They knew the fifth man, Mullah Yaqoob, to be the leader of the cell, but Yaqoob was eluding capture. Then, an event took place that no one could have expected. Mullah Yaqoob approached the Marines' headquarters, demanding the release of the other members of the cell, claiming that they had been falsely imprisoned. The Marines invited him inside, saying that they certainly wanted to discuss the matter of the IED cell accusations with him. As he entered the base, he was promptly detained. Many Afghan insurgents, having been fighting for generations and generations, are some of the toughest and hardiest warriors you could possibly meet on the battlefield, and some of them are the canniest thinkers, able to improvise and make due under conditions of extreme hardship. But the lesson from Mullah Yaqoob is that some of them were just not very smart at all.

The next major incident of retributive violence took place in the capital on October 23, 2004. A lone man wearing local Afghan attire was carrying six grenades in a crowded market area of Kabul known as Chicken Street. Chicken Street is always busy with local Afghans, but it is also a popular shopping area for international visitors from the military, United Nations, and nongovernmental organization community. The man approached two Icelandic soldiers and detonated three of the six grenades that he was carrying. The grenades were strapped to his waist and in his hands, and the explosion killed the bomber instantly. The NATO soldiers were standing outside a carpet shop. There were two International Security Assistance Force vehicles parked near the carpet shop, and three other soldiers were inside the shop at the time of the attack. The three distinct explosions from the grenade injured three of the soldiers and killed an American female who was working for Worldwide Language Resources. An eleven-year-old Afghan girl, who frequented the area to beg from passersby, was also killed. Several bystanders and shopkeepers were also injured in this attack.

Suicide bombers in Afghanistan were extremely rare. The warrior ethos of Afghanistan's history makes the self-destruction of a suicide attack not as culturally acceptable as among radical Muslims from the Middle East, which the Afghans call "Arabistan." Although reports in September and early October had indicated repeated threats of suicide bombings, few such attacks materialized. It is likely that the threats were in part exaggerated. For instance, the Afghan National Army intelligence officer Colonel Abdul Mohammed told me about a report from one of his contacts that asserted that one hundred suicide bombers were spreading out for a coordinated Election Day attack in eight major cities of Afghanistan. We assessed this report to be an exaggeration at the time, but considering the repeated threats of a similar nature, it is probable that some suicide bombers had planned elections attacks. These bombers were most likely al Qaeda foreign fighters because the indigenous insurgents had not adopted suicide attacks as a tactic of choice. The Chicken Street attack was likely a bomber who failed in reaching his Election Day target, but was determined and desperate enough to carry out the suicide bombing. One of the Icelandic soldiers was a senior officer, in command of the NATO base at Kabul International Airport, but it seems unlikely that the lone terrorist was interested in and able to target this official; rather, the shopping soldiers were likely a target of opportunity.

The most dramatic and notorious episode of postelection retributive violence took place on October 28, when three Joint Electoral Management Body employees were abducted in plain daylight from the streets of Kabul. On October 28 at 12:15 P.M. in the afternoon, three elections workers, Annetta Flanigan, Shquipe Hebibe, and Angelito Nayan, went into the Chinese Dragon Restaurant and asked the Afghan driver of their white UN SUV, Rafique, to wait for them. They remained in the restaurant for approximately fifteen minutes. Upon exiting the Chinese Dragon, they asked the driver to take them to the Intercontinental Hotel. At 12:50 P.M., their UN Toyota four-runner was held up by gunmen, and the driver was removed from the vehicle. The dirt road where the abduction took place is used very regularly to travel between town and the Intercontinental Hotel or Karte Parwan Joint Electoral Management Body office. UN vehicles were frequently on that road.

An Afghan eyewitness observed Angelito being carried to the getaway vehicle, a black or dark blue Toyota Surf with tinted windows. Later that evening, the witness relayed his account to our Elections Security office. He observed what appeared to be the latter portion of the abduction where Angelito Nayan was being carried on a perpetrator's shoulder to the getaway vehicle. The Afghan reported a number of small identifying details. The witness followed the vehicle past the *Loya Jirga* site, on to Polytechnic Road in the direction of the Malteser Hospital before losing it. The witness described the man carrying Angelito as not wearing a hat, and with a black beard. Another perpetrator was described as wearing a hat and clean-shaven. The witness made clear that he was not prepared to have any details disclosed that might lead to his identification.

The Afghan Ministry of Interior, the government's law enforcement department, reported that the suspect vehicle was bound toward Paghman, and that police were tailing it. Later in the afternoon, the Ministry reported that the suspect vehicle was abandoned, but they never gave a satisfactory explanation for the loss of contact with the vehicle.

At 4:30 P.M., a representative of Global Risk Strategies received information that someone called Annetta's mobile phone, and a male answered and stated she was unavailable. This report was unconfirmed, and it was not possible to determine whether this actually occurred. If Annetta, or any of the captives, had their phones turned on, it is surprising and disturbing that none of the security authorities used the SIM (Subscriber Identity Module) card to ascertain the captives' location. After little progress had been made on the investigation two weeks into the abduction, the Coalition Forces Command Signal Intelligence cell requested the SIM card numbers from the United Nations. I was the liaison for this request. While it was a valuable possible lead, it was weeks late. Worse, when I asked the Joint Electoral Management Body Secretariat's Security Office for the information, it was discovered that there were no UN records tracking SIM cards of their employees in Afghanistan. While the Joint Electoral Management Body Logistics Office maintained a database on phone information for each of its international employees, the database was missing the needed data on numerous individuals, including the three who were kidnapped. I raised the point to several of the UN's security personnel, strongly encouraging them to strengthen their database. However, the matter was soon dropped, forgotten, and there remained insufficient data on SIM cards of UN electoral staff in Afghanistan, and doubtless in other UN organizations worldwide.

It is a needless vulnerability that exposes these workers to added dangers in many hostile areas throughout the world.

Afghan security forces detained several individuals who were believed connected to the abduction. Sharifullah, a criminal associated with Kabul gangs, was a suspect. The Afghan National Police raided his home as well as that of another figure named Rohan. Neither of these individuals was found, but Sharifullah's brother, Toorilay, and his father, Sediqullah, were detained. Khalid, a boy of fourteen years, was detained at Rohan's house. He was a servant of Rohan. Qudbudin, Khalid's father, was also detained. The apprehension of these individuals highlights differences in the rule of law and rights of the accused in Afghanistan and Western industrialized countries. Some were likely material witnesses at best, with no closer connection to the incident. The following day, interrogations revealed that Sharifullah had visited Rohan's house with unidentified individuals. This information was most likely provided by Khalid or his father. It seemed that the National Directorate of Security, Afghanistan's investigative and intelligence arm (a combination of our CIA and FBI), was pursuing its leads independent of the Ministry of Interior, which controlled the police forces of the country.

On October 30, the kidnappers provided identification numbers that they claimed would prove they were holding the hostages. It turned out that the number they provided was the account number for a Barclay's account in Spain held by hostage Annetta Flanigan. This matter was not easy to resolve. While passports, United Nations ID cards, medical records, and other personnel information were readily available, relatively obscure financial data were unknown. Eventually the number was connected to the hostage.

Annetta was from England, and her husband Jose Maria Aranaz, was Spanish. Jose was one of the most senior members of the UN's electoral team in Afghanistan. One of the six international commissioners, Jose, an attorney, has been involved in peacekeeping missions since 1994 in Croatia, Bosnia, Rwanda, Guatemala, Russia, and Kenya. Mr. Aranaz's involvement prompted a special assignment of a Spanish counterintelligence team from the NATO International Security Assistance Force. These investigators were charged by their government to assist in the recovery of the hostages, but they were not reporting their activities to their NATO superiors to avoid compromising their investigation. While their involvement might have helped to recover information leading to the release of the hostages, it also highlights the difficulties of working in a multinational military environment.

American intelligence agencies had developed a prime suspect in the neighboring Maydan Shar area of Wardak Province. A local warlord in the area was fingered, but I will withhold his name here due to the sensitivity of the information, the nature of which will become clear as this part of the story unfolds. A contact in the United Nations informed me that the warlord in question had extensive contact with the UN Central Region political office, which had developed a detailed background report on the individual. Since

Wardak does not have an active Taliban insurgency, there was a minimal Coalition presence. This meant the Coalition had very little information on the warlord, sources of routine information in the area, or an awareness of the network of individuals that might build further leads in recovering the hostages. To respond to this need for information, I visited the UN Assistance Mission Afghanistan (UNAMA) Central Region political officer, Anne, a German female UN functionary who told me she would be leaving the country within the next few days. I had met her before. A few years older than me, she was an attractive woman with long, wavy auburn hair, high cheekbones, and clear gray eyes. She was among my contacts in Kabul with whom I collaborated for election security information, and to whom I passed along security information that would be relevant to her, although she did not work with the election project.

As I sat down to meet with Anne on the subject of this Maydan Shar warlord, she informed me of her upcoming departure. I gave her a friendly congratulation and explained to her the need for her report to help rescue her abducted colleagues. It would fill a serious information gap on a potential connection to the abduction and could lead to further information, if not, in the best-case scenario, develop suspects or the location of the hostages. As I concluded my pitch, she seemed responsive.

At that moment, her boss, the UNAMA Central Region Head of Office walked in. The official was more politician than bureaucrat, and I had met with him one-on-one several times before. He was a Brit named Trevor Martin, with dark hair, glasses, a slightly receding hairline, and he was probably in his forties. As he walked into Anne's office, he asked about the purpose of our meeting. I summarized the situation, and Trevor politely refused the request to provide his political officer's report. I was very frustrated by this reaction because I was not asking for special assistance for a military combat mission. The Coalition was responding to the UN's urgent need to recover its people safely, as quickly as possible.

The decision of the Head of Office was motivated by protecting the confidentiality of his assessment of the local warlord. Frustratingly, this trumped the opportunity to contribute to the rescue of his kidnapped colleagues. This is not to say that Trevor's priority was not a valid concern. Public discourse of the United Nations' unfavorable evaluation of this local leader would make it much harder for UN diplomats to deal with him in the future. Above all, it would be difficult to interact with a local warlord who knew that international officials were aware and disapproved of his criminal activity. So I was cognizant of Trevor's concerns, which is why I gave my assurance to protect the confidentiality of the information. I could offer a degree of anonymity, for instance attributing the report to an unnamed international organization in Kabul (after all, there were thousands of NGOs in Afghanistan, and the UN bureaucracy alone was vast). Nonetheless, my arguments and assurances were not sufficient to win Trevor's trust. I was even more frustrated because my failure to convince him was in spite of previous information-sharing that I had done to assist his needs and build trust. During each of my previous office visits, Trevor was always interested in asking what the Coalition intelligence had discovered about events in his region. As I left the office, I felt aggravated.

It did not seem worthwhile to invest more time and information-sharing into the relationship with this office. Information-sharing itself was always a risk for me. Coalition threat information had various levels of classification, and upon assuming my role in Kabul I had spoken with the Foreign Disclosure Officer at Bagram about what information could be shared with whom and under what circumstances. The Foreign Disclosure Officer was a military intelligence captain whose sole job was to protect classified information and assess what circumstances would permit sharing information with Coalition partners. He provided guidance to units and staff officers on these matters. His guidance to me was vague: "If they need the information, share it with them." So my decision-making process was very independent, and it was a significant responsibility. Releasing the wrong information to the wrong person could result in a threat group receiving situational awareness on our locations, intelligence collection methods, or plans. There is a long list of reasons to not share any information with UN officials, so selecting information that would be appropriate and helpful to share was a risky process.

The United Nations had no military forces, no action capabilities. While the information in UNAMA Central's report may not have been essential or even ultimately helpful, the possibility was there. I knew that if I did nothing, no action would come from this information. I decided I needed to act. Two days later, I returned to the office to talk to Anne to try to convince her of the need away from her boss. As her last day was fast approaching, I felt that it would be possible to prevail upon her to provide the information needed to further the Coalition investigation. Anne had been more receptive than Trevor, and given the high stakes, I thought she would be willing to share her report with me if Trevor was not there and I could provide assurances to keep it secret. I went into Anne's office, but she was not there.

I made a high-risk choice at this moment. I copied the file from her computer onto my portable USB (universal serial bus) drive. The mechanics of this were easy; it took hardly any time to locate the file, and the computer was not secured. The decision, however, was not so easy. Doing this thing would risk my future work in Kabul. Collecting information by removing it from a UN computer without permission would compromise my ability to collect any information from anyone in the future. However, lives were at stake, so the risk I took seemed minor in comparison. Until this writing, this decision was a closely kept secret that I shared only with my partner and, a few months later, with the incoming officer who would replace me. I classified the report as "Secret" and attributed it to a "reliable international organization in Kabul."

After passing the report along, I never discovered its ultimate significance. Military intelligence is "compartmented," so that no one has access to the entire picture, so in the field of intelligence, you can never expect full situational awareness. More importantly, in this situation, there were hundreds of American intelligence analysts working in Afghanistan. The process of intelligence often involves numerous people making connections and developing patterns with large amounts of data. The significance of this piece in the larger puzzle and whether my risk was worthwhile are two things I will never know for sure.

A senior civilian Army intelligence official in the Combined Forces Command headquarters who was assigned to the hostage recovery cell told me about the initial efforts at recovering the hostages. SEAL teams and other elite special forces units were active in attempting to follow leads and rescue the hostages. There were repeated raids in the early days, but with villages with no lighting, street addresses, or even common frames of reference for names, these efforts were bound to fail even assuming they were based on correct information to begin with. After three nights of fruitless raids, the special operators and planners realized that the names of their target location, "Khel," was the word for "village," which explained their failure to pinpoint the right compound in the right village. With these failed results, the general officers overseeing the hostage cell decided to retrench their efforts.

The situation was becoming increasingly urgent. The terrorists set a deadline of November 5 at two o'clock in the afternoon to behead the hostages and demanded that the Ministry of Interior cease all searches. The Kabul Multi-National Brigade (KMNB), the NATO force responsible for the capital, held a hostage crisis meeting at their headquarters at Camp Warehouse in Kabul. I attended this meeting with Scott Carney and Perry Gammon from Elections Security. Several American Special Forces officers were getting integrated in the hostage rescue effort. Major Dave Snider introduced himself and offered to exchange intelligence to this end. A slender, angular man, Dave spoke with a strong southern accent and a friendly smile and manner. He wore civilian clothes that had the paramilitary look of a private security contractor, with a bulletproof vest strapped to his chest and a pistol on his leg. We exchanged e-mail addresses on the government's classified Internet network, the siprnet. Dave would prove to be a smart, thoughtful, and dedicated member of the team in recovering the hostages.

On October 31, the ubiquitous media network Al-Jazeera reported on its Web site that it was screening a video of the three hostages. The video was circulated throughout the media, and demands began to surface about the hostages' release. The perpetrators identified themselves as Jaish-e-Muslimeen, which was a little-known Taliban splinter group. The media attention of this incident was likely an attempt to raise the profile of the group. The captors had different representatives, who insisted upon slightly different demands for the release of the hostages. Over the next few weeks, demands would vary slightly from a few spokespersons who were contacting members of the media or the United Nations in Kabul. For instance, here are two sets of demands released on October 31.

A Jaish-e-Musilmeen spokesman named Saedr Momin issued the following demands:

1. If the government did not begin negotiations by Friday, one hostage would be killed.
2. Foreign non-governmental organizations connected with Coalition Forces should be withdrawn. (Coalition Forces would not need to withdraw because they will be forced out as a result of military action against them.)
3. All prisoners in Guantanamo Bay must be released. The caller was not clear as to whether this demand referred to only Afghan prisoners or all prisoners held there.

Another unnamed Jaish-e-Musilmeen spokesman issued the following demands on the same day to a media correspondent:

1. A deadline of three days for negotiations.
2. The United Nations was to leave Afghanistan and to condemn the attack and invasion of Afghanistan. The terrorist spokesman noted that the UN works around the world for justice but in Afghanistan was supporting the invading forces.
3. All Afghans imprisoned in Afghanistan and Guantanamo Bay were to be released.
4. British and Kosovar forces were to be withdrawn from Afghanistan.
5. The Philippines must condemn the invasion of Afghanistan.

Later in the day, Al-Jazeera broadcast the video of the hostages, but there was no indication of their location. The videotape indicated that Afghans should be released from prisons (presumably Coalition ones rather than the local government prisons), and troops withdrawn along with a three-day deadline. The deadline of the wildly unrealistic demand for withdrawal of U.S. troops from Afghanistan seemed to be synchronized with the upcoming American presidential election. It seemed that the killing of the hostages before the election might be used to discredit the Bush Administration's efforts in Afghanistan. Another motivation for connecting the timeline of the hostage crisis to the American election was to attract more media attention, seemingly one of the fundamental goals of this abduction. The abduction was the first of its kind in the history of the country. While kidnappings for small ransoms are fairly commonplace, the United Nations and other international aid organizations had been unaffected. The massive influx of international funds going to Afghanistan through the United Nations and its constituent agencies, both directly through the contribution of foreign aid and indirectly through the presence of masses of relatively wealthy foreign relief workers, protected UN workers from being targeted. This money, like most transfers of wealth in a free market, goes disproportionately to the owners of capital, who are able to make increased profits by selling to, renting to, and servicing the international community. In Afghanistan, the affluent who conduct legitimate business are often the same wealthy warlords that oversee criminal networks. Thus, the possibility of criminals or warlords harming UN staff and causing a massive pullout from the country had previously been minimal.

On the other hand, abduction of locals for small ransoms was a common practice among the criminal element in Afghanistan. Rebecca Maddaford was a New Zealander and the wife of a UN security officer. A former military nurse, she served as a supervising nurse at Kabul Hospital in the center of the city. She told me of a man who arrived at the hospital in January 2005 with the worst case of gangrene she had ever seen. His feet were black and deformed, and both had to be amputated. It turned out that the man was a local school teacher from Kabul who had been kidnapped by criminals from the West of the city. The criminals hiked him through the freezing mountains during the harsh winter, which is what caused the damage to his feet. His family, unable to raise the ransom because of the meager earnings of teachers, had no choice but to leave him to his fate in captivity. The school teacher stayed with the abductors for several weeks until he was finally released. Rebecca asked him how much was the unpaid ransom that had cost him both his feet. The answer, shocking to us, was three hundred dollars.

The best lead in the first days of the incident seemed to be the driver of the UN vehicle, an Afghan man named Rafique. Rafique was the central witness to the incident. Leaving him behind was pragmatic because the mobilization of the international community would occur to secure the release of foreign diplomats rather than an indigenous driver, so there would be little benefit to the abductors to take along the driver. However, in the minds of some investigating the incident, particularly the Afghan Ministry of Interior, Rafique was a prime suspect for involvement in the abduction. His initial debriefing was conducted by Jody Clark, a security officer who often took charge of affairs involving local national staff.

Jody Clark served as an operations officer in the JEMB Security Office. During the run-up to the election, she was the Operations Officer for the Election Security Operations Center. In this role, she coordinated the shift schedules, meals, staffing, and other such matters. The role includes a bit of interaction with male local nationals, and I was curious about any difficulties that might arise from this. In a society where women are barely allowed to show their presence or interact with men, I wondered what level of mutual discomfort must emerge from this strong woman giving orders to these men.

She said that she had not experienced many problems, but if she went into the city, she wore a scarf over her head to cover her wavy auburn hair because to do otherwise would elicit an unfavorable reaction. "It's about respect," she explained to me. "I am also upfront about my expectations, and I am sure to treat everyone with respect, which usually wins people over." Jody was a command sergeant major in the Australian Army (or senior soldier, as she told me the Australians call it). After twenty-one years in logistics in the Australian military, she worked as a subcontractor for the World Food Program in Iraq, responsible for feeding two million people. When the United Nations prematurely withdrew from Iraq due to the attack on their headquarters in 2003, Jody returned home and was offered a logistics position in Afghanistan. Soon after arriving here, she transitioned to security.

Rafique told his story clearly without appearing nervous or dubious. The first moment when Rafique noticed anything unusual was when a black vehicle came alongside his own. He said that he thought it looked like an official vehicle, perhaps part of the International Security Assistance Force, so he slowed down. The black vehicle pulled up in front, and he noticed it was a Black Surf-type jeep with blacked out windows and a black official governmental plate. One man approached the driver's side window. Rafique described the man as dressed in light, cream-colored military fatigues, wearing some kind of military webbing, carrying a Kalashnikov variant weapon. Rafique initially still thought that it was someone from NATO's International Security Assistance Force because he had a shaved head and wore sunglasses. (Afghans rarely wear sunglasses.)

The man who approached asked, "Why did you overtake?" He spoke Dari with a Panshiri accent. Rafique said he immediately went to lock the doors, and his own was locked but the two female internationals in the back had not locked the back doors. (This simple precaution, for reasons I have already discussed in earlier chapters, can be extremely valuable.) Then, the back doors were opened by other men. Shquipe was carried away to the black car; the man who carried her was tall and strong enough to carry her on his shoulder. Annetta resisted slightly but was dragged away by another man. There was a moment of indecision over Angelito, which Rafique interpreted as a delay as the abductor was determining whether Angelito was Afghan. He is Filipino, so his appearance at first glance might seem Central Asian. There were five male assailants, all of whom appeared to be between twenty-five and twenty-eight years old. They were of heavy build, stocky rather than fat, and dressed in tan military fatigues, black and white face scarves, and sunglasses. They were all tall, with two slightly over six feet and the other three slightly shorter.

The men then leaned into the vehicle and unlocked the front door. Rafique was hit first with a rifle butt and then punched. Angelito attempted to resist but was also dragged out. As Rafique struggled, one abductor's Afghan black and white neck scarf was pulled down, and the man said, "I'll kill you." Rafique was thrown to the ground. The three hostages were put into the back seat of the black vehicle. Because three men got into the back seat, Rafique deduced that the abductees must have been forced into the rear storage part of the getaway vehicle. As the black vehicle drove off, Rafique said that he went back to his UN vehicle with the intention of following the kidnappers. However, the keys and a radio had been taken.

The normal driver of the vehicle took an international member of the UN staff to the central United Nations compound in Kabul, where he visited the medical clinic because of a sore throat. He said that he had had this sore throat for about a month, and a Canadian international staff member in the graphics department corroborated his claim. After returning to the electoral compound between 11:00 A.M. and 11:30 A.M., the driver was still feeling unwell, and left his keys for the dispatcher, Mustafa, to give to another driver. He then went home. He said that he did not know to whom the keys would be given. The driver did not have a planned schedule for the rest of the day, and was not the normal, assigned driver for the abduction victims. The driver knew Rafique, but not very well. Like some of the other drivers, he had been to Rafique's house in Paghman, but only once, and he could not identify it. He said that none of the other drivers have expressed anti-international sentiments, and all were shocked by what happened.

It seemed (based on the interviews that were conducted of Rafique, the other driver, and the dispatcher) that Rafique was not complicit in the abduction. However, the Afghan Ministry of Interior felt that he was the strongest lead, and tied him to a criminal network in his home area of Paghman. They interviewed him the following day, and were less convinced of his innocence. A United Nations international observed the interview, and described Rafique as extremely uncomfortable, arrogant, and shifty. The change may have been due to hostility to the law enforcement authorities, who are known to have capricious and corrupt members. The behavior, nonetheless, did not alleviate any of the suspicions about the driver.

The "principals" involved in security around Kabul held their first meeting on October 31, including the Minister of Interior, general officers from Combined Forces Command and the International Security Assistance Force, and senior civilian officers, including the Elections Security Manager, Scott Carnie. At this meeting, the Ministry of Interior was designated the lead agency in resolving the crisis. From an international military point of view, the incident was not in the best location from the perspective of jurisdiction. Kabul Province fell under the control of the NATO International Security Assistance Force, but the Coalition, with its arguably more effective covert intelligence and direct action capabilities and more aggressive posture, would be better suited to handle the situation.

The National Directorate of Security revealed that they believed Shari-fullah was responsible for the kidnapping. The agency also felt that desig-nation of the Ministry of Interior as the lead agency would hamper their investigation. They primarily focused on Paghman valley, west of Kabul, where the Kabul-area criminal elements are concentrated. Command Forces Command—Afghanistan began to track operations. The dissemination of information on this tracking was extremely limited, with a special cell being set up to monitor the recovery efforts.

On November 1, the hostage-takers reported to the media that they split up the hostages to make any rescue attempts more difficult. There were also conflicting reports about whether the militants extended the deadline for a demand to free prisoners from Afghan jails and Guantanamo Bay. The hostages were "not in one location; they are in three different locations," Akbar Agha was quoted as saying. This report was also given by another spokesman for the group. "We have separated the three hostages and are keeping them far from each other so that in case one is discovered by the authorities we have the chance to kill the other two," Mullah Ishaq Manzoor told Reuters.

The U.S. National Guard infantry battalion stationed in Ghazni Province, 3rd of the 116th Infantry, provided a report that it claimed came from two separate reliable sources. One of the subsources of the report was believed to be a Taliban soldier who operated in the Nawa area. The battalion reported that they worked with these sources on numerous occasions and they had provided reliable information in the past. They reported that a tan Landcruiser was moving through Ghazni Province, then Zabul Province, and into Pakistan. The report said that the occupants of the vehicle were the three UN hostages and five armed men. This report provided some consternation because moving the hostages into Pakistan would seriously undercut any possibility of their recovery.

On the evening of November 1, I met representatives from Scotland Yard and a high-level United Nations crisis action team, both of whom had recently arrived in country. The Scotland Yard team was dispatched by their government because Annetta Flanigan was a British citizen. The UN crisis team was composed of three individuals, headed by a retired U.S. Army colonel named Richard Manlove. Manlove was a West Point graduate, and as a former West Point cadet myself, I did not envy the man's plebe year with a name like Dick Manlove, which would attract the unwanted abuse of upperclassmen whose mission was to toughen the new trainees at the military academy by putting stress on them in whatever way was possible.

My partner, Eric Harbaugh, took the lead explaining the capabilities the American military brought to bear on the hostage crisis. Being a little dramatic, he announced that our armed forces are good at breaking things but might not be as helpful in recovering hostages. Fortunately, the other UN liaison, Lieutenant Colonel Craig Gilbert, whom we met in Chapter 1, was present on this occasion and made a slight correction to Harbaugh's assertion. He stated simply, "Ahh . . . we actually have a pretty robust direct action capability."

As I considered the extensive special forces presence in the country, it occurred to me that these soldiers conducted intensive training for just these sorts of situations. Navy SEALs, Delta Force, and other organizations hunting for terrorists among the Other Coalition Forces would play a significant role in the hostage recovery efforts. Gilbert's response was a helpful clarification of my partner's somewhat impulsive remark.

The intervention of Manlove's crisis action team was rather frustrating to other members of the UN security apparatus in Kabul because the crisis team was extremely secretive. Situational awareness on the recovery efforts soon deteriorated as the crisis team restricted access to the information. The presence of the team might not have led to the recovery of the hostages, but it did prevent midlevel security managers from tracking the situation.

Many members of the Afghan administration were convinced that influential Afghans in contact with Taliban elements in Pakistan were the main culprits behind the October 28 kidnapping of the three elections workers. As with many conspiracy theories advanced by Afghan government officials, opposition leader Yunis Qanuni was supposedly involved. Reportedly, President Karzai planned to move carefully in negotiations, but once the hostages were safe, he would aggressively pursue the culprits and the influential individuals backing them. The government did not believe the kidnappers would kill the hostages, whom the government felt were probably still in the Kabul area. However, there was a concern that the kidnappers might sell them to extremist elements such as the Taliban.

The government believed it would have been impossible to successfully carry out the attack without influential support. They characterized key suspect Sharifullah as a thug linked to Ittihad-e Islami leader and ethnic Tajik Abdul Rausol Sayyaf, indicating Sayyaf's involvement. Immediately after security forces put pressure on Sharifullah, Taliban elements in Pakistan threatened to kill the hostages if the government did not relent. The members of the Afghan administration viewed this as coordination between Sharifullah and the cross-border militants. They speculated that the influential Afghans involved were able to pass videotape and images to extremist elements in Pakistan in order to reinforce the perception that the radical fighters had the hostages, when they in fact did not.

This reasoning assumed that Qanuni and other influential opposition leaders viewed President Karzai's success in the October 9 presidential election as a threat and had backed the abduction in order to overshadow the elections and to punish the United Nations for its role in bringing about the Karzai victory. The Afghan officials felt that this was the opposition's way of indicating that major problems would take place if they were shut out of the government. Aggressive investigations against the perpetrators once the hostages were safe would demonstrate that such tactics were counterproductive. Some of these ideas might have been valid, such as local criminals holding the hostages and communicating with militants in Pakistan. However,

typical and unfounded conspiracy theories against ethnic Tajiks most likely
motivated the allegations against the opposition leaders rather than hard
facts.

By November 2, Coalition and UN security officials were assessing that
the hostages were with a criminal element rather than the Jaish-e-Muslimeen
as disseminated in the media. President Karzai convened a meeting with the
principal security leaders at the presidential palace. The American Special
Forces representatives visited our office, where we provided them personal
and medical background on the hostages. The medical information was
crucial for any rescue attempt. The chief medic, Chris Morris, was a private
contractor for the elections with a firm called Ex-Med, and his background
in British Special Operations gave a basis for his proficiency in his medical
assessment as well as in the type of information the direct action team would
need. The Ministry of Interior was continuing to follow leads, deploying
personnel to search in the Shaka Dara area of Kabul. The U.S. Embassy was
also actively involved, hosting a meeting between Deputy Chief of Mission
Dick Christiansen and senior officers from Combined Forces Command and
liaising with the British Ambassador.

On the following day, Jaish-e-Muslimeen spokesman Sayed Khalid indicated the organization might compromise on its hostage release demands.
Throughout the day, the deadline to meet the demands continued to shift
based on communications from the various spokespersons of the terrorist
group. The deadline was extended to the evening, then at 2:00 P.M. extended to November 5, then brought back to midnight on November 3,
and finally then to November 4 at 10:00 A.M. It seemed that the group was
not very organized, and indeed, they were believed to have contact with
the abductors, but not to actually have possession of the hostages. Afghan
security forces detained an individual named Mohammed Yahya, south of
Kabul in the neighboring Logar Province, but his connection to the incident
was unclear, and the hostages were still believed to either be in Kabul City
or the nearby Paghman area. Ambassador Khalilzad, who had been out of
the country, returned to Kabul. This raised expectations of a prospective
resolution because of Khalilzad's considerable network of support.

Several reports arrived on November 4 to update the situation. Akbar
Agha, the leader of Jaish-e-Muslimeen, spoke with a hostage taker in Wardak Province and directed him to keep the hostages in separate compounds
and be prepared to kill them quickly in the event of a failure to meet demands or of an attempted rescue. According to a second-hand report, the
terrorists were planning to ask for thirty thousand dollars per hostage to
gain their release. One of the female hostages was allegedly extremely ill
and had not eaten in several days. At the same time these reports were being
disseminated, Afghan security forces detained several suspects in the area
of Jalrez in Wardak Province. The Afghan National Police also released
photographs of three Toyota Surfs that had been confiscated in Paghman

District and Kabul District over the past few days. The Ministry of Interior informed us that they were investigating further to determine whether these vehicles were involved with the abduction.

In addition, a local Afghan contact of Coalition intelligence sources provided some background information. The main subject of the report was Abdul Rausol Sayyaf, an Afghan of Pashtun ethnicity who lived in Alajhahdi Village of Paghman District, Kabul Province. Sayyaf was approached by Astad Akhbery, a Taliban leader. Akhbery explained to Sayyaf that he wanted all Taliban and al Qaeda personnel released from Afghan prisons and the detention facility in Guantanamo Bay, Cuba. The meeting and planning for the kidnapping took place at Sayyaf's residence about a month before the actual kidnapping. To carry out the actual kidnapping, Sayyaf turned to his nephew Montaz, a well-known criminal in Kabul.

Montaz carried out the kidnapping with several other individuals, two of whom have been identified as Amrulli Chontaa and Dowood. After the kidnapping occurred, they traveled to Qarghah Corner in Kabul and switched vehicles. From this location, the victims and the kidnappers fled the area into Paghman District.

Sayyaf, a large Afghan, standing six feet tall and weighing 200 pounds, was a teacher. He had a foot-long salt and pepper beard and occasionally wore glasses. He lectured audiences, preaching against the Afghan and U.S. governments and the NATO soldiers of the International Security Assistance Force. Sayyaf also provided training in guerilla-type tactics and was reported to be a *mujahideen* trainer.

Abdul Rausol Sayyaf had an association with an individual named Moosa Khan that dated back to the jihadi days against the Soviet Union. Moosa had a brother in the custody of the United States, Haji Gholam Mohammed Hotak. Sayyaf felt too much pressure regarding the Afghan government's search for the hostages. Sayyaf then contacted Moosa, who in turn took custody of the hostages, to take the pressure off Sayyaf. Moosa was now holding the UN workers as hostages and planned to release them in return for his brother's release from U.S. custody.

After the kidnapping, the hostages were taken to an unknown location in Somochak Village, Paghman District, Kabul Province. The hostages were then loaded into Datsun pickup trucks by Sayyaf on the day Al-Jazeera broadcast the videotape of the hostages. The hostages were transported to Wardak Province, on a little-known road that has no checkpoints and leads to Ghazni City. At an unknown point on this little-known road, the kidnappers and hostages turned in an unknown direction and headed toward Maydan Shar, Wardak Province. The exact location of the hostages in Maydan Shar was not known, but the intelligence contact reported that he was told that the hostages were being treated like guests.

The Afghan government performed a search of Somochak Village at an unknown time, presumably on November 5, 2004. During this search, an individual by the name of Kachkol was detained by Afghan authorities. The circumstances surrounding his apprehension were unknown. This entire report was provided by an Afghan source who had established a reliable reporting record with American military intelligence in the past, but on its own, it was impossible to determine to what extent the story was true rather than conjecture or rumor.

On November 4, the deadline was again extended. Reuters quoted Sayed Khalid Agha, a spokesman for the group: "We have moved the deadline to Saturday night because the United Nations and Afghan government requested us to through a third party for negotiations." Mullah Sabir Momin, a member of Jaish's leadership council, said that Shquipe, the Kosovar, would be executed first if negotiations failed. "She is important," he said, without elaborating. Likely the fact that she was a nonpracticing Muslim was the factor that might have set this hostage aside from the others, although it was also hypothesized that any one of the hostages suffering most from ill health would be a likely candidate to be executed first.

Mullah Sabir Momin also said that the health of all three abductees had declined. "The condition of all the three hostages is very bad," Momin was quoted in a Reuters report. "They are very sick and don't take meals. We bought biscuits and bottled water from the market but their situation is deteriorating." The kidnappers dismissed the idea of showing their captives any mercy despite the Muslim fasting and holy month of Ramadan, during which good deeds are supposed to be rewarded. "These are not Muslims and whosoever confronts Muslims in support of infidels is justified to be killed," Momin said. "Hamid Karzai also claims to be a Muslim. [But] he is an American agent and enemy of Islam."

We assessed that the continued extensions of deadlines were designed to prolong media coverage of the incident. It was previously noted that the terrorists were dissatisfied with the coverage, which was earlier crowded out by the American presidential election. Alternatively, the extensions may have reflected progress in Afghan negotiations, perhaps indicating that some sort of payment would be rendered, but the details of safe exchange of the payment and hostages must still be defined. On November 5, the Ministry of Interior detained more suspects in the area of Tangi, Wardak Province. One of the suspects, a militant named Mullah Karim, was armed at the time of the arrest. Mullah Karim's house was searched, and weapons and ammunition were found.

On November 7, a media report indicated that talks with United Nations and government negotiators via intermediaries were expected in the next few days. The talks were expected to start by 1:00 P.M. at an undisclosed location. The Jaish spokesman Sayed Khalid Agha said that the deadline had been extended because of the time needed for United Nations and government negotiators to arrive, but he said the kidnappers had not moderated their demands. "We are very hopeful that our demands will be met," the spokesman said. "Our demands are the same; we have not diluted them. We hope that the delegation is capable and has the necessary authority and that the talks will not just be to buy time."

Another of Jaish-e-Muslimeen's several spokesmen said that face-to-face talks between the kidnappers and United Nations and government officials were already under way at a secret location. The kidnappers said the health of the hostages had deteriorated and they were suffering from the cold. The United Nations passed cold weather gear and other personal effects and comfort items to the negotiating team to mitigate the effects of the cold. Our office collected and consolidated these care packages.

A former BBC correspondent in Kabul notified a JEMB Area Manager that Bexhet Pacolli, a prominent Swiss-based businessman from Kosovo, arrived in Kabul on November 7. Pacolli began communicating with press contacts as well as senior UN officials in an attempt to arrange a ransom, funded from his own personal resources. It is unclear whether he planned to ransom all the hostages or focus on his countrywoman, Shquibe Hebibe. The significance of this development was not clear, but the hostage team began monitoring the activities of this businessman. At this point, the limitations of intelligence on the whereabouts of the hostages seemed to indicate that some sort of negotiated release would be the only way to avoid further harm to the hostages, who according to the medical information, were likely in poor condition at that point.

On November 8, the hostages were allowed to make calls home in the morning. Several calls were placed to Kosovo, the Philippines, and Belfast. The Ministry of Interior received its first sign that money was the kidnappers' primary objective when a demand for two million dollars arrived, along with detailed instructions of making a drop at a Kabul bank. A media source reported that the militants agreed to give the government until Tuesday to find and release twenty-six extremist prisoners. The negotiations through intermediaries with United Nations and government officials led the terrorists to announce later that they were willing to "soften" other demands if their twenty-six comrades were freed. "We gave them a list of twenty-six people we want them to release," said Sayed Khalid Agha, another self-proclaimed Jaish-e-Muslimeen spokesman. "They sought two days to find where these twenty-six prisoners are, and we agreed. We gave them Monday and Tuesday to find out about these prisoners and let us know whether they will be released. Then the second round of negotiations will start." Mullah Sabir Momin said the militants had "backed away from" some demands but did not elaborate. Agha said Shquibe Hebibi was seriously unwell because of the cold and the others were also suffering from the cold and poor food. The narrowing of the prisoner release demands confirmed earlier expectations that the hostage-takers would narrow their list of prisoners to be released, eventually to secure the release of the brother of one of the criminal leaders, Moosa Khan. Most likely two groups, with interests that may not entirely overlap, were involved in this situation. First, there was the criminal network that was likely holding the hostages and responsible for their original capture. Second, Jaish-e-Muslimeen, likely having contracted the abduction, was handling the media relations. The group was assessed to be insufficiently sophisticated to carry out this kidnapping on its own. Additionally, the available intelligence linked criminals rather than militants to the actual event.

The Kosovar businessman, who said he was a cousin of Hebibi, made a televised appeal for her release, saying she was a Muslim who came to help Afghanistan. "Shquipe Hebibi went to Afghanistan to help our brother people here," Bexhet Pacolli said on a private Afghan televison channel. "Please release her. We are waiting every day." Pacolli said he understood Hebibi was being held apart from the other hostages, not far from Kabul, and he had a sign she was still alive.

Later that evening, the International Security Assistance Force claimed that the hostages had been located in the Kabul area of operations and would be rescued hopefully in a "soft" (noncombat) rescue operation by U.S. Special Operations Forces. They stated that another possibility was that the hostages would be plainly released somewhere along Jalalabad road. ISAF stated that the lead would be the Afghan National Directorate of Security. This operation never materialized, however.

The following day, the media reported that Shquipe Hebibi telephoned a friend in her hometown in Kosovo and said she was well and not being badly treated. The call came on the eve of fresh talks over the hostages' release. Hebibi spoke to a female friend in her hometown of Pec, who passed a message on to her brother: "I feel very well, nobody has treated me badly and I hope to see you soon."

As investigators stepped up the process of looking for more information, some of the coworkers at the Joint Electoral Management Body reported that one of the victims, Shquipe Hebibi, had been threatened while working in the counting center by various observers: Qanuni, Karzai, and Mohaqiq party agents. Apparently, the Qanuni agents had been the most vociferous, but there was no further information on the content of the threat. In addition, an Afghan elections staff member had called her incompetent in an e-mail message. Threats of this nature, especially against female staff members, were common and typically not reported at the time they occurred. (These threats had also not been reported at the time.)

The long period for which the hostages were held made it unclear whether the Afghan militants were adopting new methods similar to their counterparts in Iraq, where beheading foreign hostages was commonplace. This incident was the first kidnapping of UN international workers in Afghanistan, so it was significant as a departure from previous practices. Additionally, the abduction was consistent with analyses that suggested that the Taliban would adopt methods of the Iraqi insurgents. Fortunately, this practice did not materialize as a Taliban method. The enormous amount of money being poured into the country due to the presence of the United Nations to some extent insulated the international presence here from the type of targeting that is more prevalent in Iraq, where the United Nations had long since pulled out. With popular support waning in the aftermath of the election, militants would only further alienate the population by driving out a lucrative source of industrial development, education, and employment for many Afghans.

On November 9, it was discovered that the bank designated for the two-million-dollar ransom drop would not accept the money. Negotiations were continuing, and the National Directorate of Security informed their CIA counterparts that the American Central Intelligence Agency representatives could no longer be involved in the hostage negotiation process. This might have been a sign that the Afghan government was willing to make concessions that would not have been condoned by the Americans. And then, the following day, a one-and-a-half million-dollar ransom was transferred and held at the Ministry of Interior.

The Americans strongly protested against the plan of paying the ransom, but a lesser drop was agreed to. Five thousand dollars for medical supplies and food, along with clothing, for the hostages was dropped at Shah du Shamshira Mosque on November 11, 2004. The Ministry of Interior intermediary dropped the money inside the mosque. A terrorist picked up the money and left on a motorcycle, but the Afghan security team observing failed to track him. The Deputy Director of the National Directorate of Security revealed that he planned a discussion with President Karzai and wanted the Ministry of Interior removed from investigation. Whether due to incompetence or corruption, it seemed that the lead agency on the case was unable to make any significant progress in recovering the hostages.

With the upcoming Muslim holiday of Eid al-Fitr, there was some hope that a reconciliation could be achieved by securing a release of the hostages during this important religious celebration. Eid is the conclusion of the Muslim holy month of Ramadan. Ramadan is a period of fasting and devotion, during which the faithful do not eat any food or consume any liquid from sunup to sundown. The Muslim faithful in Afghanistan are strongly committed to their religion, so observance of Ramadan is strict and common. Afghan National Army mentors from Task Force Phoenix were frustrated when they traveled on long convoys across the dangerous countryside and the Afghan soldiers insisted on halting to make their prayers. The five-times-daily prayer facing the city of Mecca is a time-honored Islamic tradition. My Afghan acquaintances in Kabul were typically hungry and tired during the holy month. Celebration of Eid is a welcome respite from the rigors of Ramadan. Hostages Angelito Nayan and Annetta Flanigan were again allowed to place phone calls to families from a previously unidentified phone

number. However, the holiday did not produce a breakthrough, and negotiations were officially put on hold for Eid.

Intelligence gathered over the next few days revealed that the victims
were bored and one was still ill. Sharifullah's brother, Toorilay, who had
been arrested in the days after the abduction, died in Ministry of Interior
custody. On November 15, the Philippine government ruled out paying any
sort of ransom to the hostage-takers. As the week progressed, more reports
surfaced on the identity of the kidnappers, and the situation was becoming
increasingly desperate for them. The abductors, indulging their opium habit,
were becoming more and more paranoid. The hostages were also showing
signs of increased stress, making demands on the criminals holding them to
"Kill us or release us!" Annetta Flanigan was reluctant to make additional
proof of life calls when offered by the hostage takers. The first indications
of violence by the hostage-holders against the hostages were also appearing
at this time.

On November 21, Rafique, the UN driver of the hostages, debriefed UN
Office of Projects and Services security personnel on his time in the prison
after he had been released from Ministry of Interior custody. He reported
that another suspect had been killed by electrocution in the next cell. This
story seemed relevant in conjunction with a press report released the same
day. Earlier that day, the Afghan Islamic Press reported that the suspect
named Kachkol, whose arrest took place several days before in connection
with the abduction, died under torture. Speaking to the Afghan Islamic Press,
"reliable sources" in Kabul said that Kachkol, who was from Zar Shakh
village of Paghman District, had died. Marks on his body supported the
conclusion that torture was involved. The report quoted the suspect's wife,
Nasrin, and a number of villagers, who said that his whole body was bruised
as a result of extensive beatings. His wife said that his nails had been pulled.
Afghan officials reportedly attributed his death to his old injuries. United
Nations personnel had mixed feelings on the credibility of Rafique. It was
still unclear whether he was actually involved in the abduction. His release
did not constitute an exoneration; indeed, the arrests of many suspects, in
my mind, did not constitute reasonable suspicion of their involvement.

While we will never be certain on the issue of Rafique, I do think there
are several points about which we can be reasonably sure regarding his in-
carceration. First, Rafique was not credible. It is difficult to know what he
was hiding, but he seemed to want to show himself in the best possible light.
Second, Rafique was not involved with the hostage incident. Allegations to
the contrary were never based on substantial evidence. In fact, the process
in which Rafique was selected to drive the UN vehicle has a sort of random-
ness that contraindicates a coordinated setup. Third, Rafique's release had
more to do with his poor health than any evidence about the abduction.
He suffers from heart problems and may have not survived further time in
the austere conditions of Afghan custody. As for the Afghan Islamic Press

report, it is likely that the report was true, but it is difficult to judge whether Kachkol was actually involved with the abduction. Several arrests had taken place in connection with the abduction, but it is unclear that there are clear pieces of evidence linking these suspects to the abduction. If Kachkol were connected with the abduction, his untimely death may indicate a frustration for Afghan interrogation efforts as valuable intelligence had not been forthcoming.

Overall, the hostage situation was becoming progressively more important among UN officials in Kabul, and its outcome was linked to planning for the National Assembly Elections to include providing sufficient staffing and the assignment of Afghan versus international responsibilities. A failure to resolve the situation in a positive and timely manner may have hampered the election process in the spring. High-level Afghan government officials continued to emphasize that some senior political figures were involved with the incident. Foreign embassies throughout Kabul were reportedly exerting pressure on the Afghan government to resolve this situation to ensure the continuity of robust UN support.

During the late night of November 21, 2004, special operators from the Kabul Compound again launched a raid, this time on a house in Kabul. I had indications that something was going down, but it was not clear what, so I went to the base to see what I could find out at the hostage recovery cell. There I found the preparations for the raid. Although this raid did not succeed in recovering the hostages, it hit close to the mark. The hostages would reveal upon their release that they heard the sounds of the commotion nearby. Apparently, the raid missed the location of the hostages by only one house. If you consider that Kabul is a city with no street signs or house numbers, the mistake is more easily understood. Even with these features of American urban navigation, I have found it occasionally difficult to find a friend's house in broad daylight. A midnight raid in the difficult conditions of Afghanistan would be so much the more difficult.

On the early morning of the following day, the hostages were finally released by their captors. Pressure had mounted, perhaps reaching a breaking point with the near miss raid from the night before. I visited the Kabul Multi-National Brigade Hospital at Camp Warehouse, where the three hostages had been transferred early in the morning. I observed that all three hostages appeared to be in good condition. The women appeared thin, but their faces were not pale and they appeared strong and healthy. At the time I left, Annetta Flanigan had just completed a physical examination and was reunited with her husband, Jose Maria Arana. Shquipe Hebibe was receiving informal counseling with the UN crisis team and was next in line to receive a physical examination. Angelito Nayan was making phone calls on his cell phone and was also awaiting his physical exam. The United Nations decided to move the three out of country as soon as possible. The hospital director told us that results of the physical exams showed some old bruising from the early days of the captivity. The two female hostages both exhibited bruises that were apparently caused by the butt stroke of a rifle based on their conversations with the medical personnel. The faded bruises indicated a few weeks of time had passed, according to the doctors. It is likely that this violence occurred early on as abductors attempted to set a harsh tone, or that a brutal individual was responsible and later restrained himself or was restrained by his comrades. The hostages indicated that there was no serious violence and that they had been well treated.

Politically, the safe recovery of the hostages was extremely good news for the United Nations Assistance Mission in Afghanistan as well as for international support to the Joint Electoral Management Body for National Assembly Elections in 2005. The degree to which concessions were made to the abductors if this was a negotiated release could be seen to provide an incentive for abduction of internationals in the future. Such a possibility could have heightened the threat of kidnapping. Even if there were no such incentives provided, the widespread public and media attention to this incident highlighted it as a future threat.

The hostages were moved to the residence of Jean Arnault, the Special Representative to the Secretary-General (known among the international community in Afghanistan as the SRSG). The hostages revealed that the captors had been friendly, and although there were some tense moments, the captors were not harsh in dealing with the UN workers. The hostages revealed that they were moved frequently between four different houses. They believed that they were never very far from Kabul, although they believed their initial movement was to Paghman. Their release appeared to be a result of a negotiation because the hostages were taken to a car and told to drive themselves. At that time, international forces linked up with the vehicle. Angelito and Shquipe seemed shocked and disappointed that they would not be returning to their work. Jose Maria Arana and Annetta Flanigan were looking forward to moving on. The United Nations was working to expedite the movement of all three out of the country.

On the late evening of November 22, 2004, several Afghan prisoners were transferred to Coalition custody. The prisoners, Jamal, Mohammed Shah, and Lais, were being released by the Afghans because the abduction incident had ended. There was one other person at the hospital who had died of his wounds, and the other prisoners referred to him as "Haji." Haji is an honorific for Muslims who have made the *hajj*, the once-in-a-lifetime pilgrimage to Mecca. It is a common title in Afghanistan, although I think some men who come to be called Haji have never left the country. (The term Haji is also American military slang used to describe Afghans in general. In my opinion, it is a mildly racist term in the same way that American servicemen have used this sort of pejorative slang for decades. In the European theater, Germans were called "krauts," and in the Pacific theater, Japanese were called "slopes," Vietnamese were "gooks" in the

Vietnam War, and in Somalia, the Somalis were called "skinnies." Haji is the next generation of this aversive labeling process.)

The Coalition team went to the third floor of Kabul Central Hospital, where the prisoners were being held. There were already several Afghan officials there, including Kabul Chief of Police General Baba Jan, General Bashir of the Afghan National Police, and one other Afghan National Police general. The leader of the prisoners, Lais, bitterly told General Baba Jan, "You're not a man. If you give me to the Americans, you're not a man."

When the Coalition convoy left the hospital an hour later, they took Jamal and Lais with them. Mohammed Shah was left at the hospital because he was not stable enough to move. During the trip back to Camp Phoenix, Lais rode in one vehicle with Major Dana Rucinski, whom I had encountered long ago when I tried to coordinate a phone card for the Afghan officer who was working with me in the Elections Security Operations Center.

Major Rucinski was a masculine female, perhaps the type of woman to be expected to serve as an officer in the Army. She was not unattractive, with dark brown eyes, and brown hair that she wore long with the civilian clothes she wore when leaving the compound. As a human intelligence officer, Dana could switch in and out of uniform as she chose without anyone questioning her. Such intelligence professionals often find it helpful to leave uncertainties about their rank and role during interrogations, so she wore civilian clothes on this occasion as she interrogated Lais on the ride back from the hospital.

Her interpreter told me the questions she asked and the responses Lais gave. While this exchange was not particularly helpful, it shows both the style and approach of a professional American interrogator and the attitude of an Afghan criminal implicated in the UN abduction. (Technically speaking, Major Rucinski was a staff officer, not a seasoned interrogator, and this might explain the ineffectiveness of her questioning, although perhaps even the most experienced questioners would not have been able to break Lais under these conditions.)

Rucinski: What's your name?
Lais: Lais.
Rucinski: What's your real name?
Lais: Lais, but at home they call me Sediq. [Sediq is a common Afghan name that means "honest."]
Rucinski: What were you doing there [where you were arrested]?
Lais: Haji and his friends [the other prisoners, including the deceased], picked me up and put me in the vehicle, and drove me away.
Rucinski: Why did they pick you up?
Lais: Because I owe him money.
Rucinski: Why do you owe him money?

| | |
|---|---|
| Lais: | Because I bought some property off of him. I'm in the real estate business and so was Haji. He should have been paid a month ago. |
| Rucinski: | Why did you go with them? |
| Lais: | Because I had no choice, they had weapons. |
| Rucinski: | Who shot at you? |
| Lais: | The locals, not the police. |
| Rucinski: | Do you know where the three kidnapped victims are? |
| Lais: | I don't know. I am a college student; I'm educated. I am not Taliban or al-Qaeda. I'm in the real estate business, and I have a store in Taimoni. I fought against the Taliban for five years before the Americans came to Afghanistan. |
| Rucinski: | If you want to make it easier on yourself, you better answer me. In about fifteen or twenty minutes the helicopter is going to come pick you up, so this is your last chance. |
| Lais: | I don't know anything about kidnapping or anything. [Every time Lais mentioned the kidnapping, he was either smiling or laughing.] |
| Rucinski: | Are you married? |
| Lais: | (Answer uncertain). |
| Rucinski: | Do you know the other guys? |
| Lais: | No. One's name is Jamal, but I don't know the others. |
| Rucinski: | If you don't know them how do you know his name is Jamal? |
| Lais: | Because I heard the doctor calling his name. |
| Rucinski: | So you don't know any of them, right? |
| Lais: | No, just Haji. |
| Rucinski: | And you don't even know him, do you? Just that his name is Haji and that you owe him one million afghanis. |
| Lais: | Yes, that's all. |
| Rucinski: | You have about two minutes left, because the bird is going to come and take you, so this is your last chance. So if you want to help yourself and help us too, you better start talking. |
| Lais: | It doesn't matter if you give me two minutes or two hours or two days, my answers are the same. Even if you ask me the same questions after one or ten years, my answer will still be the same. |

After this, Major Rucinski asked the same questions several times until the helicopter arrived. Lais told the interpreter that he should believe him since they were both Afghans, even if the American interrogator did not. Lais said that, upon his release, he would "raise his voice" and go to President Karzai to complain about his arrest.

Thus it seemed to further confirm that the captors were more likely criminal than radical. The overall description from the abductees makes it seem that the hostages were never intended to leave Kabul, although the terrorists had threatened with conflicting stories from time to time saying otherwise. The incident, while potentially catastrophic, was ultimately resolved positively. A combination of luck and intense efforts by the various security constituencies in Kabul led to the successful outcome of the abduction.

The story did not end, however, for some of the key players who had gained public notoriety. Akbar Agha, the now well-known leader of the Jaish-e-Muslimeen, was arrested in Peshawar, Pakistan. Agha reportedly expressed regret to some of his close confidants that he had claimed responsibility for the kidnapping. He revealed that he had not planned the abduction, and had only learned of it by the radio. He was involved in the negotiations for the hostages' release. The demands that he and his subordinate leaders issued were an attempt to take advantage of the situation, gain some notoriety for his group, and advance the Islamist cause in Afghanistan. Agha felt that had placed himself in danger when the hostages were released and the demands were not met, and that other Taliban leaders in Pakistan would take revenge on him. He feared for his life and did not go outdoors much. In December 2004, Agha was arrested by the Pakistani Inter-Services Intelligence Directorate (ISID). Many members of the ISID are strongly suspected to have sympathies for, or even direct links to, extremist Muslim leaders, and it is likely that Agha's arrest was made possible by the approval of the Taliban and al Qaeda community in Pakistan's border region. Several leaders of the upper hierarchy of the former Taliban regime have a fairly free range of movement in Pakistan and run radical madrassas, or Muslim schools, which train in religion and combat. There were two factors that led to his arrest: Agha's notoriety with Pakistan's Western allies for his claim of responsibility for the kidnapping as well as his notoriety with Muslim extremist key players in Pakistan for his failure to have any demands met before the hostages were released. Akbar Agha was eventually turned over to the Afghan government in January 2005, and to my knowledge, he remains incarcerated in Kabul.

The release of the hostages marked the end of terrorist efforts at post-election retributive violence. The onset of winter introduced the annual winter lull, which had taken place every year since the end of the first year of American occupation in late 2002. During the winter, fighters typically rejoin their families and suspend their insurgency for some time. In spite of a few disjointed efforts at reestablishing credibility and striking back after their strategic defeat in the 2004 election, the Taliban and the associated militants were unable to mobilize any serious activity. The winter brought the new challenge of planning for the upcoming National

Assembly Elections. Only time would tell whether these elections would also be free from violence, and perhaps that the counterinsurgency had turned a corner with the successful presidential election. Or perhaps the coming year would see the reemergence of the previous years' experience following the winter lull as the Islamists insurgents would attempt to mount a new spring offensive.

# CHAPTER 5

# The Assembly Elections

The parliamentary elections, which would eventually be referred to as the National Assembly Elections, had been repeatedly delayed from their initially scheduled date, which had originally been concurrent with the presidential election. The system for the assembly elections according to the Afghan Electoral Law was a complex series of selection processes to ultimately create a bicameral legislative body.

The upper house was called the *meshrano jirga*, and it was divided into three components: presidential appointees, district council selectees, and provincial council selectees. The district and provincial councils were a matter of confusion. These councils would be popularly elected as part of the assembly election process, but their powers—other than the selection of representatives to serve in the *meshrano jirga*—were undefined. The purpose of the district councils would be to give equal input to more remote and unpopulated areas of a province in selection of members of the upper house. The large number of districts across the country prevented the representation of each district in the *meshrano jirga*.

The lower house, or *wolesi jirga*, would be selected by a more conventional democratic election, in which voters would choose their representatives directly rather than selecting local or regional councils that would select representatives for them. The lower house election was to be more like the congressional elections in the United States with which Americans are more familiar.

The month of November was mostly a wasted month as Afghan and United Nations leaders recovered from the trying presidential election period. The complexities of the upcoming assembly elections required urgent actions, but very little occurred. Many key players from the international community were either taking leave, which had been suspended for the period leading up to the presidential election, or ending their contracts for work elsewhere in the world. The kidnapping also distracted much of the attention of both UN election officials and the Afghan central government during the month of November.

By mid-December, contacts from both the Joint Electoral Management Body and the U.S. Embassy revealed that Afghan leaders had taken some steps toward preparing for the election. President Karzai replaced the JEMB with a seven-member Independent Electoral Commission consisting of five Afghans and two internationals. These members were to be appointed by the beginning of 2005, allowing the new cabinet time to be in place. (I should remind readers at this point that the Joint Electoral Management Body was the eleven-member panel that made strategic electoral decisions. The Joint Electoral Management Body Secretariat (JEMB-S) was the body that worked with Coalition forces on operational, logistical, and security issues for the election. This larger administrative body, often simply called the JEMB, was not eliminated in the transition.)

In an unrelated development, the JEMB Secretariat was moved under the authority of the UN Office for Projects and Services (UNOPS), one of the different UN agencies in Afghanistan. In the long term, this move was likely not operationally significant because the elections project had already operated fairly independently from the remainder of the UN infrastructure in Afghanistan. The move was intended to streamline chains of command for the UN elections team and put the project under the direction of a UN organization reputed for businesslike efficiency. In the short-term, however, the move paralyzed UN support to the election process.

The Ministry of Interior deployed teams to the provinces to begin the process of assigning population settlements to districts. Rather than creating a map with district boundaries, the assignment of settlements would be more productive for the electoral officials and less politically controversial to regional leaders. However, the issue of how many districts exist in a particular province would remain a matter of uncertainty because provincial governors have legal ability to redraw the district map of their provinces. Additionally, various maps held by the government, Coalition, and United Nations did not necessarily agree on the districts across the country. The number of districts varied from 350 to 450, and the actual inhabitants of a given "district" might not recognize the name of the district that a given map represented. Many of the districts were based on tribal affiliations, but even the most creative gerrymandering would be unable to assign clear district boundaries based on tribal borders. These borders could change with seasons in the case of nomadic tribes and lack any sort of consensus between overlapping or neighboring tribal territories. This situation was routinely exposed in Coalition intelligence reports from the military tactical human intelligence collectors and the CIA field officers who provided information from local informants. The locations provided in these reports would be impossible to find because the name of the district did not reflect a name of the maps used by intelligence analysts at the headquarters or appear in available gazetteer searches.

By the middle of December, the Afghan government was becoming increasingly aware that the census was a major issue that needed to be resolved before the National Assembly Elections could take place. There were two main options: using the data from the 1979 census or using the ongoing representative household survey. Both of these alternatives had political difficulties. The outdated census would no doubt be inaccurate because of population growth, demographic movements, and two decades of warfare and refugee emigration. The representative survey could be manipulated and would be unconvincing to a society whose mathematical advancement did not allow for a strong reliance in statistical methods.

Senior State Department leaders at the U.S. Embassy seemed cautiously optimistic about the initiative taken by the host government. While there was some concern over the uncertainty of redistricting, the major concerns raised involved two points: (1) these developments were still occurring too late based on internal timelines the State Department was tracking for an election to occur on time, and (2) there still seemed to be an insufficient sense of urgency among the Afghan government leaders. The Afghan Electoral Law required that the assembly elections take place during the Islamic month of Saur, which ran from April 20, 2005 to May 20, 2005. This date was already twice delayed because the assembly elections were originally scheduled in conjunction with the presidential election, which had been delayed from its initially planned date to October 2004.

After some discussion, Embassy officials dismissed the first point because their internal timeline analysis was focused on the earliest possible date in Saur, April 23, and an election closer to the end of Saur, May 20, still seemed feasible. The second point prompted Ambassador Khalilzad to charge his senior staff to come up with a plan to identify the appropriate electoral benchmarks and corresponding Afghan key leaders so that the American officials could provide mentorship. The Ambassador or his senior deputies planned to liaise with these Afghan leaders to prompt them to expedite any particular slowpoint in the election process. This was one illustration of how the American State Department officials in Kabul provided mentorship and guidance to the highest-level officials of the Afghan government. This reflected a common practice of liaison between the Embassy and the host government. However, during one of the country team meetings I attended, the Ambassador reflected on how this process would change as the Afghans evolved from a transitional, new, and dependent government to a permanent, established, and sovereign government. The Embassy leaders had observed an increasing assertion of independence by Afghan officials, and Khalilzad found this to be an appropriate and encouraging development. However, the legislative election was a new and critical event; the presidential election was the only experience of the Afghan government and election commission. When the Ambassador departed for holiday leave, he stayed in communication on election matters with his senior deputy, the Deputy Chief of Mission (or DCM) Richard Christiansen, who was running things while Ambassador Khalilzad was gone.

Once the Ambassador returned from vacation, he met with President Karzai, who told Khalilzad that he strongly opposed any delay in the election timing due to the previous unplanned delay of the presidential election. Karzai felt that the parliamentary election must go on as scheduled. The U.S. Embassy's official position was strong support for the president. The Embassy assumed a strong stance of favoring April elections in part due to the perceived vacillation of UN officials, who at the time, in December 2004, had been suggesting various delayed dates for the election, including July 2005, September 2005, October 2005, and April 2006. The last proposal, delaying the elections for an entire year, was intended to allow for the development of political parties and democratic institutions. The Embassy was not sympathetic to the UN's logistical and operational challenges because the Embassy viewed these difficulties as self-inflicted due to the passive and reactive actions the UN electoral body had taken after the presidential election.

From the UN perspective, several points about the stance of the Afghan government and American Embassy created difficulty. First, by April 2005, the United Nations would not be able to conduct anything near the "free and fair" election that was successfully executed in October 2004. Most personnel positions were not even filled, and recruiting was not expected to even begin in many departments until January 2005. Optimistically assuming that the Ministry of Interior would delineate district boundaries by its anticipated January deadline, a massive Voter Registration Project would have to take place because voters were not currently registered by the district where they reside. While there was the advantage of having done registration already, the need to create accurate geographical reference points with the registration effort would create difficultly, especially with mobile segments of the Afghan population. (The presidential election enjoyed the logistical advantage of not needing geographical distinctions because it was a national-level election. The "home address" portion of voter registration was extremely imprecise, perhaps shortsightedly so since the parliamentary election was shortly following.) The vetting of about 4,000 candidates, and production and distribution of ballots for these candidates, would also be a massively more challenging task than the eighteen-candidate presidential election where uniform ballots were distributed countrywide.

Second, the Embassy timeline was in part a negotiation tactic to resist the UN tendency to keep slipping the election date. The Embassy was allowing for the possibility that there might be some part of the assembly elections in Saur and another follow up election, say in July 2005, but they refused to state this officially or publicly because they wanted to support President Karzai and resist any further UN attempts at delay.

Third, the election month of Saur would end on May 20, 2005. Most discussions with international election officials were fixed on the month of April 2005, but the Afghan president wanted to hold the election in Saur, not April. Western sources, to include UN officials, the Embassy, and Coalition officers, frequently alluded to the earliest possible date, April 23, or the month of April in general. I believe that this occurred because Westerners tend to think in terms of the Roman rather than Islamic calendar.

Fourth, arguments over operational conflicts, such as the ongoing disarmament of militia and enhanced counternarcotics efforts were unpersuasive to the Karzai administration because these events would likely continue throughout the summer months. I had provided Coalition officials a previous intelligence report originating from the Karzai administration that commented that the president did not expect conditions to be significantly different from April 2005 to July 2005 to merit a delay in the election.

By the beginning of February 2005, Deborah Alexander, the Senior Elections Advisor to the U.S. Ambassador, provided new estimates of the likely dates of the election. She indicated at the weekly Embassy Country Team meeting that the election could occur between July and October. At the same time, UN elections officials informed me that redistricting had made little progress. The government of Afghanistan was experiencing some degree of chaos over the redistricting process. Julian Type, an administrative expert who served as the Electoral Process and Planning Officer and would eventually be elevated to the august level of electoral commissioner, said that the government was seriously considering postponing the district elections due to the controversies. This course of action would mean that only the other two elections, the *wolesi jirga* and the provincial councils, would be held on time.

In a summit meeting on February 6, 2005, between U.S. Ambassador Khalilzad, President Karzai, the UN Special Representative of the Secretary-General Jean Arnault, members of the Independent Electoral Commission, and other senior policymakers, several electoral decisions were made. I attended the Ambassador's briefing to his Political Core staff and passed along the outcome of the meeting to Coalition military planners.

Khalilzad confirmed Julian Type's earlier report that the redistricting project had plunged into chaos. The reasons for this included that some older districts had been founded by warlords during the civil war years and that local elders across the country were attempting to create new districts to enhance their power. There was still no consensus within the government of Afghanistan on district boundaries.

This difficulty resulted in the decision to indefinitely postpone the district elections. The upper house (*meshrano jirga*) would operate with two-thirds of its membership. The consensus from the meeting was that the Afghan constitution indicated that a quorum for this house would be a simple majority, so it would be able to operate without the district council representatives. At this point, no decision was settled as to when the district council elections would be held. The Ambassador related that Jean Arnault was pushing to hold these elections with the following election cycle—in other words, after the 2005 candidates completed their terms of office—but there was no general consensus on this proposal.

There was some discussion as to the legal basis for this decision. Members of the Independent Electoral Commission argued that the electoral law gave them authority to delay and defer district elections for political, technical, and various other reasons. It was debated whether this authority applied nationwide or to only specific districts. Regardless of whether the authority currently existed or would require an amendment to electoral law, the Ambassador expressed confidence that district elections would not be held in 2005.

The controversies over the various methods used to estimate provincial populations were also discussed at this meeting. This matter was resolved by compromising between the household survey conducted by the Central Statistics Office and the previous estimate used for the Constitutional *Loya Jirga*. This compromise included representation for the nomadic Kuchi tribes, who would not be assigned to any particular province, but would have their own representatives.

A serious operational challenge remaining for the election was the extensive candidate vetting process, which was unwieldy due to the large number of candidates. This process was streamlined by removing its accompanying timeline and focusing mostly on the later stages of the election, even to the point of only vetting candidates who would have already won their election. (The difficult political ramifications of disqualifying a candidate who has already won his election were not raised by the Ambassador, so I am not sure how extensively this issue was discussed in the summit meeting.) By mid-February, the Afghan government was entertaining two proposals for the vetting of candidates. First, the Deputy Minister of Justice suggested that an existing court decree finding against a candidate would be necessary to disqualify him or her. This proposal was based on a presumption of innocence and would result in little activity in a candidate vetting process. Second, the Ministry of Interior would provide candidates with vetting forms that they would be responsible to fill out. They would take the forms to every area where they have ever lived, and local police would complete local records checks. There was a concern that this plan might encourage graft, or as Patrick Fine, the director of the U.S. Agency for International Development in Afghanistan, jokingly put it, "redistribution of income."

The difficulties of replicating the refugee vote that was accomplished for the presidential election presented a serious challenge to the elections process. Out-of-country voting in Iran and Pakistan constituted a sizable minority of voting in the presidential election. The difficulty ensues from the fact that refugees are not actually citizens of a particular province or district. Their birthplace or their last place of residence could be possible ways to define local citizenship, but the registration process would be difficult enough in Afghanistan without attempting to replicate the process in refugee camps or other expatriate centers in the neighboring countries. Additionally, with the limited technological resources of the Afghan people and the low literacy rate, disseminating information on regional political candidates would be very difficult. The outcome of the meeting confirmed that there would be no refugee vote. However, refugees were to be encouraged to return to their home provinces to vote and would be afforded an extended voter registration process to last until days before the actual election.

Even though the month of Saur was closing in fast, there was still no consensus on electoral timing. There was a decision to begin voter registration and civic education in one month. The feasibility of implementing this decision seemed unrealistic due to the sluggish progress of the UN electoral team in recruiting and planning.

By mid-February, the United Nations had selected a Director of Elections for Afghanistan. A respected electoral expert, Peter Erben, was nominated for this position. Although the organization of the new electoral team was somewhat different than that of the presidential election, Erben's position was comparable to the previous Chief of Operations, David Avery. Erben had worked on several developing country elections before, including expatriate voting in Afghanistan's presidential election and the highly successful January 2005 Iraqi election. He spent several days in Afghanistan after his appointment, making observations, and meeting with key leaders. He returned to New York and made several arguments to Secretary-General Kofi Annan and the senior administration of the United Nations.

According to Erben, it would be impossible to hold fair elections without precinct lists for each polling station to prevent multiple voting and voting in the wrong constituency. He argued that the problems of the presidential election would be more acute because of the smaller regional constituencies. If these policies were to be adopted, it would force a delay in the elections until late September. (The date for the election had not yet been announced.) Erben stated that he would not return to the position in Afghanistan unless the elections would be conducted in this manner, which he claimed is the standard for developing country elections.

This concern by a well-respected official threw the electoral process into some uncertainty. The president weighed in for provincial rather than polling station voter lists, and the U.S. Ambassador seemed uncertain and willing to consider the matter. Many United Nations Assistance Mission Afghanistan staff seemed unwilling to accept the proposal. The UN mission players were in favor of not delaying the election because it would interfere with current staff contracts, budgeting, and logistical planning, which at the time were anticipating that the election should be complete by, at the latest, August 2005. Erben would later return to Afghanistan without the reassurances he had demanded in New York, although it was speculated in Kabul that his maneuvering would insulate him from criticism should the election fail to win the acclaim that the previous presidential race had earned.

Another development occurred to facilitate the electoral process in the middle of February. The contract was awarded for the private security company to support the national assembly elections. The company, an American company called Kroll, was selected to replace Global Risk Strategies, the company that supported the presidential elections. The contract was funded by The Asia Foundation (a nongovernmental organization) that received funding for this purpose from the State Department's U.S. Agency for International Development.

Many key players in the process were disappointed that Global Risk Strategies' experience in the presidential election would no longer be available during the upcoming election. The connections of local-level Global operators with local officials and tribal elders, and the experience of leaders and information officers in the capital, were lost due to the outcome of the contract bid process. Although Kroll seemed relatively new in the business of international private security consulting, it was unclear whether the company would be better or worse than Global. The successful experience of the Global team, however, who contributed effectively in the presidential election, seemed to be a loss for the National Assembly Elections.

The next developments coincided with changes of responsibility in the foreign militaries operating in Afghanistan. NATO turned command of its International Security Assistance Force over to Turkey in February 2005, which in itself was historic for several reasons. First, a Muslim country would have responsibility for the foreign occupants of a fellow Muslim country in the Global War on Terrorism. Turkey has been hailed as a model of a modern and secular Islamic state. Second, Turkey is at a crossroads between the Western world and the Islamic world. Its attempts to enter the European community in a more integrated way—most notably its bid to join the European Union—have met with resistance by the older, more powerful nations of Western Europe. Turkey's assumption of leadership of one of the largest NATO endeavors worldwide was a significant development for the Islamic "wannabe" European nation.

## GOING ON THE OFFENSIVE

A month later, Combined Joint Task Force-76 (CJTF-76), the American-led Coalition headquarters of Operation Enduring Freedom-Afghanistan at Bagram Air Base transitioned from the 25th Infantry Division to the Southern European Task Force (SETAF). The SETAF commander, Major General Jason Kamiya, took over and introduced a command philosophy that placed a new focus on development and nation building. He argued that the presidential election was a culminating moment in the "hot war" on insurgents in Afghanistan, and that this success must be consolidated by "winning hearts and minds." It is ironic how popular that phrase is in the contemporary military since it originated with Vietnam, an episode in American military history from which today's officers continue to draw and share lessons of caution.

My personal opinion of this new strategy was that it would actually change little in how small units of soldiers in the countryside conducted their missions. Building infrastructure and providing social assistance to local communities were already large pieces of the mission of Operation Enduring Freedom. While the "Other Coalition Forces" black operations units did not care about development and never engaged in such types of missions, General Kamiya had no influence over such units anyway because they fell outside of his headquarters' chain of command. So, in sum, I felt that the new commander's vision was a way for him to articulate his philosophy and priorities without finally resulting in any actual changes.

It turned out that I was right, but not for the reasons I expected. Shortly after he took command, General Kamiya received General John Abizaid, the commander of United States Central Command. General Abizaid had been hailed in various press accounts over the past years. An American of Arabic descent, fluent in Arabic, he had been popularly hailed as the perfect man to direct the American wars in Afghanistan and Iraq. The U.S. regional commands are joint military headquarters that combine the naval, air, and ground services along with intelligence collection assets and other military capabilities. The regional commander is responsible for a huge amount of military power. Pundits have labeled these officers as America's proconsuls or viceroys because they orchestrate the global projection of American power.

After a meteoric rise through the ranks, General Abizaid was perfectly positioned for such a role. He even reportedly turned down an offer from Defense Secretary Donald Rumsfeld to take over as the Army Chief of Staff in order to assume this role. I knew General Abizaid from my cadet days at West Point. Merely a one-star general at the time, John Abizaid led a significant transformation effort to make the Military Academy more focused on combat readiness and less susceptible to the meaningless types of hazing that had evolved over the years. West Point was founded in 1802, and it is an institution notoriously resistant to change. Nonetheless, through well-thought-out policy, clear communication, and sheer force of will, General Abizaid left lasting changes after his three-year tour as Commandant of Cadets. General Kamiya was about to meet both this strong, uncompromising determination coupled with the focus on direct combat that I had encountered at West Point eight years earlier.

General Kamiya presented his superior with the new strategy and focus that he had introduced to the rest of the task force. I was not present for these meetings because my work at the time was in Kabul, not Bagram. However, officers from the headquarters who attended these briefings reported to me on the tension between the two senior officers as it became increasingly clear that Abizaid did not share Kamiya's outlook on the strategy for the Afghan campaign. At first, General Kamiya futilely tried to articulate his arguments and his reasoning for them. However, General Abizaid was not persuaded and directed Kamiya to focus the task force on combat actions to counter the threat of the insurgency. While he shared the assumption with Kamiya that the presidential election entailed a decisive setback for the insurgency, his conclusions could not have been more different. Rather than changing the focus away from the insurgency, Abizaid felt that their defeat presented an opportunity to go on the offensive and prevent their resurgence. At the same time, he was concerned that the insurgents would remobilize for the assembly elections and attempt to derail the democratic process at an even more vulnerable time. An aggressive, combat-focused counterinsurgency campaign would prevent this from occurring.

Thus, the elections security process was de-emphasized as General Kamiya put out his new guidance. I traveled across the country meeting with different election liaison officers in Kandahar, Herat, and various Provincial Reconstruction Teams. I quickly learned that these officers had other priorities. Soon after Peter Erben moved back to Kabul to take over as the new Director of the Afghan Election Project, a date for the election was finally announced: September 2005. The significance of this date, now that the Coalition military had a strong combat orientation, was that the election could wait as a new counterinsurgency mission was launched under the name Operation Determined Resolve. (I thought that the name was a bit redundant, but these operations usually have two words in their names.)

These strategic developments coincided with my own move away from the Elections Security team in Kabul to Khost, a southeastern province bordering the wild Waziristan region of Pakistan that sheltered numerous Taliban insurgents and al Qaeda foreign fighters. The last element of the 25th Infantry Division to leave Afghanistan would be Task Force Thunder, the brigade headquarters at Forward Operating Base Salerno, the home to Regional Command East. The main focus of this command was the border region and the infiltration of fighters across the border. The Units' departures were at staggered times to make a smoother transition. So while Major General

Olsen surrendered command to Major General Kamiya in March 2005, my new unit would remain in place until June.

One major difference from the headquarters units in Bagram and Kabul was a greater integration of the special forces units in the Combined Joint Special Operations Task Force and the Other Coalition Forces. For me, this presented a new attitude of working together with the conventional forces of which I was a part. I think there are a few reasons accounting for the greater cooperation. First, the proximity to the border and the focus on the insurgents infiltrating made the missions of the two types of units more complementary. Second, the headquarters in modern militaries are bloated, bureaucratic, and inefficient. The front-line soldiers are more concerned with getting things done, while the rear echelon units are concerned with considerations of their parochial turf. Particularly, the natural inclination of the officers in these units to protect sensitive information becomes an end in itself in rear echelon headquarters. On the front line, this imperative is one of many, and it falls subordinate to more urgent priorities. So this phase of the mission gave me new awareness of the missions, priorities, and tactics of these special operations units.

Our own mission, Operation Determined Resolve, also provided ample reason for conventional forces to coordinate actions with their special operations counterparts. The new emphasis of CJTF-76 was targeting and neutralizing enemies. It was an exaggerated offensive mindset that started with the two-hundred-person intelligence staff at Bagram Air Base. General Kamiya had tasked his intelligence headquarters staff with identifying the most dangerous terrorists operating throughout the country so that subordinate units such as ours could capture or kill these terrorists. Having worked in that intelligence headquarters under General Olsen's command, I was familiar with how the process worked for situational development, targeting, and reallocation of intelligence collection assets.

In general, military planning begins with using existing databases of information to generate new plans and their constituent intelligence, logistical, communications, and other components. So the intelligence headquarters consulted the existing databases as a baseline. The problem was that identifying terrorist targets in a country of twenty-four million people is not an easy task. There were about one hundred active target packets, meaning that Coalition forces had developed varying degrees of information on individuals connected to various extremist movements such as al Qaeda, the Taliban, Hezb-e-Islami Gulbuddin, and others. However, most of these targets were not "actionable," meaning that there was insufficient information on the current location of the target to do anything about him. Some information came from second or thirdhand human intelligence contacts, while other information came from signals intelligence intercepts. In the latter case, the name of the target was often not known, only the language he used and the people with whom he associated. His name for the purposes of Coalition intelligence was a code name, usually an American city such as Philadelphia or Louisville. (Technically, the code name referred to a "hand set," or cell phone rather than an insurgent himself.)

The intelligence officers at Bagram scrambled to develop new intelligence to update target packets and produce new targets. They began to consult old information stored in files and computers in the top secret Sensitive Compartmented Information Facility (normally called a SCIF) at the head-quarters at Bagram. Soon they were ready with a detailed outline of the key targets, their relationships with one another, and their locations. They distributed the information to us and to the other subordinate commands throughout Afghanistan. It was now up to each command to develop further information on the targets, fill in the details, assign intelligence collection assets to confirm or deny the intelligence, and pass the assignment along to the subordinate maneuver battalions. The only problem was that our research found that many of the targets did not exist.

The centerpiece of General Kamiya's new effort was an offensive in the Tora Bora mountains, the towering range in southern Nangarhar Province along the border with Pakistan. This was a sexy target for the new com-manders who had recently arrived in Afghanistan. Everyone knew the Tora Bora. They were among the most famous terrain features in Afghanistan, the rugged range through which Osama bin Laden himself had escaped into Pakistan after the failed cordon of Operation Anaconda. To strike at ene-mies hiding in the Tora Bora mountains would be like striking at the heart of terrorism itself. Unfortunately, the information pointing to the Tora Bora was years old, dating to 2002.

My staff, with over fifty soldiers, was also capable of intensive research. They began to find names of terrorist leaders on our higher headquarters' enemy situational template who had already been captured or killed or had fled to Pakistan. So while General Kamiya was developing an understanding of the battlefield that indicated that the enemy was moving into Afghanistan in large numbers through the Tora Bora mountains, the information upon which these conclusions were based was outdated and contradictory. Rather than infiltrating through the forbidding mountain passes, Islamic militants had fled through the passes in their desperation after the initial American-led invasion. In addition, their presence in the mountains was no longer indi-cated by current intelligence. On the contrary, as we continued to develop the situation further, it became clear that in late March 2005 after what had been an extreme winter, the mountains at their high altitudes were still cov-ered with snow. The area afforded no realistic shelter or infiltration routes.

The discussions between our commander, Colonel Gary Cheek, a thirty-year career officer who had spent the last eleven months in Afghanistan, and the commanding general became more and more heated and contentious. Without directly attacking the shoddy work of the general's intelligence advisors, Colonel Cheek brought up some contradictory pieces of informa-tion, such as the dead targets on the enemy situation slides, the current temperature in the area, and the results of our own ongoing intelligence collection showing the areas where enemy radios and phones were used and where they were not. General Kamiya, recently chastened by his own commander, General Abizaid, for lacking aggressiveness in the Afghan counterinsurgency, was unwilling to listen. To General Kamiya, Colonel Cheek's reluctance was likely a sign of his own lack of aggressiveness and unwillingness to adapt to the new command vision. Colonel Cheek's conversations with the general, via videoconferencing, were some of the most politically agile discussions I have ever heard. With every point General Kamiya made, Colonel Cheek was quick to agree in principle while pointing out a few contradictory factual points. On the other hand, Kamiya seemed unwilling or unable even to understand the points that Colonel Cheek was making. Ultimately, it was a textbook communication failure and resulted in no changes in policy. So Task Force Thunder was charged with the unenviable task of hunting the ghosts of the Tora Bora mountains.

Task Force Thunder, the headquarters of Regional Command East, was responsible for three and then four subordinate infantry battalions. The first was 1st of the 509th Parachute Infantry, a unit from Fort Bragg that had arrived as part of the 82nd Airborne Division, relieving the Hawaii-based 2nd of the 29th Infantry. This unit was responsible for the southern part of Regional Command East, primarily the province of Paktika. The second battalion was a National Guard unit called 3rd of the 116th Infantry Battalion in the central Ghazni Province. Policing the main thoroughfare of Ring Road, or Highway 1, and preventing the placement of improvised explosive devices were the main responsibilities of this reservist battalion. In the eastern part of the Region, from Khost Province, where our headquarters was located, to Konar Province further north, 3/3 Marines, or "America's Battalion" was in charge. Another Marine battalion was scheduled to replace them in the near future. The fourth battalion was the 1st of the 504th Parachute Infantry, which was taking over the Khost portion of the 3/3 Marine territory in the spring.

The 3/3 Marine Battalion was preparing to leave Afghanistan after the end of their six-month tour to return to their home station of Kaneohe, Hawaii. Their replacements would begin arriving in the next week, and some of their equipment had already been shipped away. So the timing of Operation Determined Resolve could not have been worse for this unit. The Marines were selected as the main effort for the mission, having familiarity with the area since it had been their responsibility for the past six months. In addition, the additional combat power of a Marine infantry battalion made them better suited than their Army counterparts. (A Marine infantry battalion has almost twice as many soldiers as an Army infantry battalion.)

The Marines were to relocate their headquarters from Forward Operating Base Salerno near the border city of Khost to the eastern metropolis of Jalalabad. Jalalabad was the capital of Nangarhar Province, the home of the Tora Bora mountains. Setting up a new base in Jalalabad during the late spring was a major effort in itself. New tents and buildings needed to be constructed, new latrine and shower facilities installed, and generators needed to be transported and set up to cool the tents, which could reach temperatures in excess of one hundred degrees Fahrenheit during the day in this intemperate part of the country. (This was especially intolerable for those Marines who pulled night shift duty. Imagine trying to sleep in a sauna tent, which is what the sleeping tents in effect were until the generators arrived to power the air conditioning units.)

Operation Determined Resolve was ultimately a mission with a two-pronged approach, with the main effort pursuing terrorists in the foothills north of the Tora Bora range in Nangarhar Province and the supporting effort in neighboring Laghman Province. I led a small team of intelligence analysts who were attached from the brigade, or Regional Command, head-quarters to support the Marines as a Deployable Intelligence Support Element, or DISE.

In addition to visiting a new part of the country, this trip allowed me to renew contacts with Afghan friends I had met in Kabul. Murad was now living in Jalalabad, having found work for the United Nations in that city. He and several of his cousins came to visit me at our compound, and I spoke with them for a couple of hours. Murad's cousins were somewhat self-conscious in their English abilities and were at first hesitant to speak. He brought a couple of gifts, including a jar of olives from a Jalalabad olive factory where his father worked. I was also able to speak to Sahar on the phone. In Khost, I was limited to e-mail communication because the Afghan cell phone company, Roshan, had no coverage in that remote region. I was able to call Sahar almost everyday in Jalalabad and learned more about her from our phone conversations. One day, she asked me suddenly and shyly, "Are you my friend?" I was not sure what exactly she meant or why she asked, but of course I reassured her, "Yes."

In Jalalabad, our team's main concern was finding targets, particularly in Nangarhar, due to the attention that General Kamiya and his staff were devoting to the region. As hot as it was in the low-lying city of Jalalabad, the mountain passes of the Tora Bora were still frozen and impassable at that time of the year, making infiltration of new insurgents from Pakistan as yet unlikely. Our imagery and terrain analysts had put together a detailed overview of the mountain passes, which were coupled with signal intelligence hits from airborne communication intercept platforms to track movement through the mountains. The movement seemed sporadic and insubstantial, and since there were no translations available for these intercepts, we had not confirmed that the communications were even from anyone connected to any insurgent groups. What was more likely was that most, if not all, of the communications we had observed were from traveling merchants or other migrants.

Nonetheless, there was considerable pressure to conduct a mission in the Tora Bora. This was part of the ongoing conversations between General

Kamiya and his superior, General Abizaid, who was responsible for about 200,000 soldiers engaged in the campaigns in Afghanistan and Iraq. Revealing that the entire plan was based on nonexistent intelligence was not a realistic option. So, *Catch-22* fashion, we searched for terrorists to make the intelligence fit the mission. Human intelligence agents fanned out, broaching their sources for any possible insurgents who might be hiding out in southern Nangarhar Province. It turned out that we were able to identify three low-level players. We would send human intelligence collectors with each of two Marine companies that would insert by helicopter into the foothills of the Tora Boras and then travel north. As they traveled along these twin routes, they would meet with village elders, identify development projects that could be implemented, such as repairing schools or digging wells, and attempt to piece together more intelligence on the location of the three insurgent targets. The operation would also be a show of force in an area that had historically been unreceptive to Coalition presence.

Unfortunately, as the mission prepared for launch, the target whose location was most reliable was captured in a raid by the Combined Joint Special Operations Task Force. This was the routine work of the special forces units in Afghanistan, and when this low-level insurgent presented himself through reliable intelligence reporting, the Special Operations Task Force went about their business in a quiet, routine way. This was in contrast to the bells and whistles that accompanied Operation Determined Resolve. At the same time, sources began reporting that the second identified target had fled to Pakistan, perhaps prompted by the increasing questions being asked about insurgents in southern Nangarhar Province. Reporting on the third target was somewhat dated, with his last known location coming from two months before. As they say in theater, "The show must go on."

So in spite of there being little probability of actually meeting the intent of the operation by capturing or killing any enemies, the operation continued as scheduled. In briefings to subordinate leaders, the midlevel field grade commander, Lieutenant Colonel Norm Cooling, whom we met in Chapter 4, explained this with a certain logic: "We are just going to do the same mission we have been doing for the past six months. We are just going to do it in a different area. We are going to meet locals. We are going to put on a good impression of American Marines. We are going to find projects for our civil affairs guys to work on for these people." Cooling's approach, focused on winning over the civilian population, is surprising for the commander of Marines whose unit would less than a year later have returned to combat in Iraq and face charges over Heditha, the most serious massacre of innocent civilians by Americans in the Global War on Terror.

As I had remarked when Major General Kamiya first launched his change of emphasis a couple months before, there was no significant change by the time it got filtered down to the units actually conducting the missions. The mission ended without clear results, and I returned to Khost. After spending about two weeks in Jalalabad with 3/3 Marines, I had been relieved by another intelligence captain, a reservist in the Marines named Marcus Stennett. Marcus stayed with them for the last week of the mission, and then he was stuck in Jalalabad for about ten days after the mission actually ended because air travel happened to not be available.

Marcus was one of my good friends in Afghanistan. He was always cool and collected, had a great sense of humor, and was extremely insightful about the environment around him. Marcus was black with a shaved head. He was married and was not exactly happy about being in Afghanistan because he knew he would be heading to Iraq immediately after returning to his home in Florida. Shortly after Marcus returned to Khost, the two of us received an invitation to an Afghan wedding from our human intelligence agents. One of their favorite local Afghan interpreters, affectionately known as "Bob," was getting married and had asked some folks from the military task force to attend the wedding reception.

Marcus and I first had to convince our risk-averse boss to allow us to leave the compound. The major was apprehensive to even fly in helicopters because of the occasional aircraft crashes, so he was somewhat reluctant to allow us to venture off the compound. His own boss would not be sympathetic if something happened to us. Convincing the major took some doing and resulted in him telling us in an exasperated explosion, "All right, if you guys want to go, then go." We didn't wait around for him to change his mind.

For Marcus, this was a fairly new opportunity to explore something outside the limits of the secure headquarters compounds. For me, it was an opportunity to enjoy the experience I had earlier in Kabul—to put on civilian clothes, get out of the compound, and again connect with the locals to learn more about the country I was visiting. Wedding parties in Afghanistan are segregated. Men and women gather separately, dancing and socializing during a celebration that lasts several days. Ann Jones, the author of *Kabul in Winter*, was a journalist in Afghanistan volunteering to educate teachers in Kabul even at the same moment as I was visiting this wedding in Khost. She describes cultural differences revealed by her class: "Once, after I explained what blind date meant, a woman said, 'Like my wedding.'"

Of course, Afghans do not drink alcohol, so this is another major difference between wedding celebrations in the Western world. We did not actually see Bob's wedding ceremony, but spending several hours at his family's home with their friends and relatives for the reception party was an enriching experience.

The human intelligence team leader, Rudy, organized our trip to the event. It was an opportunity for me, in the capacity of my professional responsibilities, to ride with his team and observe their performance as well as expand my own knowledge of the work they did. Rudy was a slightly overweight reservist who was about six months into his Afghanistan deployment. He had a thick but neatly trimmed beard, wore glasses, and usually wore jeans, a T-shirt, and an Afghan scarf and packhol hat. I have also seen Rudy wearing the traditional loose Afghan men's pants and long shirt. The shirt hangs past the knees, and despite his beard, Rudy could not be mistaken for a native. So Rudy, like myself in my previous work as a civilian-clothed intelligence collector, more often chose Western clothes with a more subtle nod to the Afghan stylistic tastes.

Rudy's team consisted of six other soldiers who wore civilian clothes and collected intelligence from local human sources. These soldiers were also reservists. There was even a female soldier on the team. "Walk-ins," those Afghans who arrived at the base to deliver information, would often ask for "Red" by name. She was the young female reservist with whom Afghans from a misogynist society could interact because talking with Western women from the international military or the United Nations did not have the social taboos that existed against interacting with local women.

The reservists seemed to be smarter and have less discipline and more common sense than their active duty counterparts. A Cuban infantryman named Randy provided security to the team. He was a reservist from a special forces unit in Miami, and he was the typical young infantryman. Not the smartest guy you would ever meet, but friendly, loud, jocular, and quick to get himself in some sort of trouble if not supervised. Randy definitely looked the part with jet black, curly hair, a long beard, and dark skin. He wore local Afghan dress and wore it convincingly. Miguel, the base's interrogator, was another member of the human intelligence team at Forward Operating Base Salerno. He rarely left the base because he was mainly responsible for interrogating prisoners. He had lighter skin, brown hair, and a more closely trimmed beard. He told his Pashtun prisoners in the interrogation room that he was an Arab, however. This was plausible and did much to start the relationship with his detainees.

Other American guests to the wedding party included our Category II linguists, Americans of Afghan ancestry who possessed a security clearance for classified translations. In addition, there was an ethnic Hazara interpreter who worked for the civilian logistical contractor KBR (whose involvement in the war is perhaps better-known by the American public under its parent company's name, Halliburton). The Hazara, a tall man with Asiatic features and a neat moustache, was able to demonstrate his graceful dancing skills at the feast. Dancing at these events is done in large unisex groups or as a performance for onlookers. The soldiers did not dance, of course. The other linguists included Freddy, a tall bearded man who was friends with everyone. Finally, there was John, a computer science professor at Saint John's College in New York City. He wore a neatly trimmed gray moustache, shaved his head, and was withdrawn and intelligent. John was also an excellent chess player, and he and I occasionally passed time at Salerno playing. John usually won.

We sat around the floor for the feast, as Afghans use carpets, blankets, and pillows on the floor rather than tables and chairs. I was hesitant to partake of the food because of a bad gastronomical experience during my service in Kabul with the United Nations. John did not eat at all; he was more obvious than me just picking at my food and avoiding the meats. John sat back and demurred saying he was ill, so I thought my first impulse was wrong. In cultures such as Afghanistan's, not eating at a meal can be an insult and a grave social error, so I was doing my best to take small portions and eat slowly. After seeing John, however, it seemed okay. A few days later, the other interpreters would complain to me about John feigning sickness and not eating. They felt he was not a team player and considered himself better than other Afghans.

## TRANSITIONS

The next focus for Task Force Thunder was a realignment of forces to add a new battalion of combat power. The conviction of the headquarters at Bagram that there were hoards of enemies entering Afghanistan through the eastern part of the country in the vicinity of the Tora Bora led them to add another maneuver battalion to Regional Command East. A battalion that had been previously scheduled to move to Oruzgan Province in Regional Command South, 1st of the 504th Parachute Infantry, moved to augment Regional Command East in late April 2005. So, by the end of the deployment, our headquarters had four infantry battalions. This would be short-lived, though, because the National Guard battalion would be leaving without replacement before the end of the year.

We were also planning for our own handover, or transition of authority (abbreviated among soldiers as the TOA), with 1st Brigade of the 82nd Airborne Division. The 82nd Airborne was coming from Fort Bragg, North Carolina, because the SETAF from Italy did not have sufficient combat power to provide forces to man the entire task force for which they were responsible. The storied 82nd Airborne was providing an infantry brigade headquarters to replace Task Force Thunder along with three infantry battalions to replace three of the 25th Infantry Division battalions that had returned to Hawaii. The 82nd Airborne is recognized for being an elite unit with strong discipline. Although modern interventions in Grenada, Panama, and even Iraq saw paratroopers drop into combat zones, combat parachuting has not been a strategically significant capability since the Second World War. In spite of this, airborne infantry consider themselves as a select breed, and they enjoy some stature from others in the Army as well as from the general public. Because of its capability and reputation to deploy on short notice, the 82nd had been a unit of choice for previous rotations in Afghanistan and Iraq. The brigade commander was experienced in combat and a smart leader, familiar with the issues and places in Regional Command East, and quickly getting more familiar as we provided him further information.

It was easy to notice changes as soon as authority over Forward Operating Base Salerno turned over to the new unit. Soldiers were no longer allowed to play sports during the day. The basketball hoops were taken down. Soldiers could not run on the base without carrying their rifles with them. (In the past, it was permissible to ask a friend to watch your weapon while you showered or worked out.) In the past, on Sundays, soldiers had been allowed to wear their physical fitness uniforms during the day. The new rule stated that physical fitness uniforms could only be worn for exercising or going to take a shower. If someone is working thirteen hours a day for seven days a week for a year, small concessions in lifestyle such as being able to wear shorts and a T-shirt once a week make the conditions more livable.

On the other hand, much of this, particularly playing sports, is a benefit not primarily for the headquarters' soldiers pulling daily shift work at Forward Operating Base Salerno. The infantrymen stationed at the base routinely went out on dangerous, stressful patrols into the countryside. Upon returning from these physically and mentally demanding missions, it seemed to me (although I was never a grunt on patrol in Afghanistan) that relaxing in the secure compound was a well-deserved respite for those soldiers as they awaited the next mission. Ultimately, these decisions had little relevance to the outgoing soldiers of the 25th Infantry Division's Task Force Thunder. We had spent a year in Afghanistan, so spending the last week or two according to the senseless rules of the incoming unit was merely a nuisance. It was also a cloud with a silver lining, since the new rules meant that the 82nd Airborne was taking over the base, exactly what they needed to do for us to be able to return home. After a year in Afghanistan, most soldiers from our unit felt we could spend the final week standing on our heads if the 82nd asked us to.

When I flew to Bagram to prepare for departure, the Southern European Task Force staff assigned me a driver and a white SUV to travel around the post. It happened that the driver was a soldier from the 82nd Airborne Division who had been detached from his parent unit to provide extra manpower to the CJTF-76 headquarters. I mentioned the rules changes at Forward Operating Base Salerno. The soldier, a young buck sergeant of about twenty-one years of age, responded that he was familiar with those types of policies. He was self-assured, confident, and had the hard edge of a professional soldier. He explained to me that these types of restrictions were necessary to maintain the discipline for which the elite 82nd Airborne Division was renowned. I did not argue with him. After all, what sense is there in disillusioning an idealistic young noncommissioned leader proud of himself and his unit? Even if it would be possible, it would not be desirable to put doubts in his mind.

For me, however, sufficient discipline is created by the hardships inherent in the austere conditions of an outpost in a war zone in a third world country and in the separation from friends, family, and loved ones. I do not mean to imply that I do not support discipline. Even the Rangers, a unit still more elite and selective than the 82nd Airborne Division, seemed to enjoy the comforts that were possible in the combat zone whenever I visited their compound. In fact, when I was a company commander in Hawaii before the Afghanistan deployment, I enforced strict accountability and high standards, especially in the field. But I do believe that there is a point where excessive hardship in the name of discipline may hurt morale, and more importantly, the long-term retention of servicemen and women, many of whom will have visited Iraq and Afghanistan more than once over the course of their careers. There is no question that the war on terrorism has put strains on the military personnel system. Usually, U.S. political leaders get the blame. I think the leadership closer to the front line can share more accountability for not mitigating difficult conditions when possible and even sometimes making conditions worse.

One of the major responsibilities of the intelligence soldiers I supervised at Salerno was to provide force protection analysis on the base. In simple terms, this means to help prevent attacks on the base or to be ready for a rapid counterattack should prevention fail. Our base was fifteen miles away from the Pakistani border. This border was only significant to the insurgents hiding in Pakistan because it was significant to the Coalition. Coalition forces could not go into Pakistan for patrols or searches. We could, however, counterattack into Pakistan, and the select and shadowy Other Coalition Forces could enter a limited distance across the border in pursuit of their high priority targets. For the most part, however, Pakistan was a sanctuary from which Taliban elements and their allies could launch attacks into Afghanistan. The close proximity of the large base at Salerno, housing some 2,000 soldiers, made it an attractive target for these insurgents. They could fire rockets on our base without ever leaving Pakistan. Since we could counterattack after receiving rocket fire, this was far from an invulnerability among the radical fighters. However, it did give them the edge and the initiative for these sorts of attacks, making it a serious vulnerability for us and the neighboring Forward Operating Base Chapman, which housed special forces units and the Khost Provincial Reconstruction Team.

The first week after I arrived in Salerno, we received rocket attacks, one of which hit the Regional Interrogation Facility, completely destroying the corner of the brick building that housed insurgents captured during fighting or raids. It became clear to me that the tents and wooden structures that constituted most of the base's buildings offered little safety.

The Regional Interrogation Facility was the first location to house prisoners before evacuating them to the headquarters at Bagram Air Base and eventually to Guantanamo Bay, Cuba. At each stage in the process, there was a procedure to manage decisions on releasing prisoners, holding them at the local facility, or evacuating them to the successive larger facilities that would eventually mean Guantanamo. After a firefight or a raid, the unit in the field would determine whether or not the Afghans (or foreign fighters as was often the case) should be detained.

There were specific criteria that made things very clear for the soldiers in the field, such as the individual being a foreign fighter (terrorist affiliation with al Qaeda was the reason Arabs, North Africans, and "immigrants" from a few other countries of origin could be found in Afghanistan). Another criterion was actually firing on American soldiers or Afghan civilians. Some cases were less clear, especially in the context of raids, or "soft knock" operations, where American forces would enter a compound in search of high priority terrorist or insurgent targets. One of the intelligence analysts in our section, a young Sergeant Marshall who had served in Kandahar after the initial invasion of Afghanistan at the end of 2001 and beginning of 2002, told me about a twelve-year-old boy who had been detained in the Kandahar facility at that time. However, age was not always easy to document, as Marshall also related a story of a white-bearded old man who was detained. When interpreters asked the old man's age, he said he did not know. This is reasonable in the culture of frontier Pashtunistan, where there is little literacy or organized government records of any kind. The interpreter pressed him to make a guess, and the old man answered "150." So, for a time, the Kandahar Regional Interrogation Facility held a 150-year-old man, even according to its official records.

In many cases, soldiers in the field could release detainees who clearly did not belong in captivity. However, it made more sense if there was a question for them to bring the detainees back to Salerno and let the interrogators decide. Detainees brought to Salerno in this way could remain there for seventy-two hours for processing. After this, they had to be released or sent to Bagram for further processing. The shadowy "Other Coalition Forces" could hold detainees in the regional facility for up to fourteen days. This additional time was allotted to them because their mission of tracking Osama bin Laden and other high profile terrorist leaders could require more scrutiny of detainees and result in more important follow-up operations.

When Task Force Thunder first moved to take over Forward Operating Base Salerno, the interrogation facility was in sorry shape. There were no systematic procedures for processing and safeguarding detainees. Soldiers could carry weapons into and out of the facility, presenting an unnecessary threat. Recordkeeping was poor. The facility was not secure. The noncommissioned officer in charge (or NCOIC) of our intelligence section, a forty-year-old master sergeant from Hawaii named Chris Medeiros, took over the prison. As the new "warden" of our interrogation facility, he made numerous improvements, professionalizing the facility and leaving a much better system in place by the time we left. Detention facility operations were a major concern all along the chain of command because the recent fiasco at the Abu Ghraib Prison in Iraq was still at the forefront of most people's minds. Master Sergeant Medeiros gave me a tour of the facility and explained the improvements he had made, which gave me confidence that no such scandal would be replicated at Salerno. However, the prisoners were still unhappy to be there, and especially wanted to avoid Guantanamo. On some level, it was not entirely bad treatment for them, as the food was good and many received in American custody the first shower they had ever taken in their lives. Anxiety for their future was the major matter of concern. During my fifteen-minute tour of the twenty-cell facility, only one cell was occupied by an old man who shouted the word "Allah" into the air over and over again. As we walked through the facility, you could hear a loud nasally voice through the hallway, "Allah ... Allah ... Allah." Apparently the detainee had taken to doing this as a form of protest and prayer for deliverance.

Because the facility was small and detainees did not stay long, the end of the building hit by the rocket attack was empty. However, the attack itself was an introductory indication for me that rockets were a popular question in intelligence briefings. It was common for the commander to interject in intelligence briefings: "So, when is the next rocket attack going to be?"

As the second in charge of fifty-four soldiers in the brigade's intelligence section, some tasks and some analyses were to become my personal responsibility. This was one of those situations. I had been trained in the study of envisioning alternative future scenarios at the University of Hawaii's futures studies program. A maxim of this program is that the future does not exist. What does not exist cannot be predicted. It only can be envisioned in a plurality of scenarios and created through our present choices. This is particularly true when we are talking about something like a threatening attack, which we have a strong motivation to prevent. Consider if analysts had predicted the attacks on the World Trade Center on September 11, 2001. If the analysis had credibility, surely authorities would have moved to avert the attacks. Consider, for example, grounding all aircraft on 9–11. The World Trade Center would surely still stand on September 12, and perhaps even longer. But there would be no certain, irrefutable evidence that the attack was prevented. There would be only the certainty that the predicted attack did not take place and then a suspicion that the original prediction was mistaken.

So, rather than "predicting" one future, we envision alternative scenarios of various future possibilities and determine the factors over which we have influence that will lead to the favorable scenarios and avoid the unfavorable ones. Colonel Gary Cheek was pretty tolerant and his curiosity even mildly kindled by my exposition on these concepts of forecasting. However, it was soon down to business. While my exploration of "philosophy" was interesting, "we need to know when the most likely rocket attack will be."

We had fed all kinds of data into the analysis, and I had anticipated Cheek's interest would be on the more pragmatic aspects of the problem. So we continued the presentation of our findings. Based on information that had been compiled since the base was built in 2002, terrorists seem to like attacking Forward Operating Base Salerno on Tuesdays or Thursdays. They favor early evenings for short-range rocket attacks, hitting before the sun sets. For long-range attacks, sometime after 8:00 P.M. during times of the month when most of the moon's face is illuminated seemed likely. Weather was important because clouds could obstruct visibility to target the base. Rain was an important factor because it could make it harder to aim, throw off the accuracy of rockets once launched, and just make it less pleasant for an evening insurgent outing. The U.S. Army infantry have a saying, "If it ain't raining, we ain't training," and soldiers will often revel in hardship created by the natural elements. But all things being equal, I think the Islamists will just wait for a clear night. In addition to these factors, our own actions, such as helicopter patrols near the historic points of origin of rocket attacks, practice fire of artillery howitzers, and other activity could make an attack less likely. Rumors spreading among Afghans, which could be measured by a spike in absenteeism among the hundreds of local workers needed to run the base, could also be an indicator of a possible attack.

Finally, traditional intelligence collection activity was factored in. This included imagery from satellites or aerial vehicles indicating unusual movements near the firing points. Signals intelligence, which involved intercepting, translating, and decoding radio messages and cell phone calls, was often inconclusive. Intercepting a call on an upcoming wedding, feast, or gathering could signify a code word for an imminent attack or it could merely be an actual wedding, feast, or gathering. Often, an increase in communications hits in a particular area could be more helpful to prevent attacks than the content of the messages themselves. Finally, human intelligence provided clear, if not entirely reliable, information on plans for attacks. This information was clear in that some Afghan or Pakistani would report that he or a contact of his—and I use "he" and "his" not to be chauvinistic, but because to my knowledge these sources were always male—had information that an attack was planned "in the next few days," or "next Thursday," or "soon." It was unreliable because you could never know the honesty or credibility of the report's ultimate source. Since intelligence information is compartmented, our analysis team would often be unaware of the position or reporting pattern of the source of information, except for a cryptic and less than helpful notice, "the source of this information has reported reliably in the past" and "had first- [or second-] hand access to the reported information." Lastly, countersurveillance efforts would sometimes reveal observation of the base, another indicator of preparation for an attack.

In any case, all of these factors would come together to raise the alert on some upcoming days and times. The colonel would dispatch helicopters, fire artillery rockets, and take other preventative measures to avert attacks. Sometimes, even these efforts would not pay off. One such day occurred on Tuesday, April 19, 2005. As expected, Tuesday was a preferred day for attacks. (Gore Vidal's essay on 9-11 was titled, "September 11th, a

Tuesday.") Intelligence indicated that an attack was likely. And it turned out to be a very large attack.

As I previously discussed, Colonel Cheek was responsive to good intelligence, which is more than one can say for many commanders. He already had his howitzer crews running targeting drills against the historical launch locations, and helicopters were in the air to conduct patrols. So when the rockets hit, the artillerymen were able to respond within minutes. Attack helicopters quickly moved in to observe and adjust fires and to take their own fight to the enemy. Colonel Cheek prompted the Air Force's liaison officer, and we found out that A-10 fixed wing aircraft were flying and available to divert to the fight. Thus, a major rocket attack by the Taliban fighters ended up leading to no Coalition casualties or damage, and the combined arms attack by the artillery, Army aviation, and Air Force planes resulted in fifty confirmed kills. That was the last rocket attack on Forward Operating Base Salerno during my tour in Afghanistan.

Whenever a new unit comes in, it is almost a cliché to remark that they are more energetic and aggressive than the fatigued, seasoned, and relatively more cautious unit being replaced. However, this is exactly what happened with respect to the rocket attacks. Our models were much less sophisticated than the types of quantitative analyses I have seen in the corporate and academic world outside of my military experience. In spite of the relative simplicity of the analysis, analysts will not focus on areas that are not priorities for commanders. It became clear that the rocket attacks on Salerno would not receive the interest from the 82nd Airborne that they received by Task Force Thunder. Even in June, we were still conducting aggressive counter-rocket measures that seemed clear to me would be consigned to some transition folder and not looked at again, or at least not looked at until after the next attack.

In our last week in Khost, Colonel Cheek and his officers attended a luncheon at Forward Operating Base Chapman, which was the special operations outpost about two miles from our installation. It was an opportunity to eat and socialize with the border patrol forces with whom we had worked over the past months. The border of Khost Province and Pakistan is monitored by a series of border checkpoints. These checkpoints are manned by Afghan mercenaries in a unit called the Khost Protective Force (KPF). The unit is funded by the CIA and supervised by contractors from the private security firm, Blackwater Security. Mercenaries from the KPF are paid well; a private in that mercenary force earned more than three times the monthly wages of a private in the Afghan National Army. The Khost Protective Force was not popular among citizens of Khost Province, and its existence and higher salaries could be seen to undermine the professionalism of the nascent Afghan military. This is one way in which American policy can undermine itself—at the same time as Task Force Phoenix was working hard to build a credible Afghan military and the Coalition forces were working to disarm private militias, the CIA and its adjunct Blackwater Security were creating a private militia to perform the security role of a national military. However, Blackwater Security itself could be seen as an institution that performed such a deleterious role with the U.S. armed forces by attracting the most trained and competent elite special forces soldiers from the U.S. military's NCO corps to work for payments in the neighborhood of five hundred dollars a day.

The border checkpoints do receive some of the heaviest fighting in the country, and perhaps this heavy fighting created reservations among leaders that the Afghan Army was up for the challenge. In addition to rocketing our base and Forward Operating Base Chapman, militants living on the Pakistani side of the border find the Border Checkpoints to be particularly attractive targets and have often engaged them with direct attacks. Overrunning a checkpoint, which the insurgents had done on rare occasions, is seen as a particularly momentous symbolic victory.

The KPF was commanded by Colonel Gafaar, a tall, bearded warrior with intense eyes and stony features. At the conclusion of our lunch, Colonel Cheek presented a plaque to the Afghan commander, calling him a brother in arms and thanking him and his men for their vigilance on the border. Gafaar similarly thanked Cheek, whose artillery, aviation, intelligence, medical, and logistical support provided invaluable support to the border checkpoints. He presented Colonel Cheek with a turban with long scarves that hung down, a black vest with brightly colored decorative embroidery, and a finely woven Afghan carpet. The men embraced, and we parted ways, the Americans to prepare for their return to Hawaii and the Afghans to their border vigil.

## THE ASSEMBLY ELECTIONS

As I prepared for departure in June 2005, the upcoming assembly elections again became the main focus of the Coalition as the remaining months closed in. After our departure, there was a rise in attacks, but it was possible that this was part of the normal pattern of late spring and early summer. In fact, factional violence related to small-scale local disputes exacerbated by the stakes of the electoral process seemed more likely than insurgent activity focused on the provincial elections. It turned out that the rise in violence could in fact be attributed to normal patterns of activity. As NATO took over the security of Afghanistan in the months following the 2005 elections, a radical increase in attacks would make Afghanistan the most dangerous it had been since the initial invasion after September 11.

The process of nominating candidates was the first major challenge for the reconstituted elections project staff. In May 2005, some 6,000 Afghans filed petitions of candidacy. About one-tenth of these were women. After the Independent Electoral Commission review, only seventeen candidates were disqualified from running. The reasons for these exclusions included links to illegal armed groups, insufficient signatures, and, in one case, holding a prohibited public position. A few hundred more candidates withdrew on their own. After the ballot lottery to determine the order of the candidates' names on the ballots, the JEMB designed newspaper-style ballot papers with the candidates' photographs, names, and unique symbols. Because some provinces had hundreds of candidates running for office, ballots extended as long as seven pages.

An election security conference was held in Kabul in June. The principal leaders again convened to prepare for the election as they had begun doing almost a year before. Later in the month, the JEMB conducted voter registration for Afghans who had not registered to vote the previous year. A million and a half new voter registration cards were issued, almost half of which to women voters. Peter Erben noted that "the absence of a reliable voters' registry and the consequent absence of an exact voters' list for each polling station was without doubt one of the most significant inherent weaknesses of the electoral process, seriously affecting accurate logistics planning and the ability to counter electoral fraud."

The lack of a precise voter registry made estimating the voter turnout in specific locations impossible. Thus, to ensure there were sufficient resources to conduct the election, the JEMB printed forty million ballots for the sixty-nine different elections. The total election budget was about $159 million, of which the United States contributed over $60 million.

The turnout was somewhat lower than that of the presidential elections. Several reasons can account for this. First, the idea of voting had lost some of its novelty since this was the second election. In addition, parliamentary elections typically result in lower voter turnouts. Continued voter intimidation by antigovernment forces might have deterred voters. The single nontransferable vote and absence of political parties gave people a bewildering number of candidates from which to choose. Finally, the failure to screen out candidates with links to armed groups or human rights abuse gave people a poor choice. They must select between candidates who were unknown or notorious, or as Human Rights Watch observed, "nameless or shameless."

Although the national turnout was lower than for the presidential election, a higher proportion of voters were female, and turnout increased in seven provinces (including Nuristan, where the turnout nearly doubled) and among the Kuchi population. Election officials hypothesized that more polling stations distributed across the country allowed more voting in the countryside.

# CHAPTER 6

# Prospects for Afghan Democracy

The Afghan presidential election was hailed in political and media circles as a stunning success for Afghan society and its various international benefactors. Working as the Director of Intelligence for the Afghanistan Election Security Operations Center, I was able to observe the efforts of the Center's constituent groups—the United Nations, the Afghan National Army, the NATO International Security Assistance Force, the U.S.-led Combined Joint Task Force-76, and others—to prevent threats to the election and to overcome the logistical and operational challenges to bringing a modern democratic election to one of the most impoverished countries in the world. By any measure, the election was a successful event. With high voter participation in spite of the new and foreign concept of elections and in spite of the prospect of terrorist violence, the Afghan people demonstrated a civic commitment surpassing that of the safer and more mature democracies of their American and European benefactors. The anticipated violence did not materialize, in large part due to the efforts of international and indigenous security forces. Finally, electoral experts from across the world observed the nascent democratic process and declared that the election was "free and fair."

Splashing cold water on the heady excitement over Afghanistan's democratic progress, research from decades of democratization theory argues that more than an election is needed to make a democracy. Afghanistan's history of violent unrest is only one factor that calls into question the prospects for long-term democracy. The reliance on narco-trafficking to fund the country's meager national income and the presence of powerful regional warlords, often connected to the opium crop, are also strong counterindications of democracy. Ethnic divisions and an active insurgency by remnants of the fundamentalist Taliban regime also pose daunting challenges. In order to explore the issue of whether democracy will "catch" in Afghanistan, it will first be necessary to define the elements needed in democratization, then to apply them to Afghanistan, and finally to discuss the prospects for overcoming the challenges.

## DEMOCRATIZATION

There is some disagreement among theorists about what makes a democracy. For instance, democracy in discussions of modern government does not denote the direct rule by the people that ancient Athenians practiced. The most fundamental, or minimalist, definitions of democracy are based on Joseph Schumpeter's democracy, a system "for arriving at political decisions in which individuals acquire the power to decide by means of a competitive struggle for the people's vote." Broader definitions of democracy have included Robert Dahl's influential concept of polyarchy requiring political competition and participation as well as civil liberties (such as freedom of speech, press, and others) and pluralism to allow meaningful expression of political preferences.

Popular current conceptions of democracy have evolved from merely electoral to broader liberal democracy. These conceptions include features of governance beyond elections themselves. The United States Department of State International Information Program has promoted a similar view in its *What is Democracy?* publication. Most theorists have recognized democracy as a series of governmental forms, individual rights, and institutional effectiveness to secure political freedom. The United Nations Human Development Report 2002, *Deepening Democracy in a Fragmented World*, asserted that elections are necessary but not sufficient criteria for democracy, and provided a wide range of indicators in order to capture as many as possible of the aspects of social organization that permit democratic governance. As the report explained:

> Democratic governance in this fast-changing environment is about more than people having the right to vote. It must be about strengthening democratic institutions so that they keep pace with the changing distribution of economic and political power. And it must be about promoting democratic politics that make participation and public accountability possible even when the relevant power and processes lie outside the formal institutions of the state.

The indicators in the UN report are broad, drawn from various sources, and tend to overlap to some extent. In order to provide clarity and avoid redundancy, I will focus on two categories drawn from Freedom House indices: political rights and civil liberties. These measures form the basis of Freedom House's annual report on the status of democracy throughout the world and are extensive enough to capture a broad range of democratic institutions. Political rights include free and fair elections for offices with real power, freedom of political organization, significant opposition, freedom from domination by powerful groups, and autonomy or political inclusion of minority groups; civil liberties include freedom of expression/belief, freedom of association, rule of law and human rights, and personal autonomy and individual rights. Table 6.1 spells out the questions used to determine the extent to which these rights exist. In the next section, I will walk through this model to assess the prospects for democracy in Afghanistan.

## AFGHANISTAN'S CURRENT SITUATION

### Electoral Process

President Karzai won the recent election with an acceptable mandate, although his margin of victory was not as high as expected and the election was marred by some procedural irregularities. In spite of these incidents, the losing candidates eventually conceded the election, endorsing its outcome as fair and legitimate. Numerous independent electoral observers noted that despite these incidents, the election was free and fair for a significant majority of the eight million people who turned out. In addition, a specially appointed panel of electoral experts accepted and investigated all candidate complaints. The panel ruled that the election was ultimately free and fair, far beyond the expected level of procedural justice for a country of a comparable state of development. The legislative elections also exhibited a dedication to freedom and fairness in spite of serious problems for repeating the level of electoral effectiveness that the presidential election enjoyed. As discussed in the last chapter, the assembly elections magnified the intricacies of the presidential election by seventy times.

The supervision of the United Nations has supported the development and execution of fair laws. In addition, the scrutiny of the international community, which closely monitors the outcome of its massive flows of foreign aid into Afghanistan, provided support for transparency and honesty in the election. It is notable that the election process was far too expensive for the country to afford on its own. This fact makes it extremely difficult to continue with the fair polling and ballot tabulation that Afghanistan enjoyed in 2004 and 2005. The hundreds of millions of dollars spent on the election far exceed Afghanistan's prospective budget allowance for such events in the future. The slim government funds must be devoted to security against lawless violence and providing basic infrastructure and services.

**TABLE 6.1**
Freedom House Measures of Democracy

*Political Rights*

Electoral Process

1. *Is the head of state elected through free and fair elections?*
2. *Are the legislative representatives elected through free and fair elections?*
3. *Are there fair electoral laws, equal campaigning opportunities, fair polling, and honest tabulation of ballots?*

Political Pluralism and Participation

1. *Do the people have the right to organize in different political parties or other competitive political groupings of their choice, and is the system open to the rise and fall of these competing parties or groupings?*
2. *Is there a significant opposition vote, de facto opposition power, and a realistic possibility for the opposition to increase its support or gain power through elections?*
3. *Are the people's political choices free from domination by the military, foreign powers, totalitarian parties, religious hierarchies, economic oligarchies, or any other powerful group?*
4. *Do cultural, ethnic, religious, and other minority groups have reasonable self-determination, self-government, autonomy, or participation through informal consensus in the decision-making process?*

Functioning of Government

1. *Do freely elected representatives determine the policies of the government?*
2. *Is the government free from pervasive corruption?*

*Civil Liberties*

Freedom of Expression and Belief

1. *Are there free and independent media and other forms of cultural expression?*
2. *Are there free religious institutions, and is there free private and public religious expression?*
3. *Is there academic freedom, and is the educational system free of extensive political indoctrination?*
4. *Is there open and free private discussion?*

Rule of Law

1. *Is there an independent judiciary?*
2. *Does the rule of law prevail in civil and criminal matters? Are police under direct civilian control?*
3. *Is there protection from police terror, unjustified imprisonment, exile, or torture, whether by groups that support or oppose the system? Is there freedom from war and insurgencies?*
4. *Is the population treated equally under the law?*

Personal Autonomy and Individual Rights

1. *Is there personal autonomy? Does the state control travel, choice of residence, or choice of employment? Is there freedom from indoctrination and excessive dependency on the state?*
2. *Do citizens have the right to own property and establish private businesses? Is private business activity unduly influenced by government officials, the security forces, or organized crime?*
3. *Are there personal social freedoms, including gender equality, choice of marriage partners, and size of family?*
4. *Is there equality of opportunity and the absence of economic exploitation?*

## Political Pluralism and Participation

The people's right to organize in different political parties is limited by the underdeveloped status of political parties in the country. In the run-up to the assembly elections, this was a central concern about the prospects for success. Political parties, as they existed in 2005, were centered in Kabul and had not yet made it into the outlying country. Claire Le Claire, a political officer in the U.S. Embassy at Kabul, told me that the parties were holding meetings and saying the right things, but their influence remained uncertain. The elections themselves, which established legitimate *meshrano* and *wolesi jirgas*, have advanced the future power and influence of political parties.

There does seem to be a significant opposition constituency, best personified in the presidential candidacy of northern warlord Yunis Qanuni. The other two candidates who broke into double digits, Rashid Dostum and Mohammed Mohaqiq, like Qanuni, each represented one of the significant minority ethnicities. Afghanistan is divided along ethnic lines, with the majority Pashtuns, the tribal group of both President Karzai and the Taliban, currently economically and socially marginalized. Despite being the language of the majority of the Afghan population, Pashtun is not spoken for most official government, educational, and commercial activity. Karzai, with a strong perceived backing of the United States and the international community, was the only candidate who was able to reach out to a significant portion of the population who did not share his ethnicity. While this ethnically based minority opposition is not necessarily "undemocratic," it does raise concerns about the role of ethnicity in the prospective democracy, recalling similar dilemmas in Bosnia and Iraq. Without the presence of a unifying figure like Karzai, it is easy to envision a situation in which ethnic differences come to dominate the society. While non-Islamic minorities are suppressed to the point of apparent nonexistence, the minority Hazara people are able to practice Shia Islam without the hostility exhibited in other Sunni Muslim nations.

The question on whether people's political choices are free from external domination is extremely "loaded" when considering Afghanistan's democracy. On the one hand, people enjoyed the privacy of a truly secret ballot, and their personal choice was thus unencumbered by any outside influence. However, foreign military powers are thoroughly enmeshed into Afghanistan's political environment. The United States has exerted influence above all of the foreign military and diplomatic presences in Afghanistan. People view Hamid Karzai as closely tied to American interests. His frequent appearances with American Ambassador Zalmay Khalilzad, and Khalilzad's residence in the presidential palace, promoted this perception. Aside from the other thirty foreign military powers present in Afghanistan, the Islamic religious hierarchy can also be reasonably said to dominate Afghan politics.

Supporting a stronger central government is one matter that has become a delicate balancing act for both the United Nations and the American-led military forces in Afghanistan. I spoke with Ajmal Ahmady, a Californian of Afghan descent who served as the deputy finance minister during the election period. Mr. Ahmady was responsible for the national budget in the country, and he explained that foreign powers were undermining the state by not allowing it to budget the massive international aid flowing into the country. In my observation, the American military was attempting to improve its support of government authority. For instance, the large base at Bagram was sustained in large part through the construction, maintenance, and cleaning labor of locals. Rather than choosing these workers themselves, the Americans required Afghans to solicit employment through the governor of Parwan Province, the region in which Bagram is located. Even though Bagram Air Field was perhaps the largest employer of Afghans in the province, the government was able to exercise the considerable influence that came with selecting the prospective workers for employment. Similarly, many local reconstruction projects throughout the country were coordinated with the local governments by the Provincial Reconstruction Teams, and the governments' requests were most often the decisive factor in determining which type of project should be implemented.

## Functioning of Government

Corruption is a problem to some extent in most governments of developing countries, and Afghanistan is no exception. The background of much of the country's wealthy and elite in the opium trade is problematic and may result in a more pervasive corruption problem as the counternarcotics effort progresses. I have personally observed low-level corruption by security officials or persons posing as security officials, collecting illegal tariffs from drivers on the road. At the same time, the very international presence in Afghanistan that restrains some of the government's independence is able to restrict corruption at all levels. At the higher levels, UN and U.S. State Department advisors are able to use the massive inflows of international aid to leverage government decisions that will reinforce effective and scrupulous governance.

## Freedom of Expression and Belief

I spoke with a UN media expert, Dora Cheok, about the extent of the free press in Afghanistan. Dora is a producer for CNBC in Singapore and had taken a leave of absence to serve in Afghanistan. She explained that while there is a free press, it has little influence. In a country where the literacy rate is among the lowest in the world, the government has little interest in restricting the printed news media, which is in fact occasionally critical of the government. Television media similarly has little influence on a population that largely does not enjoy electricity. Radio has made inroads among the general public, and popular programming has been growing. The media is free and independent, largely unobstructed by government interference.

Religious freedom in the Islamic Republic of Afghanistan is by its nature restricted. In the context of the previous Taliban administration, religious freedom in Afghanistan has made remarkable progress. However, relative to the secular Western world, there is no genuine Afghan freedom of conscience. As I have already discussed, practicing Christianity (and any other non-Islamic faith) is against the law. While this law is not stringently enforced, laws in Afghanistan are generally not stringently enforced due to the government's limited power and the nascent development of the rule of law. The existence of the law indicates the limitations on freedom of religious expression in the country.

The Taliban enforced an extreme interpretation of Islam. Kite flying, which is sometimes known as Afghanistan's national pastime, was outlawed by the Taliban. The king's tomb is a landmark in Kabul City. It stands as a shattered monument on a hill in the center of Kabul overlooking the city. It is a popular destination for visitors, so I traveled there with UN workers or visiting Coalition soldiers several times. The sky was filled with kites as children once again pursued the pastime that had been outlawed under the Taliban.

Photographs were also outlawed because it was believed that representing a person's image is sacrilegious. Some of these radical beliefs have relaxed, and people enjoy seeing pictures of themselves. I visited a refugee camp in Kabul with some UN workers, and the Afghans enjoyed having their photographs taken, particularly if you showed them the image on the digital camera or provided prints after developing or printing the pictures.

A controversy in the presidential campaign arose when Supreme Court Chief Justice Fazl Hadi Shinwari declared presidential candidate Latif Pedram to be insufficiently Islamic to run for president. This followed Pedram's comments in favor of women's equality and against the practice of polygamy. Despite the court's ruling in September 2004, Pedram remained on the ballot. However, the ruling itself indicates that the religious atmosphere in the country is far from free even if it is much improved over the previous regime.

Afghanistan does enjoy academic freedom, and the educational system that exists is free of indoctrination. The appointment of the former Finance Minister Ghani as the President of Kabul University is a significant step forward for the higher education system. Ghani's unpopularity among the Afghans prevented his appointment to another term at a high-level cabinet position. However, his credibility among the international community and his effective management of Afghanistan's developing economy speak well for the prospects of his leadership of the university.

Open and free private discussion, another important factor in freedom of expression, seems to exist. My own experience conversing with Afghans, coupled with secondhand information from other internationals in Afghanistan, indicates that open and free discussion is widespread. State Department, United Nations, and media employees frequently engage Afghans and have even been successful soliciting candid opinions from women. Social stigma against women expressing their opinions, predominantly in the south of the country, is an area where free discussion could improve.

## Rule of Law

There is an independent judicial branch of the government. However, its influence is not as strong as in other democracies. For instance, when the court declared one of the presidential candidates "un-Islamic" and disallowed his candidacy, the ruling was ignored and the candidate still appeared on the ballot. Similar historical showdowns in the United States actually had similar results. Franklin Roosevelt's threat to "pack the Court" ultimately cowed the Supreme Court, and even the famous *Marbury v. Madison* ruling, which established the American principle of judicial review, also found in favor of Thomas Jefferson's administration.

A more recent blow to the court's power and independence in Afghanistan might be the alleged involvement of one of the justices in the August 2004 car bombing of an American security firm, DynCorp, discussed in Chapter 2, and the justice's subsequent arrest in January 2005. In late 2004, two suspects, Mohammed Haider (a Tajik) and another man, were arrested in connection with organizing both the DynCorp bombing and the October 2004 suicide bombing on Chicken Street in Kabul, which was discussed in Chapter 4. Judge Naqibullah had belonged to a faction of the *mujahideen*, or holy warriors, which fought the 1980s Soviet occupation and then the Taliban from the late 1990s, helping U.S.-led forces topple them in 2001. Naqibullah was serving as head of the Primary Court of Panshir Province, north of Kabul, and was a member of the Afghan Supreme Court. NATO International Security Assistance Forces and Afghan National Directorate of

Security agents discovered explosives during a raid on Naqibullah's house, and the judge acknowledged that the suspected organizers of the attack had previously stayed at his home.

The rule of law does not always prevail, although police are under direct civilian control. The Minister of Interior during my deployment, Ali Ahmad Jalali, was actually an American citizen who served as a broadcaster for Voice of America before moving to Afghanistan in 2002. His family still lived in Maryland, and Jalali has since returned from his ancestral land to his American homeland. He was strongly influential over the Afghan National Police and other law enforcement forces. His background in the United States legal system gave him credibility among the international community in Afghanistan to provide oversight of the police forces. Jalali's American citizenship caused controversy after the 2004 election because cabinet members in the permanent government were legally required to renounce foreign citizenship. Jalali refused to do this, but President Karzai retained him due to his effectiveness in his role. This decision was thus simultaneously a setback and an accomplishment for the rule of law in Afghanistan.

The rule of law is not regarded in the same way as in Western countries. For instance, I described the traffic conditions already. One day, my partner and I were driving our Afghan guide, Khoshall Murad, to his home in Kabul after he had completed some instruction to us in the Pashtun language. We were driving along one of the divided roads in the city, and a car was moving the wrong way, toward us, in one of the lanes of the roadway. In a shocked and dismayed voice, our Afghan comrade exclaimed, "That's illegal!" That was only one of many instances we observed of a local driver violating expectations of decorum on the roadway, but it was impossible to conceptualize any traffic law mechanism to promulgate and enforce such a law. After all, drivers are not licensed and traffic police are very rare, to be found only in the busiest of intersections. Much of the population is not literate. So our Afghan friend, among the most ready to accept the Western concepts of democracy and law, seemed far ahead of the practical reality of his society at the time.

Another way to consider the rule of law is the process of buying and selling, which differs in some fundamental ways from American or European experience. At a bazaar in Kandahar, I found myself negotiating for a cheap jewelry set before I even realized I had the slightest interest in it. Such is the nature of private commerce in Afghanistan. The shopkeepers are persistent and aggressive. The best I could do was (truthfully) claim that I did not even have the cash he was asking for the jewelry. The amount was not even close. I had hoped this would extricate me from this bargain for a piece of merchandise that I really didn't even want. I even flashed the wad of cash in my pocket, which was certainly not near the amount the shopkeeper had asked. My bluff was called, so to speak, when the merchant accepted the "offer" that I did not realize I was making. So perhaps I had some inadvertent negotiating talent, winning the jewelry set for less than half its price. But more credit goes to the merchant, whose fast moves allowed him to sell his merchandise to a customer who never had any intention of buying.

The differences between American retail and the Afghan bazaar system go beyond the negotiable prices and aggressive merchants of Kabul, Kandahar, and the other smaller cities of Afghanistan. There is an implicit credit system that is part of the Afghan culture. My negotiation in Kandahar hinted at this when the shopkeeper offered to have me take the jewelry and pay him at an undetermined, future date. Only after I made it clear that this alternative was unacceptable did he lower the price. But afterwards, I came to realize that making future payments for small purchases such as this was a common practice. My Afghan friend, Khoshall Murad, took me and my partner shopping in the local districts of Kabul. We stopped by a store where he had purchased some china dishes a few weeks before. Now he was coming to claim his purchase. Apparently, he had paid the shopkeeper but had declined to pick up the china until this later time. Without any written record of such transactions, relying on the honesty and the accurate memory of both parties, private commerce routinely takes place across Afghanistan.

Unfortunately, there is not sufficient protection from police abuses, unjustified imprisonment, or torture. There are indications that police use inappropriate tactics and that due process is not sufficiently developed in the legal system. Abdul Mohammed, the Afghan lieutenant colonel who worked with me in the Election Security Operations Center, provides an example of this. I received a CIA report on two black pickup trucks with certain license plates being used for car bombs for the election. Without revealing the source of the report, I disseminated the license plates and the description of the vehicles to the other members of the ESOC. A half day later, Abdul Mohammed told me that cars with license plates matching those from my report had been detained in Jalalabad. He said that they were sedans, not pickup trucks, and that the colors did not match. He also said that no explosives or anything suspicious had been found, but the cars were in impoundment and the owners being held in jail. He asked me what to do. I responded that I would contact the source of the report and get back to him. So I contacted the point of contact listed on the report. Of course, since it was the famously unhelpful CIA, I never even got any response at all to my inquiry. The following day, Adbul again asked me what to do. Having received no further advice from the CIA field office that had generated the report, I was not sure what to tell Abdul. Depending on the original information that led to the report, the vehicles in detention might reasonably be dangerous. On the other hand, the source of the report might not be as confident in the numbers on the license plate, but he might have been sure of the color and make of the car bomb vehicles. So I revealed the original source of the report as an Afghan National Directorate of Security contact, so that Abdul could inquire with his Afghan contacts, without saying that it was a CIA report. Then I told him that my personal inclination would be to release the vehicle, but this was an Afghan matter and it must ultimately be resolved by Afghan, not Coalition, authorities.

The kidnapping investigation discussed in Chapter 4 also reveals the presumption of guilt that pervades the Afghan law enforcement system. This approach, rather than the presumption of innocence that forms the bedrock of American jurisprudence, has significant implications for everyday Afghans. Law enforcement in general can be said to strike a balance between security and liberty. In the United States, we often err on the side of liberty, perhaps releasing guilty criminals if the state cannot meet its burden of proof or if a procedural error is made in pursuing the investigation. In Afghanistan, where there is not sufficient security to even guarantee a meaningful enjoyment of liberty in many parts of the country, law enforcement errs on the opposite side. Abraham Lincoln famously defended his defiance of Supreme Court Chief Justice Roger Taney's decision in *Ex Parte Merryman* in 1861, asserting the presidential prerogative to suspend citizens' constitutional rights as guaranteed by the writ of habeas corpus in times of war and emergency: "Are all the laws, but one, to go unexecuted, and the government itself to go to pieces, lest that one be violated?" Late Chief Justice William Rehnquist titled his 1998 book on the history of civil rights during wartime *All the Laws But One* in allusion to the Lincoln quotation. For Afghanistan, the perpetual state of crisis and war in which the country finds itself makes this tension much more acute. The arrests, detentions, and likely incidents of torture described in Chapter 4 indicate the dangers posed by these circumstances.

Technological limitations restrict the ability of the system to function effectively and preserve rights to the extent that Western countries do. More problematically, the ongoing Taliban insurgency threatens the rule of law, especially in the southern and southeastern provinces. Criminal influence persists throughout the country, and the widespread presence of private militias reinforces the "might makes right" principle upon which the warlord system is based.

The population is not always treated equally under the law due to the power that warlords exercise, especially in areas of the country that are not yet completely under the influence of the central government. The degree to which privileged segments of the population enjoy special treatment under the law may be tested as the country pursues its counternarcotics campaign. At a micro level, I have seen examples and heard firsthand accounts of minor bribes to win special treatment from traffic police and similar low-level law enforcement. The ethnic diversity in Afghanistan has not resulted in the tensions noted in some other countries. Part of the reason for this is the majority Pashtuns, who are the poorer and less educated part of the population and have been historically repressed, are now represented by the Pashtun President Hamid Karzai. This is significant because the Taliban were primarily Pashtun, prompting the possibility of a backlash by the wealthier minority ethnicities. That this backlash never materialized is instrumental in equal treatment and in the relative stability the country currently enjoys.

## Personal Autonomy and Individual Rights

The state is not the main source of restriction of citizens' personal autonomy. The state is not overbearing in Afghanistan. On the contrary, it is the limits of the state's influence that goes to the heart of the problem for Afghan democratization. However, the limits of the state's influence provide good prospects for personal autonomy, including freedom of travel, choice of residence, and choice of employment. Cultural convention, however, rather than the state, restricts the rights of women. Economic hardships and the weakness of the state against danger and lawlessness also provide challenges for citizens to actually enjoy these rights.

There is a right to private property. There is an organized criminal element, centered around the historical military warlords and opium traffickers. The government is working to reduce the influence of this element, but it unfortunately continues to dominate portions of the private economy. Bazaar merchants on international military bases share their proceeds with powerful warlords. American and NATO military forces thus reinforce these warlords, but in the absence of other power structures and organizations of civil society, there is no one else to deal with in coordinating basic needs from the local economy. This has been slowly improving as the official government has been able to replace these informal power centers.

Personal social freedoms, including gender equality, choice of marriage partners, and size of family, remain underdeveloped although much improved since the Taliban regime. The status of gender equality is still largely restricted. There was a saying that it would be better to be a donkey than a woman in Taliban Afghanistan. As I have had a chance to see those overburdened and mistreated animals roaming the streets of Kabul, that saying gained added meaning. While women's rights have made great strides, it is surprisingly common to see the blue burkha on women in the streets of Kabul, which is one of the most cosmopolitan areas of the country. Arranged marriages are still common.

The treatment of foreign women is an interesting way of looking at the gender issue in Afghanistan. When foreign military or UN women meet Afghans in social settings, they can either mingle with the males or females. (Foreign and Afghan males can never mingle with the Afghan females.) Foreign women are treated like men in that they will interact like equals. (Military women in Afghanistan typically wear uniforms and do not interact with locals. However, military human intelligence specialists wear civilian clothes and do interact with locals. More often, especially in the capital, foreign women are nonmilitary UN or aid workers.) Afghan men also seem to enjoy relating to these women in ways that would be unacceptable with Afghan women. When I visited Jalalabad City, the Army counterintelligence team told me that one of their young female soldiers frequently received marriage proposals from Afghan men. Further south, in Khost, Afghans reporting information to the Coalition forces frequently requested to speak with the young female soldier on the counterintelligence team. In Kabul, the UN media worker, Dora Cheeok, told me that an elderly Afghan man pinched her bottom in the market and others leered at her. Since then, she never traveled unescorted. Thus, Afghans are able to adapt to a different view of women, more reminiscent of my travels in Mediterranean Europe or Latin America than in the Muslim world.

However, I am not as confident that such adaptability with foreign women will be able to transform Afghan gender relations in their domestic society. One of the most frightening examples of the difficulties women still experience occurred early in my time in Afghanistan. Jody Clark from the Elections Security Operations Center was asked to assist in bandaging the horrible wounds of a burned young Afghan woman. The fifteen-year-old woman had been riding a public bus in Jalalabad, and the bus driver sexually assaulted her. When the girl returned home in tears, her parents threw her out of the house, saying she was a harlot and no longer welcome there. The girl traveled to Kabul, trying unsuccessfully to make it on her own. Desperate and without hope, she poured gasoline on her vagina and lit it aflame. She chose this incredibly painful way to commit suicide to purify herself and to redeem her lost virtue. The girl survived. Jody, with a choking voice and tears welling in her eyes, recounted to me that she was asked to dress the wounds because males would not be permitted to do so. It was a terrible incident that drives home the extreme morals and their importance in Afghan society.

Equality of opportunity and economic exploitation are two other issues that are progressing slowly in Afghanistan. Microcredit programs, especially those directed at women, have become popular to expand economic opportunity. However, it is common to see powerful businessmen, often with warlord backgrounds, skimming a good portion of the wages paid by the military and international organizations to Afghan employees.

Karl Maddaford was one of the security officers in Kabul during the National Assembly Elections. A New Zealander, or Kiwi, he had worked in the Demobilization, Disarmament, and Reintegration (DDR) program in 2004, and was recruited to work in the election in 2005. Karl's wife, Rebecca, worked as a nurse in one of the hospitals in Kabul. Living together in Kabul, Afghanistan, as newlyweds was certainly a unique marital experience. They both had served in the New Zealand Army, so perhaps this had prepared them for the adventure and hardship of work in Afghanistan. Rebecca gave me a tour of her hospital, which showed how far Afghanistan needs to go in terms of public health.

Rebecca reminds me of Minnie Driver. She has the same facial features and accent, but with remarkable blue eyes. She told me that she does not mind this comparison and admitted that she had heard it before. Karl and Rebecca's first home was a house on Flower Street in Kabul. This is a popular market area for internationals visiting. It is difficult to navigate the street, though, as an international visitor because there are numerous indigent people asking for handouts. I tried to bring candy bars for the children, but there are just too many people. And if you give out money or anything else at the beginning of your trip, you will be seen as an easy customer and will not be able to make it down the street for the crowd of beggars trying to ask for their share. It is always better to give handouts on your return after you have finished all your stops in stores. Otherwise, if you stop in a store, a crowd will gather and await your departure, making it that much harder to proceed.

There are certain beggars on Flower Street who are regular fixtures, and it is easy to remember them because of their distinctive features. There are a few preadolescent boys ready to offer their services as bodyguards. I knew them by name by the time I left Kabul. There are some preadolescent girls who say that they want to be your girlfriend. The children speak English well and are happy to guide you to the type of store you are looking for, to keep away other beggars, and to carry shopping bags. I do not think these beggar children really need money; as near as I can determine from talking to them, they are the shopkeepers' children and ask for money for something to do and for the challenge more than for any other reason. There are other more serious hard-luck cases. Over Christmas, I stayed in Karl and Rebecca's house on Flower Street to watch the house for them. It let me experience Afghanistan differently than I had living on a military compound. Across the street from their house was a man who slept in a bed on the sidewalk in front of a store. His bed was in the same spot everyday. He woke up around 10:00 A.M. each day, so he was somewhat more lax than the average Afghan whose disciplined schedule allows for the five daily prayers required by the Koran. There was a young pregnant woman with beautiful striking eyes. There must have been something illicit about the pregnancy because the woman would otherwise have had some sort of familial support structure rather than needing to beg on the street. There was an extremely old woman with wrinkled leathery skin that looked like dark parchment. She had one tooth in her mouth and a child who must have been a grandchild, and who was apparently in the care of the old woman.

Rebecca, or Minnie, as I liked to call her, told me that she met this old woman on Flower Street and gave her money from time to time. I knew exactly who she meant; as I said, many of the street people on Flower Street are as regular as the shopkeepers. Rebecca gave the woman a doll for her child and continued walking down the street. The woman chased her down and finally caught up with her. She softly put her weak, wrinkled hand on Rebecca's arm. She smiled at Rebecca with a toothless grin and handed her an orange. In the Book of Mark, Jesus describes a poor widow who gave two pennies, and because she gave everything she had, exceeded the much larger gifts of rich donors. Rebecca actually experienced this as one of the most destitute people she had ever met gave her a piece of fruit that was more a share of her possessions than what most of us have ever given to anyone.

## CHALLENGES FOR THE FUTURE

Afghanistan is by no means on an unobstructed path to democracy. Numerous challenges face the country. Culturally, Afghanistan shares many similarities with the European medieval societies that preceded modern industrialized democracy. Ann Jones in *Kabul in Winter* remarked that "Afghanistan follows the Islamic calendar that counts the days from the Prophet's flight to Medina, so that in Afghanistan at that time the year was 1380. Until that moment the different calendar had seemed to me a cultural curiosity, like an alternative system of bookkeeping, but in the Welayat [a Kabul prison] the fourteenth century became real." This makes it a challenge to implement the sort of multiethnic democracy with which many developed nations still struggle. More problematically, the country faces several difficulties that may derail it from the track to full-fledged democracy. First, the narcotics industry is booming. This threatens the government, whose options to restrict the drug trade are limited due to the fragility of the Afghan economy. Second, the underdeveloped economy itself is among the challenges facing democracy in Afghanistan. The lack of education, technology, and civil society present impediments to democratic progress. Third, warlordism presents a significant problem for the peaceful and lawful society needed for a successful democracy. Finally, ethnic and religious divisions are prominent, and while they do not currently manifest serious tensions, they cast an ominous shadow over Afghanistan's nascent democracy. These ethnic divisions are especially troubling when compared to other multiethnic developing democracies that have never escaped violent rivalry.

### Narcotics

Afghanistan, by some surveys the poorest country in the world, enjoys one flourishing sector in its economy: opium. The singular voice of Christopher Hitchens can be relied upon to present a divergent view, as he did in an article advocating sustaining the opium crop, "Let the Afghan Poppies Bloom," in *Slate* in December 2004. Hitchens argued that the opium export from Afghanistan could be redirected to the more constructive production of analgesics, replacing longtime poppy exporters from countries such as Turkey. The Senlis Council, a British think tank active in Afghan affairs, advocated this approach as well and has been critical of American and British security and counternarcotics policies in Afghanistan. The approach is problematic, for reasons aside from the fact that Turkey, which assumed leadership of NATO's International Security Assistance Force mission in Afghanistan in 2005, would probably not like to lose the millions of dollars from its own export trade.

We cannot realistically expect the poppy crop in Afghanistan to be pushed toward more legitimate and less profitable pursuits for similar reasons that the land on which the poppies are grown cannot be easily redesignated for other crops. The narcotics industry is not only central to the Afghan economy, generating revenues far beyond any other possible industry in the impoverished nation. It is also central to political and military power for an important segment of society. While not as far degenerated as Colombia, Afghanistan's growth in drug trafficking in the years since the Taliban's overthrow has brought the country to the brink of imminent danger from the domination of these narcotics forces. In fact, some U.S. Embassy officials were reportedly urging President Karzai to visit the Colombian president to better understand these dangers.

In December 2004, a research paper from the World Bank, "Drugs and Development in Afghanistan," documented the growing opium problem. Opium has taken more and more a foothold in the Afghan economy, and its domination of the political and social fabric of the country poses a serious threat. Accounting for over 40 percent of the economy, there are few options besides restructuring the agricultural sector. Merely reapplying the poppy crop to legitimate trade would lead to relapse if not mere continuation of the illicit narcotics traffic. And doing nothing would be disastrous. There are more nuanced arguments on how to combat the opium trade, accepting the premise that it must be combated. Most Afghan government officials hope to avoid complete and immediate destruction of the poppy fields. American policymakers, on the other hand, have been faster to advocate a strategy of eradication. The Afghan approach may make more sense to avoid unintended consequences of a war on drugs that does not include rehabilitation of this large sector of the economy. The major negative consequence is the creation of a class of former poppy growers who will be suddenly impoverished and infuriated by harsh government action. This could infuse the Afghan insurgency with a new source of recruitment and popular support. This contingency is particularly dangerous because the rural south and east are the areas where the Taliban was most dominant and the insurgency is most active. Thus, the narcotics situation threatens the nascent democracy and civil society because it empowers the most lawless and dangerous elements of society. However, the developing war on drugs also poses a danger as it reorders the society and removes the largest source of national income.

When I visited the Provincial Reconstruction Team (PRT) in Farah in Western Afghanistan, the civil affairs noncommissioned officer, Segeant Farrands, informed me that they frequently reported poppy fields during their travels. The poppy crop is more prevalent in the south of the country, but it can be found in the southwest Farah Province as well. There are several indications of the scope and depth of the problem. First, the reporting requirements for the PRT indicate that team members must report the existence of fields greater than one hundred meters by one hundred meters. However, it is much more likely for patrols to find ten thirty by thirty meter fields. This is a problem for two reasons. The smaller, more numerous fields are much harder for tracking and intervention. In addition, the reporting requirements make it less likely to arrive at an accurate picture of the problem. During the time I was in Afghanistan, American military forces, including the development-focused PRTs, were not to get involved with eradication. This was somewhat controversial due to the significant threat posed by the narcotics sector of the economy. In late 2004, the PRT would warn local farmers that poppy growing was illegal. This in itself was probably helpful in at least a small way. Communicating the laws in a country with a weak government, widespread illiteracy, and little electricity was an important step. The PRT also distributed newspapers to people through its psychological operations division, which promoted a poppy-free Afghan future. An Afghan farmer actually informed the Farah civil affairs team that he was happy about eradication because the poppy prices rose from a hundred dollars a bushel to three hundred dollars a bushel. To get an idea of how much poppy was in Farah, which was not the most significant producer of the crop, a six- to eight-hour patrol would typically result in finding fifteen to twenty fields. Another practice that complicates the problem is that fields would often have a border of wheat, which is a taller plant, surrounding the lower poppy crops. The PRT noticed this during talks with farmers and they were on the look out for it afterwards.

## The Economy

Afghanistan, as one of the poorest countries in the world, is in many ways unsuited to independent democracy as it is understood in modernized nations, if only because of economic constraints. International media coverage of the movement of ballots via donkeys presented a stark example of this concern. While industrialized nations enjoy nearly instantaneous results due to electronic technology, Afghanistan's presidential election took weeks before the final outcome was clear. This delay occurred even with the majority of ballots being moved by U.S. and other allied military lift aircraft. In addition, few Afghans have access to computer technology. Working with senior Afghan military officers in the Election Security Operations Center, I found out that exchanging e-mail addresses would be meaningless because it is a technology that they just do not use. Because of the United Nations' involvement in the election, the Afghan electoral body enjoyed the use of computerized databases and foreign computer experts to tally the results of the vote. However, this is not an approach on which the country could rely without the huge international presence in Afghanistan. Finally, the bill for the election itself, in the hundreds of millions of dollars, is not something Afghanistan alone could support as a national expenditure. The economic constraints on the technical conduct of the election do not necessarily contraindicate democracy. American and European democracies flourished for a few hundred years before the advent of the computer, albeit with populations much smaller than their current levels. However, it should be noted that the economy poses significant technical challenges to democratic processes and governance.

The next point relevant to the economic condition of Afghanistan is the level of education and literacy. An uninformed electorate is one of the major concerns in American democracy. In a country where the *CIA World Factbook 2004* reported that the literacy rate was only 36 percent, ensuring that the public is aware of the issues and the candidates becomes even more difficult. While the challenge is severe, especially in light of somewhat unimpressive efforts of national voter education projects in Western democracies, there are points of encouragement. The Afghan people are extremely gifted in linguistics. Much of the country is bilingual, speaking the Pashtun language of the southern ethnic majority as well as the Dari language used by the government and most commercial enterprises. Some speak Urdu, which is a related language used by peoples living in Pakistan. In addition, many people speak English. Certainly, most who do so speak more fluently than my beginning efforts into Pashtun. Many people speak Russian due to the decade-long invasion of Soviet forces in the 1980s, and the ability to read, if not speak, Arabic is common among literate Afghans because of the Muslim custom of reading the *Koran* in the original Arabic. I went to a marketplace to buy some scarves, and a French soldier was negotiating with the shopkeeper, who was speaking fluent French. I came behind him, and the shopkeeper spoke to me in fluent English. Based on the surprising facility of the people with languages, I suspect that educational efforts will make significant progress in teaching reading and writing. Nonetheless, this will be a long-term effort and will need to be followed by the development and expansion of the media.

The most problematic implication for democratization of the underdeveloped economy is the impact on civil society. Perhaps the most important element in democratic society according to most democracy theorists, civil society refers to the voluntary associations that enrich public participation in democracies, such as professional associations, religious groups, labor unions, private clubs, and citizen advocacy organizations. Due to the harsh realities of survival, such private association cannot be a priority in Afghanistan. Additionally, the problem of illiteracy prevents connections through the written media. The technological underdevelopment of the country prevents effective communication and transportation, along with the forbidding rugged terrain. Finally, the lack of computer technology prevents any sort of Internet connectivity, which has arguably been the most significant boon for civil society in the West and other parts of the world in recent history.

## Warlordism

The fact remains that for much of the country, "might makes right." While the inauguration ceremony in November 2004 signaled the transitional government's succession to a new government, many parts of the country are still outside the reach of the government. In these areas, local warlords continue to hold sway over the communities. An organized disarmament process, Demobilization, Disarmament, and Reintegration (DDR), has been underway to reduce the capabilities of armed militia forces and thus reduce the power of local warlords. The DDR program has boasted of progress since it was first implemented in late 2003. However, the program was too narrowly scoped, preventing it from reaching the heart of the problem. DDR has been limited to organized Afghan Militia Forces, which were independent militias nominally under the control of the Ministry of Defense. Private militias were not involved with this disarmament process. Thus, the most unaccountable and dangerous parts of the warlord system have not even begun any disarmament process. Additionally, the DDR process was largely focused on heavy weapons, but small arms, including rifles and light machine guns, were often left untouched. Anti-air implements, mortars, rockets, and heavy machine guns are more frequently seized in the disarmament process. Part of this is because of a "gun culture" in Afghanistan, where it is not only a pragmatic need to possess a weapon, but owning a firearm is also connected with an individual's sense of independence, capability, and manhood. All of this creates an environment of potential violence that could be threatening for democratization, especially due to the connection of warlords to the narcotics problem.

The tensions between democratization and warlordism are revealed in an e-mail I received from Murad in early 2007. Murad still lives and works in Afghanistan, in a small village outside of the major city of Jalalabad. He titled the subject line of the message, "zama malgari wrowr salaam," which I translate from the Pashtun as "my friend and brother, hello."

...As you have already informed that life became difficult for me in Jalalabad, so, for a long time I lived in Khugyani district with my wife and my in laws family.

A few months ago I got a job as a language assistant with U.S. forces in south Afghanistan after 3 months my family were informed so my father called me to leave the job because of danger and I did.

After that I was not looking for jobs every where because still some of the candidates and local commanders are threatening me that why I did not help them in the election and why I have been working with foreign forces, but I will not change my mind and I will do more then that for the stability, peace, freedom and security in Afghanistan....

I understood from his letter that the candidates themselves are the local strongmen who oppose the international forces in Afghanistan. It seems that young Afghan men cannot escape threats from local officials when they choose to work with the international soldiers in the country trying to stop insurgents and develop the infrastructure of Afghanistan. One can also understand from my friend's message that thuggish pressure is being applied by candidates to enlist help in the election. Perhaps the strongmen revealed in Murad's letter are similar to the political machines of early American democracy, such as Tammany Hall in New York City. The account is revealing about how, in the near term at least, democratically elected officials will not replace the warlords and militia commanders of the past. The election process will merely allow those power players to exercise their control in a different system.

## Ethnic Divisions

The Pashtun people are the largest ethnic and linguistic community of the ethnically diverse country. About half the population is Pashtun, and they are concentrated in the east and south, the former stronghold of the Taliban. The Dari-speaking Tajiks are the second-largest community, making up about a quarter of the population. The Tajiks account for most of the educated elite and possess substantial wealth. They wield considerable political influence, and are related to the inhabitants of the neighboring Tajikistan.

Tensions between the Pashtuns and Tajiks complicate efforts at multi-ethnic democracy. The Pashtuns are by far the largest ethnic group in the country, but their political and economic disenfranchisement threatens a backlash against the wealthier and more powerful Tajiks. At the same time, Tajiks, possibly threatened by such a prospect, may use their position of advantage to maintain their influence in Afghanistan. In fact, all of the minority races may still feel resentment and apprehension toward the Pashtun majority, from which the repressive Taliban regime was comprised.

About 11 percent of the population are Turkic, mostly Uzbek and Turk-men, who live in the northern plains as farmers and herders. These Turkic races are related to the former Soviet republics of Uzbekistan and Turk-menistan that border the north of Afghanistan. Finally, the Hazara, a Mongoloid people of central Afghanistan, are a sufficiently large minor-ity to wield noteworthy amounts of power.

A significant point about the Hazara is that they are part of the Shia sect of Islam, while the rest of the country is largely Sunni. The differences between Shia and Sunni Muslims in Afghanistan do not seem to currently motivate the serious sorts of divisions that they do among Middle Eastern Muslims. In the time of the Taliban, the Hazara were particular targets of oppression, which Rory Stewart documented in his *The Places in Between*. Today, the Hazara area of the country is one of the most stable and free from violence. However, given historical Shia-Sunni tensions and the contemporary ten-sions elsewhere in the world, religious persecution of the Hazara minority remains a potential threat.

## SETBACKS IN THE YEARS SINCE

In 2007, the Senlis Council released a report entitled *Countering the In-surgency in Afghanistan: Losing Friends and Making Enemies*. The report noted, "With a rapid rise in violent insurgency, southern Afghanistan is at tipping point," and strongly criticized the allied military efforts in the coun-try, arguing that they have been too focused on counterterrorism and not sufficiently engaged with development and reconstruction. In the same year, Anthony Cordesman of the conservative Center for Strategic and Interna-tional Studies think tank provided testimony to the House Committee on Foreign Affairs and released a report entitled *Winning in Afghanistan: The Challenges and the Response*. This report was much more upbeat, placing significant store in a December 2006 poll conducted by ABC News that found strong support for American presence among the Afghan people and strong disfavor for the Taliban militants. Cordesman argued that the mili-tants have been successful only through their sanctuary in Pakistan rather than being sustained by popular support as in a traditional insurgency. These findings contradict the Senlis Council's perspective, which argues that the Afghans have lost faith in the international community and are turning back to the Taliban. I am hesitant to accept the opinion poll at face value, particu-larly as it avoided the provinces of Zabul and Oruzgan for security reasons, which seems to be an indicator that some others of the more remote areas of the country may not have been reached. I am uncertain as well about the dismal forecast of the Senlis Council. The truth, perhaps, lies somewhere in-between. What is irrefutable, however, is that the year 2006 was a signif-icant setback for the government of Afghanistan and its U.S. and coalition allies. The militant activity has increased, causing fighting to reach its highest intensity since the initial invasion, according to the comments of the commanding general of Combined Forces Command, Lieutenant General Karl Eikenberry, during a presentation at Harvard University on May 5, 2006. In order to look at how the environment has changed since my departure from the country in June 2005, it is important to first describe the degree to which the violence in Afghanistan increased in the following year. Second, it will be helpful to understand the key reasons for this change—a shifting reliance on NATO forces and increased freedom of movement for insurgents in the Pakistani tribal areas. Finally, it will be important to understand how this changing environment impacts the prospects for democracy given the four major challenges of narcotics, the economy, warlordism, and ethnic divisions.

There has been a significant increase in insurgent activity in Afghanistan across a variety of metrics. Direct and indirect attacks almost tripled from 2005 to 2006. Direct attacks, involving direct rifle or machine-gun fire, increased to about 4,500 attacks in 2006 from about 1,500 in 2005. Indirect attacks, which consist mostly of rockets, but include mortars as well, increased from almost 600 to over 1,500. Improvised explosive device attacks doubled from almost 800 incidents to over 1,600. At the same time, the International Security Assistance Force was able to kill over 250 IED operators, including fifty cell leaders. Attacks on the international military almost tripled, going from over 1,000 in 2005 to almost 2,900 in 2006. Attacks on Afghan forces almost quadrupled, perhaps in part to the nascent expansion of these forces. There were 830 attacks on Afghan forces in 2005, but in 2006, this number increased to over 3,500. Finally, suicide attacks, which had not been as prevalent in Afghanistan as they have in the Middle East, increased by more than six times: 27 in 2005 to 139 in 2006, killing 15 coalition soldiers and 206 Afghan civilians, and wounding 460 Afghans. The year also resulted in a major increase in local fighters recruited in remote areas where the government of Afghanistan holds little sway.

The limits of NATO's ability to operate in a high-stress combat environment have been made clear through the experience in Afghanistan. The Bush Administration, and particularly the Rumsfeld Defense Department, received strong criticism after their decision in 2001 to invade Afghanistan with an ad hoc coalition rather than accepting the offer of NATO allies to mobilize the collective security alliance for the invasion. Many detractors suggested that it was a case of cowboy diplomacy needlessly snubbing allies. This is perhaps an overstatement, but I do agree with the critics that the more difficult call for allies in Iraq might have gone more easily had there been a greater sense of cooperation in Afghanistan when it had been offered. On the tactical and operational level, however, the decision to avoid a NATO command structure has been validated as extremely beneficial.

Many of the problems in the NATO International Security Assistance Force that I observed during the kidnapping crisis have emerged on a much larger scale throughout the country. There are issues more problematic than those I noticed in the abduction investigation involving conflicts of interest between country loyalty and loyalty to the NATO command. Caveats restricting the soldiers' responses under certain conditions prevent many of the soldiers from responding to the most critical situations in the country, or from responding in a timely manner. These issues threaten the capability for good work of the entire international community in Afghanistan. NATO's Undersecretary for Political Affairs, R. Nicholas Burns, noted in 2007 that the viability of the entire organization was threatened by this ineffectiveness, comparing it to failures in Kosovo that NATO leaders vowed never to repeat. He stated, "When you have 26 allies in Afghanistan and you have four countries doing the majority of the fighting—Canada, the Netherlands, the United Kingdom, and the United States—it is right for us to ask the other allies to make a greater effort to remove the military restrictions so that everybody can be called upon to make the kind of sacrifices that need to be made." Thus, the divided command structure and the thousands of soldiers ill-equipped, unready, or unable to get into the fight have doubtlessly contributed to the Taliban's resurgence.

More important than the deficiencies of NATO is the increased sanctuary that threat groups were able to find in the Northwest Frontier Province, the Federally Administered Tribal Areas, and Baluchistan. The Pakistani government, which had earlier been engaged (if not entirely effective) in patrolling the wild area of the country, has retrenched. The most notable accomplishment of the Pakistani military was the capture of Khalid Sheikh Mohammed in 2003. Mohammed was the number three man in al Qaeda and responsible for planning both the 9-11 attacks and the earlier 1993 attack on the World Trade Center and is currently being held in U.S. custody.

The previous mixed success of Pakistan in monitoring the area occurred for at least three different reasons. First, the area has never been controlled by any government. The British failed to win full control over this mountainous and ethnically Pashtun region in the colonial times, and Pakistan has never asserted full control over it either. (As a Pakistani investment banker, and good friend of mine, pointed out, after years in Baghdad, the U.S. military has failed to control the insurgency there. The Pashtun tribal region is much larger and less trafficable than Baghdad, making the situation extremely difficult.) The area has retained some degree of autonomy under the Pakistani system of government, and most of the Pashtun tribal leaders consider themselves independent and do not recognize the Pakistani government's authority, nor the border separating them from the Pashtun lands in Afghanistan. The swath of land covering southern and eastern Afghanistan and northwestern Pakistan is thought of by many as a greater Pashtunistan. Further complicating the matter, during my time in Afghanistan, many local people told me about the Durand Line, a border established by the British to divide Pakistan and Afghanistan at the end of the colonial period. There are

a number of independence movements on the Pakistani side of the border—
as well as Afghans on the other side—who believe that the Durand treaty
was set to expire a hundred years after its establishment in 1893. This would
have major ramifications for the Global War on Terrorism, particularly if
the Pashtunistan areas fell under Afghan control. I have been unable to confirm what I was told in Afghanistan, however. It seems that there was no
such time limit established when the Durand Line was originally set. Regardless of the legal status of the treaty, resistance to the boundary among
Pashtuns who populate both sides of the border present serious difficulties
in preventing terrorist and insurgent infiltration into Afghanistan.

The second reason for difficulties in monitoring extremists in the region
is the end game of the Pakistani Inter-Services Intelligence Directorate, the
agency most responsible for counter-terrorist activity on the Pakistani side
of the border. As I have already discussed, the ISID is known for the extremists who serve in its ranks. This makes successful raids such as the Sheikh
Mohammed capture seem extremely unlikely. On one hand, two-thirds of
al Qaeda's leadership has been captured or killed in the first two years after
the World Trade Center bombing according to the White House's *Progress
Report on the Global War on Terrorism* released in September 2003. This
could not have been accomplished without the strong support of the Pak-
istanis. On the other hand, the highest profile targets, including al Qaeda
leaders Bin Laden and Ayman al-Zawahiri and Taliban leaders Mullah
Mohammed Omar and Jalaluddin Haqqani, have remained at large. It has
been argued (particularly based on the precarious situation with the Pashtuns and the border controversy in the country) that Pakistan desires a weak,
unstable Afghanistan. The ISID, according to this line of thinking, enables
the Taliban movement in the frontier region in order to intentionally disrupt
Afghanistan.

Finally, Pakistani President Pervez Musharraf has tried to find a balance
between supporting the Americans in the Global War on Terror and arous-
ing his own downfall in a country prone to extremism. Having survived
numerous assassination attempts, some coming perilously close to ending
his life, President Musharraf cannot risk too much in supporting the war.
He revealed the pressure in his 2006 memoir, *In the Line of Fire*, relating
that the United States had made it abundantly clear that he must aban-
don the Taliban and support the American effort: "In what has to be the
most undiplomatic statement ever made, [the then Deputy Secretary of State
Richard] Armitage . . . told the director general [of the ISID] not only that
we had to decide whether we were with America or with the terrorists, but
that if we chose the terrorists, then we should be prepared to be bombed
back to the Stone Age."

With this double bind, Musharraf has walked a fine line. The Pakistani
military had been engaged in a conflict with Pashtun forces led by former
leaders of the Taliban government in the border region. Facing impressive

battlefield victories by the Pashtun fighters and the manifest diminishing American power demonstrated in both Afghanistan and Iraq throughout 2006, the president extended a peace agreement with tribal leaders in North Waziristan Agency on September 5, 2006. The agreement required that Taliban-associated leaders in the agency no longer support foreign fighters and no longer conduct movements into Afghanistan. There is little reason to believe that the militants will follow the treaty, given that there are no enforcement mechanisms and the Taliban's military leader, Jalaluddin Haqqani, is the senior figure of authority in the agency. Haqqani and other Taliban leaders have essentially established a state-within-a-state, calling their realm the Islamic Emirate of Waziristan and ruling with the harsh justice of the former Taliban regime, strictly enforcing their interpretation of *sharia* law and beheading offenders.

Thus, in 2006, the madrassa bases in Pakistan seem to have been able to provide even better staging areas for incursions into neighboring Afghanistan than before, and the international forces under NATO command have not demonstrated the readiness to confront the challenge. In particular, the situation in Pakistan does not seem likely to improve soon with the Pakistani withdrawal from Waziristan. With intelligence indications of plans for a major spring offensive to be launched from Pakistan, the U.S. government responded by quietly raising troop levels by over 3,000 soldiers in January and February of 2007 in response to requests from the U.S. Combined Forces Command. At the same time that the surge in Iraq sparked contentious debate in Congress and in media circles, the increase in Afghanistan received less attention. In the short term, I am concerned that the situation may further deteriorate. Containing crossborder attacks from Pakistan while being unable to disrupt supply lines, staging bases, and command and control nodes will present increasing difficulties for the international military in Afghanistan. From a longer-term perspective, the increased pressures on the security situation from the mounting Taliban insurgency will place pressure on the Afghan government's efforts to restrain the drug trade, which is inextricably linked to the growing Taliban presence in Pakistan. It will also hamper government efforts to combat poverty because of the destructive effects of the insurgency on the country's infrastructure and economic activity. Ethnic tensions may heighten because of the Pashtun context in which the effort is being launched. The resurgent Taliban will exacerbate the serious challenges confronting Afghan democracy. Controlling the Afghan side of the border with Pakistan will be the key to mitigating this developing threat.

## PARTING THOUGHTS

Among the citizens of the country, Afghanistan is progressing toward democracy with a popular enthusiasm that is very encouraging for outside observers. However, such optimistic appraisals must be tempered with an understanding of the very real challenges the country faces. With an incredible voter turnout in 2004 and a diminishing terrorist presence in the aftermath of the election, Afghanistan took giant first steps toward democratization. These political developments must be coupled with social reform to reduce the influence of armed warlords and economic improvement to provide the country with the resources it needs to sustain democracy. With continued support from the international community, Afghanistan will be able to make progress toward these goals.

In many ways, the country is at a unique crossroads. It has the potential to return to a more egalitarian, wealthier, and freer society. Before the Soviet invasion, Afghanistan was not the dangerous, impoverished, and extremist country that it has been for the past twenty-five years. Whether it can recapture the encouraging path to development that it previously enjoyed remains to be seen. The threat of narcotics and lawlessness are among the most pressing issues, but the shadow of the former Taliban government still remains. Seeing women walk the streets in burkhas and continued factional violence by religious militants contribute to fears of this possibility.

Democratic development is a hope and a vision that can be realized with the cooperative efforts of many constituencies and leaders. Hamid Karzai has proven himself an invaluable leader, and his legacy as the "father of his country" in the model of George Washington is assured if the country can continue to walk along the path he has found for it. Other political leaders are providing the discourse necessary for self-governance in a free society. Foreign leaders, such as the former Ambassador Zalmay Khalilzad and the European and American military officers, have proven vital allies in a fight that is a war for the survival of a nation itself. Khalilzad moved on to Iraq, which proved an even more dangerous and threatening situation, to devote his considerable talents to constructing a viable peace. Ultimately, I feel that the ambassador was unable to make the progress in Iraq that he did in Afghanistan because of his own Sunni Muslim background. The very characteristic that won trust among the Afghans stoked suspicions among the Iraqis, among whom the Shiite denomination comprises a majority. To me, however, he is a true hero of Afghanistan's early development, and when I was in Afghanistan, the man himself was a symbol of cooperation between nations and how politics can secure peace and development.

Individual contributors in many roles and at many levels also demonstrated incredible commitment to realizing the dream that is a democratic Afghanistan. The teenage Minnesota National Guardsman whose initiative led to repairing the young Afghan girl's disfigured face is in a small, and perhaps strategically insignificant way, a hero. However, the repetition of such gestures of goodwill throughout the country builds bonds of trust and shows the benefits of a society designed around the concepts of mutual respect. UN officers such as Scott Raesler, bringing their experience from hotspots around the world, provide inspiration to the Afghans with whom they work. Other internationals are also helping reconstruct the society in numerous ways. For instance, Rebecca Maddaford, who accompanied her husband on his UN tour to Afghanistan, tirelessly worked in a Kabul hospital, attended to the most serious injuries and sicknesses of Afghan locals in the most austere conditions. United States military officers throughout the country, such as Major Tim Barrick in the Election Security Operations Center and Major Greg Hall in Task Force Phoenix, provided mentorship and coaching that will have effects for years to come. Finally, the Afghans themselves are the most important contributors in this process. Colonels Abdul Mohammed and Aziz Hassan courageously defended the ideals of their new nation. Perhaps most importantly, Afghans such as Khoshall Murad—the twenty-five-year-old man who loves his country and hopes to see it become a better home—are standing up for what they believe in and for what they hope their country can be.

The military intervention in Afghanistan's first presidential election was thus a promising step forward and an example of the exciting possibilities of cooperation among many different players in building a better future. While Osama bin Laden eludes capture as of this writing, he can see the changes in Afghanistan from whatever remote cave or village he has secreted himself. Rather than exploiting a people in their worst moment for their own destructive ends, as the foreign legions of al Qaeda did in the late 1990s, today's foreign visitors cooperatively work toward a better future for Afghanistan. The American invasion was by no means altruistic. Taliban Afghanistan, in cooperating with the al Qaeda terrorist organization, presented an intolerable threat to American national security. However, American intervention has been mutually beneficial. Together, Americans and Afghans can achieve national security for Americans today while building a better future for Afghanistan tomorrow.

# INDEX

25th Infantry Division, 22, 23, 125, 126, 134, 135

Abduction. *See* United Nations
Abizaid, General John, 38, 125–26, 129, 131
Air Force. *See* U.S. Air Force
Akbar, Agha, 102, 115
Alexander, Deborah, 55–58, 121
al Qaeda, 1, 20, 22, 38, 40, 59–61, 63–65, 68–70, 72, 74, 75, 82, 92, 105, 114, 115, 126, 127, 137, 165, 166, 169
al-Zawahiri, Ayman, 64–65, 166
Armitage, Richard, 166
Australia, 82, 85, 100

Baluchistan, 60, 165
Bamiyan, 60, 68–69, 80
bin Laden, Osama, 13, 40, 61–64, 69, 128, 137, 166, 169
Blackwater, 41, 140–41
*Blowback*, 65. *See also* Johnson, Chalmers
*The Bookseller of Kabul*, 5, 9. *See also* Seierstand, Åsne
Bosnia, 20, 60, 71, 94, 147
Bush, George W., 60

Canada, 165
*Caravans*, 5. *See also* Michener, James
Central Intelligence Agency (CIA), 11, 33, 40–42, 45, 53, 65, 109, 119, 140, 152–53
Chechnya, 13, 60
Cheek, Colonel Gary, 22, 23, 128–29, 138, 140–41
Christiansen, Richard, 56–57, 104, 120
Combined Joint Task Force-76 (CJTF-76), 14, 15, 17, 20, 21, 22, 24, 25, 30, 38, 39, 41, 48, 54, 70, 76, 125, 127, 135, 143
*Corporate Warriors*, 41. *See also* Singer, Peter

Defense Human Intelligence Service (Defense HUMINT Service, DH), 40–41
Defense Intelligence Agency (DIA), 41
Dostum, Rashid, 80, 83, 147
Drug Enforcement Agency (DEA), 40–41, 53
DynCorp, 41–42, 44, 47, 63, 150

Egypt, 13, 19–20
Election, 2004 U.S., 1, 63, 98, 106
Erben, Peter, 123–24, 126, 142

*Fatwa*, 13, 63
Federal Bureau of Investigation (FBI), 40–41, 94
Federally Administered Tribal Area (FATA), 60, 165
Fine, Patrick, 122
Flanigan, Annetta, 92, 94, 102, 109–12
France, 19, 20, 25, 37, 70, 160

Germany, 7, 15, 33, 95, 112
Global Risk Strategies, 14, 41–4, 66, 80, 93, 124
Great Britain, 25, 34, 41, 98, 104, 158, 165
Gul, Siddiqa Sahar, 2, 4–8, 130

Halliburton; KBR, 133
Haqqani, Jalaluddin, 68–70, 166–67
Haqqani, Siraq, 69
Hassan, Aziz, 7–8, 65, 169
Hebebi, Shquibe, 92, 100, 106–8, 111–12
Herat, 23–24, 30–31, 33, 38, 65, 83, 88, 126
Hezb-e Islami Gulbiddin (HIG), 66–67, 71, 127
Highway 1, 32, 45, 68, 129. *See also* Ring Road
Hitchens, Christopher, 157
Hosseini, Khaled, 73. *See also The Kite Runner*

Improvised explosive devices (IEDs), 45, 65, 66, 68, 69, 73, 76, 77, 79, 89, 91, 129, 164
Interrogation, 14, 40, 73, 94, 111, 113, 114, 133, 136–37
*The Interrogators*, 40. *See also* Mackey, Chris
Inter-Services Intelligence Directorate (ISID), 115, 166
Iran, 2, 17, 23–25, 33, 70, 82, 123
Iraq, 6, 12, 15, 25, 41–42, 63–64, 71–72, 91, 100, 108, 109, 123, 125, 131–32, 134, 136–37, 147, 164, 167–68

Jaish-e-Musliman, 70, 97–98, 104, 106–8, 115
Jalalabad, 65–67, 71, 73, 77–78, 129–32, 152, 155, 161, 162
Jalali, Ali Ahmad, 151
Jan, Baba, 113
Japan, 12, 16, 112
Johnson, Chalmers, 53, 65. *See also Blowback; The Sorrows of Empire*
Jones, Ann, 53, 132, 157. *See also Kabul in Winter*

*Kabul in Winter*, 53, 132, 157. *See also* Jones, Ann
Kamiya, General Jason, 125–31
Kandahar, 8, 9, 23, 25, 30, 35, 38, 66, 68–74, 76–77, 79, 126, 137, 151–52
Kaplan, Robert, 37. *See also Soldiers of God*
Karzai, Hamid, 3, 9, 15, 24, 31, 41, 42, 47, 53, 59, 62, 63, 65, 69, 73–76, 78, 80–85, 103–4, 106, 108–9, 114, 118, 120–21, 147, 148, 151, 153, 158, 168
Kashmir, 60
Kha, Zali, 1–3
Khalilzad, Ambassador Zalmay, 53, 56, 57, 63, 83, 104, 119–21, 148, 168
Khan, Fahim, 76, 83
Khan, Ismail, 23–24, 65, 78, 83
Khan, Rozi, 38–39
Khost Protective Force (KPF), 140–41; Gafaar, Colonel, 141
Kidnapping. *See* United Nations
*The Kite Runner*, 73. *See also* Hosseini, Khaled

*Laaf*, 73
Lais, 112–14
*Loya Jirga*, 15, 62, 93, 122

Mackey, Chris, 40. *See also The Interrogators*
Maney, General Patt, 55–57
Marine Corps. *See* U.S. Marine Corps
Martin, Trevor, 95

Massoud, Ahmad Shah, 75–76
Massoud, Zia, 74, 76
Mazar-e-Sharif, 42
*Meshrano jirga*, 117, 122, 147
Michener, James, 5. *See also Caravans*
Ministry of Interior, 83, 93–94, 97, 99, 101, 104–7, 109–10, 118, 120, 122, 151
Mohammed, Abdul, 2, 7–8, 10–12, 92, 152, 169
Mohammed, Din, 66
Mohaqiq, Haji Mohammed, 80, 83, 108, 147
Morris, Christopher, 88–89, 104
*Mujahideen*, 64–65, 105, 150
Murad, Khoshall, 2–4, 6, 81, 130, 151–52, 161–62, 169
Musharraf, Pervez, 166

Naray, 69
National Directorate of Security (NDS), 32, 66, 73, 76, 94, 101, 108–9, 152
North Atlantic Treaty Organization (NATO); International Security Assistance Force (ISAF), 14, 19, 21, 24, 29, 33, 40, 47, 62, 70, 92, 94, 97, 100, 101, 105, 124, 141, 143, 150, 154, 158, 164–65, 167
North Korea, 12, 16

Olsen, General Eric, 22, 23, 39, 127
Omar, Mullah Mohammed, 60, 67–68, 166

Pakistan, 7–8, 10, 13, 17, 20, 22, 32, 37, 40–41, 60, 63, 66–71, 76–79, 84, 89, 102–3, 115, 123, 126, 128, 130–31, 136, 139–41, 160, 163–67
Palestine, 60
*Pashtunwali*, 61–62
Pedram, Latif, 82, 149
Peshawar, 7, 69, 71, 115
Philippines, 98, 107
*The Places in Between*, 9, 163. *See also* Stewart, Rory
Provincial Reconstruction Team (PRT), 29–33, 35, 159

Qanuni, Yunis, 80–84, 103, 108, 147

Ring Road, 32, 45, 68, 129. *See also* Highway 1
Rumsfeld, Donald, 30, 58, 125, 164
Russian invasion, 64, 78, 160

Sayyaf, Abdul Rausol, 103, 105
Seierstand, Åsne, 5, 9. *See also The Bookseller of Kabul*
September 11th, 12, 22, 60, 64, 74, 75, 138, 139, 141
Sharifullah, 94, 101, 103, 110
Singer, Peter, 41. *See also Corporate Warriors*
*Soldiers of God*, 37. *See also* Kaplan, Robert
*The Sorrows of Empire*, 53. *See also* Johnson, Chalmers
Southern European Task Force (SETAF), 125, 134, 135
State Department. *See* U.S. State Department
Stewart, Rory, 9, 163. *See also The Places in Between*

Taliban, 1–2, 4–6, 8–9, 14–15, 18–23, 34, 38–39, 44, 59–77, 81–84, 86, 90, 95, 97, 102–3, 105, 108–9, 114–15, 126–27, 136, 140, 144, 147, 149–50, 153–54, 158, 162–63, 165–69
The Asian Foundation (TAF), 54, 124
Traffic incidents, 44–45, 47–52, 151
Turkey, 20, 124, 158
Type, Julian, 121

United Nations, abduction of workers and, 92–115; Joint Electoral Management Body (JEMB), 66, 77, 78, 82–84, 99, 107, 118, 142; United Nations Assistance Mission Afghanistan (UNAMA), 84, 95–96, 112, 124; United Nations Development Program (UNDP), 49; United Nations Office for Projects and Services (UNOPS), 4, 5, 7, 118

U.S. Air Force, 87, 140; pararescue jumpers (PJs), 87
U.S. Marine Corps, 16, 49–51, 54, 81, 90–91, 129–31
U.S. Military Academy. *See* West Point
U.S. State Department, 58, 63, 119, 124, 148, 150; U.S. Agency for International Development, 29–30, 33, 122, 124; U.S. Embassy, 21, 41, 44, 50, 53–57, 61, 86, 104, 118–21, 147, 158

Vietnam War, 13, 22, 35, 42, 59, 112, 113, 125

West Point, 12, 24, 26–27, 37, 102, 125–26
*Wolesi jirga*, 117, 121, 147

## About the Author

MATTHEW J. MORGAN is a graduate of the U.S. Military Academy at West Point and has completed graduate work at Harvard Business School and the University of Hawai'i. He served six years in U.S. Army intelligence, including a tour of Afghanistan in which he was awarded the Bronze Star, and he currently works as an Associate at McKinsey & Company. Morgan has served in a variety of teaching appointments at various institutions since 2002, including Assistant Professor of Government at Bentley College and Lecturer of Organizational and Political Communications at Emerson College. He is the author of over thirty articles on strategic and organizational issues and of the forthcoming book, *The American Military after 9/11* (2008).